Abel
17.98

Multistory Housing · Mehrgeschossiger Wohnbau

Karl Wilhelm Schmitt **Multistory Housing**

Mehrgeschossiger Wohnbau

Frederick A. Praeger, Publishers, New York · Washington

BOOKS THAT MATTER

Published in the United States of America in 1966
by Frederick A. Praeger, Inc., Publishers
111 Fourth Avenue, New York 3, N.Y.
All rights reserved
Copyright 1966 by Verlag Gerd Hatje, Stuttgart
Library of Congress Catalog Card Number: 66–12990
Printed in Germany

Translation into English by E. Rockwell

Preface

"Genuine New Building has not yet begun" said Gerrit Rietveld in January 1964, shortly before he died. This is also the message which this book tries to convey. The reader may complain that too much effort has been spent on so modest an objective: he may prefer formulas or practical specifications. Of such specifications, however, hundreds are now available and are being applied to the construction of millions of dwellings every year – as will also be borne out by many of the examples shown here. That is not inconsistent with the objectives of this book, since any step into unexplored territory must be preceded by a survey of present conditions.

No doubt, the old practices still prevail in Paris and Moscow, in New York and London, as much as in Berlin and elsewhere: but they do not do justice to urban life in the latter part of the twentieth century.

Our thesis is therefore that the plan of a dwelling as well as that of an urban settlement should be governed, from the outset, not only by purely technical considerations but by due regard to all aspects of human life. What is important is not so much the dwelling as such, but the facilities offered to the residents to live as freely and individually as possible.

According to an old masons' rule, it is Wisdom, Strength and a Sense of Beauty which must be the godparents of a fine building. At present, this trinity is endangered by a predominance of "Strength" in the mechanical sense.

Critical observations, even if sharply or polemically formulated, might help to support the two other pillars of building construction. My thanks are due to all those who helped me to produce this book – especially Miss Gisela Rahne and Miss Irmgard Mann who were responsible for most of the drawing work.

Berlin, 1st August, 1964   Karl Wilhelm Schmitt

Vorwort

»Das echte Neue Bauen muß noch beginnen«, sagte Gerrit Rietveld im Januar 1964, kurz vor seinem Tod. Die gleiche Einsicht will dieses Buch vermitteln. Der Leser mag einwenden, der Aufwand sei zu groß für ein so niedrig gestecktes Ziel; Rezepte und Details, wie man es machen solle, seien ihm lieber. Doch diese Art von Rezepturen sind in hunderterlei Form im Gebrauch und werden jährlich beim Bau einiger Millionen Wohnungen angewendet, wie es auch manches der hier gezeigten Beispiele erkennen läßt. Das steht nicht im Widerspruch zu der Zielsetzung des Buches, denn eine Bestandsaufnahme muß jedem Schritt in unerforschtes Neuland vorausgehen.

Gewiß, die alten Praktiken nähren ihren Mann in Paris wie in Moskau, in New York oder London ebenso wie in Berlin oder anderswo; dem Leben in den Städtegebilden des ausgehenden zwanzigsten Jahrhunderts werden sie nicht gerecht.

So fordern wir denn, die Arbeit am Wohnungsgrundriß und Stadtplan nicht nur unter rein technischen Gesichtspunkten, sondern unter Einbeziehung aller Bedingungen menschlichen Lebens zu beginnen. Nicht das Haus ist wichtig, die Möglichkeit zur freien Entfaltung seiner Bewohner ist wichtiger.

Eine alte Steinmetzregel besagt, daß nur mit Weisheit, Kraft und Schönheitssinn ein guter Bau entstehen kann. Das Übermaß maschineller »Kraft« droht derzeit dieses Gleichgewicht zu zerstören.

Die manchmal hart oder polemisch formulierte Kritik möge dazu beitragen, die beiden anderen Grundpfeiler des Bauens zu stützen. – Ich danke allen, die mir bei der Arbeit an diesem Buch behilflich waren, insbesondere Fräulein Gisela Rahne und Fräulein Irmgard Mann, die den größten Teil der Zeichenarbeiten übernahmen.

Berlin, am 1. August 1964   Karl Wilhelm Schmitt

Contents

Inhalt

Structural Considerations

As a critic, I would not dare to postulate whether a building with a clearly recognisable structure should be preferred to one where the structural design is completely relegated to the background so as to reveal all the more clearly the meaning and purpose of the building. The choice between these solutions depends on far too many variables – on the environment, for example, or on the early antecedents – to permit statements of general validity. It is an essential ingredient of Man's freedom of choice that this decision should be made afresh on each occasion. Some hundred years or so ago, it was still possible to rely on clearly defined, static criteria. To-day, we are in the midst of a highly fluid development where standpoints are shifting and therefore extremely difficult to locate, observe and define. With a structure that is always deliberately designed with the future in mind, the possibilities of combination – and therefore the potential sources of error – are multiplied if the design is to be based on conceptions that are still fluid. It is not mere coincidence that more and more projects are encountered for dwellings which are placed on floating concrete islands or suspended from skyhooks, and which are clearly not intended to last.

It is not so long ago that courageous revolutionaries among architects accused their contemporaries of hypocrisy, pompousness and snobbery, and proclaimed compliance with the nature of the materials as the one and only truth. Purposefulness – functionalism – was discovered as an objective in its own right, and architecture was freed from the fetters of petrified tradition, from slavish adherence to an obsolete social order.

But yesterday's truth is to-day's falsehood. Just as an insect must go through each stage of transition, architecture too must apparently go through the chrysalis stage of purism. At many places where the old social order has not yet been overcome, the orderly element of purism, which abhors pretentiousness, is still not out of place. It is not the external appearance which can be regarded as the decisive criterion in judging the quality of housing construction; the true criterion is the liberation of the residents from built-in constraints. Their dwelling should not be just a shelter for them; it should enable them to live a full life of their own. This freedom has many names.

In 1928, the German Pavilion at the Barcelona Exhibition, designed by the Berlin architect Ludwig Mies van der Rohe, was hailed as a work of liberation. To-day, Sergius Ruegenberg, once in charge of the construction of this building which has meanwhile been demolished, would decline the invitation to assist in its resurrection – an onyx wall is no longer regarded as an expression of contemporary truth. Even Mies van der Rohe himself would, to-day, regard a new and different design as more appropriate.

A knowledge of structural potentialities is, after all, the basis of the art of building construction. How would an architect-cum-technician fare without technical knowledge? Those interested in housing construction may like to be reminded of certain basic principles which will make it easier for them to find their way about in the necessarily specialised and refined discipline of structural analysis.

Anything that is artificially raised above the ground is under the sway of gravity, and the first and foremost task is to cope with this all-pervading, all-important force with the materials available. Next comes the task of coping with the horizontal forces such as wind forces above ground or seismic forces below ground; did not even the ancient Chinese warn against high building for fear of the vengeful sprites of the air?

In housing construction, the practical possibilities of covering or bridging wide spans are limited. Even if, for once, money should be no object, there are limits to the size of the individual rooms in a dwelling. If a room is too large, it ceases to be intimate and assumes the character of a public building. The horizontal parts of residential buildings can therefore generally be designed as statically uncomplicated slabs or beams and can transmit their loads to posts or walls. In multi-storey housing, vaults, shell structures and similar more complicated structural forms are the exception. The most usual types of structures are those where the load is borne by longitudinal walls, by cross-walls, by stanchions, or by a combination of these elements. All the examples shown here can be reduced to these basic designs.

Key to plans see page 213
Legende zu den Grundrissen siehe Seite 213

1 Type of flat with load-bearing longitudinal walls, with precast concrete panels. Partial plan of undulating block of flats at Pantin near Paris, architect Emile Aillaud
2 Type of flat with load-bearing cross-walls. Maisonettes at Cumbernauld, Scotland, 1 in 500 (see Fig. 8, Block D)
3 Alternation of cross-walls and stanchions. Ground floor plan of a ten-storey block of flats at Nowe Tichy, Poland, 1 in 500

1 Längswandtyp bei einer Bauweise mit vorfabrizierten Betonplatten. Grundrißausschnitt aus dem schlangenförmigen Haus in Pantin bei Paris, Architekt Emile Aillaud
2 Querwandtyp. Maisonettewohnung in Cumbernauld, Schottland, 1:500 (siehe Bild 8, Haus D)
3 Wechsel von Querwänden und Stützen. Erdgeschoßgrundriß eines zehngeschossigen Hochhauses in Nowe Tichy, Polen, 1:500

Konstruktion

Als Kritiker wage ich nicht zu sagen, ob ein Bau mit einer klaren, erkennbar zutage tretenden Konstruktion einem Bau vorzuziehen ist, dessen Konstruktion völlig zurücktritt hinter dem ideellen oder materiellen Zweck, dem er zu dienen hat. Ob die eine oder die andere Lösung vorzuziehen ist, hängt von zu vielen Voraussetzungen ab – von Landschaft und Geschichte, dem Zeitpunkt der Entscheidung usw. –, als daß man Festlegungen treffen könnte, die ein für allemal gültig sind. Es liegt im Wesen menschlicher Entscheidungsfreiheit, daß eben diese Freiheit fordert, die Entscheidung jeweils neu herbeizuführen. Vor etwa hundert Jahren konnte man noch mit in sich ruhenden, »statischen« Werten rechnen, heute stehen wir mitten in einer Entwicklung, die die Ortung, Beobachtung und Festlegung des in Bewegung geratenen »Stand«-Punktes außerordentlich erschwert. Bei einem Bauwerk, das immer in die Zukunft hinein konzipiert ist, vervielfachen sich die Möglichkeiten der Kombination – und der Fehlerquellen –, wenn nach den im Fluß befindlichen Gegebenheiten ein Fundament gesetzt werden soll. Nicht rein zufällig mehren sich die Projekte, auf schwimmenden Betoninseln oder schwebend im Gestänge über der Erde Behausungen zu schaffen, die nicht für alle Ewigkeit gedacht sind.

Es ist noch nicht allzu lange her, daß mutige Architektur-Revolutionäre ihren Zeitgenossen Falschheit, Prunk und Protzentum vorwarfen und daß sie die Materialgerechtigkeit als einzig anzuerkennende Wahrheit auf ihre Fahne schrieben. Die Zweckhaftigkeit, die Funktion, wurde entdeckt und befreite die Architektur von der Last der historisierenden Betrachtungsweise, dem Anhängsel einer erstarrten Gesellschaftsordnung.

Doch die Wahrheit von gestern ist die Lüge von heute. Wie bei einem Insekt jede Verwandlungsstufe notwendig ist, erscheint auch für das Bauen der Purismus als eine notwendige Zwischenstufe. An vielen Orten, die in ihrer Entwicklung die alte Gesellschaftsordnung noch nicht überwunden haben, ist das ordnende, dem falschen Schein abholde Element des Purismus heute noch durchaus zeitgemäß. Entscheidendes Kriterium für die Beurteilung des Wohnungsbaues kann nicht die äußere Form sein. Maßstab ist die Befreiung der Bewohner vom einengenden Zwang. Sie sollen im Wohngehäuse nicht nur vegetieren, sondern leben können. Diese Freiheit hat vielerlei Namen. 1928 war der deutsche Pavillon in Barcelona des Berliner Architekten Ludwig Mies van der Rohe eine befreiende Tat. Heute würde es Sergius Ruegenberg, der Bauleiter dieses inzwischen abgerissenen Bauwerks, ablehnen, bei der Wiederaufrichtung zu helfen; eine Onyx-Mauer entspricht nicht mehr der heutigen Wahrheit. Auch Mies van der Rohe erscheint heute ein anderer, neuer Bau sinnvoller.

Das Wissen um die Möglichkeiten der Konstruktion ist immerhin die Grundlage des Bauens. Wie sollten Arche-Techniker ohne Technik auskommen! Das Zurückgehen auf einige Prinzipien soll dem am Wohnungsbau Interessierten hier nur das Zurechtfinden im notwendigerweise spezialisierten und verfeinerten Geäst der Statik erleichtern.

Alles künstlich vom Boden Abgehobene unterliegt der Erdanziehung und alles Bemühen geht zunächst dahin, den Ausgleich zu dieser wichtigsten und stärksten Kraft mit den gegebenen Materialien zu finden. Horizontale Kraftstöße, oberirdisch zum Beispiel als Windkräfte, unterirdisch als Erdbebenwellen angreifend, stehen an nächster Stelle; warnten doch einst die Chinesen wegen der »rachsüchtigen Luftgeister« vor dem Höherbauen.

Im Wohnungsbau ist nur eine beschränkte Anzahl der technischen Möglichkeiten, große Räume zu überdecken oder zu überbrücken, ausnutzbar. Auch wenn die Kosten einmal keine Rolle spielen, sind der Größe der einzelnen Räume in einer Wohnung Grenzen gesetzt. Ein zu großer Raum verliert seine Intimität, fordert Öffentlichkeit. Der »living-room« im amerikanischen Bungalow wird zum »partyroom«. Die waagrecht gespannten Bauteile im Wohnungsbau können daher meist als statisch unkomplizierte Platten oder Balken konstruiert werden und ihre Last auf Stützen oder Wände abtragen. Gewölbe, Schalen und andere kompliziertere Bauformen sind im Mehrgeschoßbau die Ausnahme. Längswand-, Querwand- und Stützensysteme in reiner und gemischter Form sind die gebräuchlichsten Konstruktionsarten. Alle hier gezeigten Beispiele lassen sich darauf zurückführen.

9

4 Slab-shaped tower block with stanchion type structure in the Cerro Grande District of Caracas, Venezuela
5 Project for "suspended" blocks of flats, architect Heinz Rasch, 1930 (cf. Fig. 22)
6 Cross-wall principle applied to pre-fabricated flats in Hamburg (cf. pages 78 f.)

4 Scheibenförmiges Hochhaus mit Stützenkonstruktion im Quartier Cerro Grande, Caracas, Venezuela
5 Hängehausprojekt aus dem Jahr 1930, Architekt Heinz Rasch (siehe Bild 22)
6 Querwandprinzip bei Montagehäusern in Hamburg (siehe Seite 78 f.)

Load-bearing Longitudinal Walls

Before the age of industrialisation and concrete construction, the layout of a dwelling used to be governed by the normal span of the timber beam, 15 ft. or so. The outer walls, solid anyhow, were load-bearing, and the depth of the house was increased to 33 ft. or so by placing another longitudinal wall in the centre. If the identical depth of the rooms on either side of the house was a disadvantage, this was matched by the advantage that the party walls could be placed at will, a feature particularly valuable in large dwellings with long street frontages.

Due to inertia, the introduction of a new building material is not immediately followed by adapting the design to the new structural possibilities. Although wood joist floors are now rarely used in multi-storey buildings, the system of load-bearing longitudinal walls is but slowly giving way to other structural systems. With slab construction methods, which can be regarded as imitation-masonry with larger bricks, the small window openings typical for load-bearing outer walls are re-appearing, as the prefabricated floor slabs are frequently supported by all the four walls of the room (Fig. 1).

Load-bearing Cross-Walls

Maritime countries, borrowing their terms from ship-building, talk of bulkhead construction methods. With the advent of concrete floor slabs, the earlier difficulties with terrace houses due to the timber joist recesses in the crosswalls were overcome and this led, after the Second World War, to a more widespread adoption of this structural principle. For the architect, it is not easy to reconcile the demands on a dwelling with a rigid layout plan. The difficulties were particularly great during the early period of low-rent housing construction, when the attempt was made to accommodate each of the small dwelling units, with kitchen and bathroom on the outside, within a single cross-wall compartment of about 20 ft. span, using a minimum of building materials. It was therefore necessary to adopt make-shift solutions for the bedroom, in the form of bed-sitting rooms, or beds built into sleeping bunks at their head or foot (cf. Fig. 25, page 32; Spandauer Damm, scale 1 in 200). Floors made of prefabricated components, slabs or beams, available on the market in hundreds of varieties, were found to be too expensive for smaller spans, compared with in-situ cast concrete floors. It was only when it became possible to build dwelling units of a somewhat larger size that a more flexible layout could be adopted. The flexibility of the layout based on a cross-wall system is demonstrated by a group of flats designed by London architects for Cumbernauld New Town, Scotland (Fig. 2, 9–11). A typical feature is the continuous ribbon of windows, extending from wall to wall (Fig. 12). Even with a low window lintel, the relatively low rooms therefore still receive sufficient daylight in depth. A difficulty arises at the connections between window front and cross-walls where heat transfer is apt to occur. A possible means of insulating these wall heads is indicated by Senn at the Hechtliacker tower blocks, Basle, (cf. detail drawing 1 in 10 page 156). Projecting parts of the crosswalls are exposed to the risks of thermal stresses within the wall. They should therefore remain within the insulated part of the flat. Experience with light-weight concrete claddings for the protection of exposed wall or floor parts has not been encouraging. Even when filled with putty, the joints were not adequately sealed.

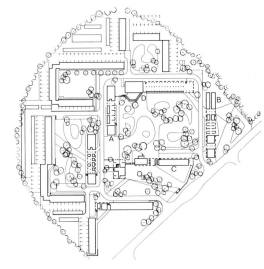

 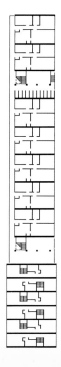

7 Kildrum, Cumbernauld, Block D with access galleries on the north side
8 Kildrum, Cumbernauld, layout plan, 1 in 5000, Architects Gillespie, Kidd & Coia
9 Block B, plans, 1 in 1000

7 Cumbernauld-Kildrum, Haus D mit den Laubengängen an der Nordseite
8 Lageplan, 1:5000, Cumbernauld-Kildrum, Architekten Gillespie, Kidd & Coia
9 Haus B, Grundrisse, 1:1000

4th, 3rd floor
Ground floor

4., 3. Obergeschoß
und Erdgeschoß

Tragende Längswände

Bis zur Industrialisierung und Verbreitung der Betonkonstruktionen bestimmte die mit Holzbalken in normalen Dimensionen zu überbrückende Distanz von etwa 4,5 m die Wohnungsgrundrisse. Die ohnehin schweren Außenwände wurden als Tragwände herangezogen und mit einer Mittelwand die Haustiefe auf etwa 10 m Außenmaß vergrößert. Dem Nachteil der gleichmäßigen Raumtiefe an beiden Hausseiten steht eine Freizügigkeit in der Anordnung der Querwände gegenüber, die bei großen Wohnungen mit breiten Straßenfronten wertvoll ist.

Die Gewohnheit bringt es mit sich, daß ein Wechsel in den Baumaterialien nicht sogleich zu einer Anpassung an neue konstruktive Möglichkeiten führt. Holzbalkendecken werden nur in seltenen Fällen noch im Mehrgeschoßbau verwendet; das Längswandsystem weicht dagegen erst langsam anderen Konstruktionsprinzipien. Bei Plattenbauweisen, die als Mauerwerknachahmungen mit vergrößerten »Steinen« aufzufassen sind, tauchen die für tragende Außenwände typischen Fensterlöcher wieder auf, denn die vorfabrizierten Deckenplatten werden häufig von allen vier Raumwänden getragen (Bild 1).

Tragende Querwände

In Küstenländern wird in Anlehnung an den Schiffsbau von der Schottenbauweise gesprochen. Die Schwierigkeiten, die beim alten Reihenhausbau durch das Hineingreifen der Holzbalken in die Brandmauern entstanden, fielen mit dem Aufkommen der Betondecken fort und förderten nach dem zweiten Weltkrieg die Verbreitung dieses Konstruktionsprinzips. Für den Architekten ist es nicht leicht, die Starrheit der Grundrisse mit den Wohnforderungen in Einklang zu bringen. Besonders in der ersten Zeit des Kleinwohnungsbaues hatte der Versuch, mit geringstem Materialaufwand bei 6,0 bis 6,5 m Deckenspannweite die kleinen Wohneinheiten mit außenliegenden Küchen und Bädern jeweils in einem Querwandabschnitt unterzubringen, zur Folge, daß für den Schlafraum nach Ersatzlösungen gesucht werden mußte: Wohnschlafräume oder am Kopf- und Fußende in Schlafkojen eingebaute Betten (Seite 32, Bild 25). Die in hundertfachen Variationen angebotenen Decken aus Fertigteilen, -platten oder -balken erwiesen sich bei geringeren Spannweiten als zu teuer gegenüber der Ortbetondecke. Erst die Möglichkeit, die Wohnungen etwas größer zu bauen, brachte eine Auflockerung der Grundrisse mit sich. An einer von Londoner Architekten geplanten Wohnhausgruppe in der neuen schottischen Stadt Cumbernauld läßt sich demonstrieren, wie wandlungsfähig die Auslegung des Querwandsystems ist (Bild 2, 9–11). Typisch sind die von Wand zu Wand durchlaufenden Fensterbänder (Bild 12). Bei einem niedrigen Fenstersturz erhalten so die relativ niedrigen Räume in der Tiefe noch genügend Tageslicht. Schwierig ist der Anschluß der Fensterwände an die Köpfe der Querwände, da leicht Wärmebrücken entstehen. Die mögliche Isolierung dieser Wandköpfe zeigt Senn bei den Hechtliacker-Hochhäusern (Detail 1:10 auf Seite 156). Nach außen herausragende Querwandteile sind gefährdet infolge der Temperaturspannungen innerhalb des Mauerwerks. Sie sollen deshalb in den gegen Wärmeverluste geschützten Bereich des Hauses einbezogen werden. Brüstungsplatten aus Leichtbeton, die vor die Wand- und Deckenteile gehängt wurden, bewährten sich nicht. Auch mit Kittfüllung blieben die Fugen nicht ausreichend dicht.

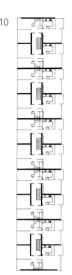
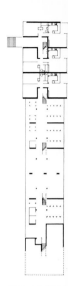

10

1st, 2nd, 3rd floor
1., 2., 3. Obergeschoß

Ground floor
Erdgeschoß

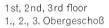
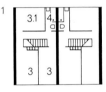

11

2nd, 4th floor
2., 4. Obergeschoß

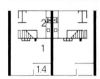

Ground floor
Erdgeschoß

1st, 3rd floor
1., 3. Obergeschoß

10 Block A, plans, 1 in 1000
11 Block C, plans, 1 in 500
12 South front of Block D (see plans, Fig. 2)

10 Haus A, Grundrisse, 1:1000
11 Haus C, Grundrisse, 1:500
12 Südseite Haus D (siehe Grundrisse Bild 2)

Stanchion Systems

The highest degree of freedom in design and of flexibility in layout is offered by the stanchion systems. Rarely has this freedom been used as consistently as in Friberger's Gothenburg experiment where Germany's latest prefabrication rationales were anticipated by thirty years. The flexibility aimed at by Gottwald in his block of flats at the Hansa District, Berlin, and by William Ohlsson in another experimental building at Gothenburg, is here already present. The removable "dwelling unit" can be completely remodelled without changing the stanchion or floor structure. With the exception of the installation points, any of the units within the building site can be reduced or enlarged in size (Figs. 15–18). At the same time, the separation of the structural from the heat insulating floor offers a maximum of sound protection. The indifferent quality of some of the layouts is immaterial; a first, courageous pioneering effort cannot be expected to reach an optimum. With this housing unit, a way was shown to a future sphere of building construction which lies beyond the conventional practice of adopting external designs laid down once and for all. In conjunction with economic construction methods such as the "lift-slab" system which has meanwhile proved its worth many times over, such stanchion system may well join the ranks of the economically favourable building systems.

With stanchion type flats of more conventional design, it is often only a variation in the outer walls which provides a slight indication of the freedom permitted by the system (Latis's building in Milan, Figs. 13/14). In the case of small dwelling units, the benefits obtainable from this mode of construction are limited by the solid party walls between dwellings. But the flexibility of the layout can already be enhanced by an alternation of load-bearing walls and rows of stanchions (standard house at Nowe Tichy, Fig. 3).

Suspended Structures

Heinz Rasch who had pleaded the case for suspended structures since the nineteen-thirties, never lived to see the results of his painstaking pioneering efforts (Fig. 22). It was only the generation after him which was able to take advantage of his work. It may be symptomatic that the first suspended housing structure was built in open-minded South America (Figs. 19–21). As far as the Continent of Europe is concerned, our experience is at present still confined to the experiment, suspiciously watched by the fire protection authorities, with the town hall turrets at Marl which does not yet permit of any conclusions regarding practical value, costs, etc.

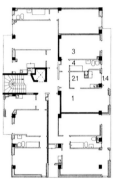

2nd, 4th, 5th, 7th floor   1st, 3rd, 6th floor
2., 4., 5., 7. Obergeschoß   1., 3., 6. Obergeschoß

13 Building in Viale Liguria, Milan, Architect Vito Latis
14 Plans, 1 in 500. The stanchion system permits variations in the plans

13 Haus in Mailand, Viale Liguria. Architekt Vito Latis
14 Grundrisse, 1:500. Das Stützensystem ermöglicht die Variationen in den Grundrissen

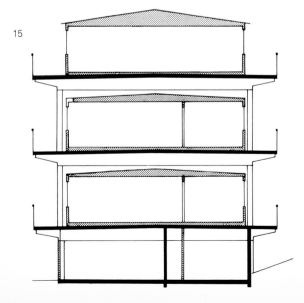

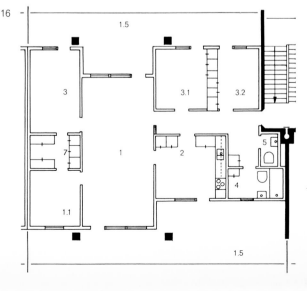

Stützensysteme

Die größte Freiheit im Aufbau und in der Veränderung des Grundrisses bieten Stützensysteme. Selten ist diese Freiheit so konsequent genutzt wie im Göteborger Experiment von Friberger, der die hierzulande gegenwärtig angestellten Vorfertigungsüberlegungen bereits vor dreißig Jahren vorweggenommen hat. Die sogenannte Flexibilität, die Gottwald im Hansaviertel-Wohnhaus und William-Olsson in einem anderen Göteborger Experimenthaus zu erreichen suchten, ist hier vorhanden: das demontable »Einfamilienhaus« kann ohne Veränderung der Decken- und Stützenkonstruktion völlig erneuert werden; innerhalb des »Bauplatzes« sind mit Ausnahme des Installations-Anschlußpunktes Verkleinerungen und Vergrößerungen möglich (Bild 15–18). Die Trennung der konstruktiven und der wärmedämmenden Decke bietet ein Höchstmaß an Schallschutz. Die unterschiedliche Qualität der einzelnen Grundrisse ist unerheblich; bei einem ersten wagemutigen Experiment kann die Bestform noch nicht erreicht werden. Mit diesem »Haus« ist die Tür aufgestoßen zu einem zukünftigen Bereich des Bauens, der jenseits der einmalig festgelegten äußeren Erscheinungsformen liegt. In Verbindung mit kostensparenden Herstellungsverfahren, zum Beispiel dem inzwischen häufiger erprobten Lift-slab-System, rücken derartige Stützensysteme vermutlich in den Bereich der wirtschaftlich günstigen Bauweisen.

Übliche Stützenhäuser lassen oft nur im Wechsel der Außenwände ein wenig von der im System liegenden Freiheit spüren (Latis' Haus in Mailand, Bild 13/14). Bei kleinen Wohnungstypen schränken die massiven Wohnungstrennwände die Ausnutzung der Vorteile sehr ein. Ein Wechsel von tragenden Wänden und Stützenachsen kann wenigstens eine Auflockerung der Grundrißanordnung bewirken (Typenhaus in Nowe Tichy, Bild 3).

Hängekonstruktionen

Heinz Rasch, der seit den dreißiger Jahren für Hängehäuser geworben hat, ist nie in den Genuß seiner mühevollen Terrainsondierungen gekommen (Bild 22). Erst die nachfolgende Generation konnte aus seinen Überlegungen Nutzen ziehen. Es ist symptomatisch, daß im unvoreingenommenen Südamerika das erste Wohnhaus mit einer Hängekonstruktion gebaut werden konnte (Bild 19–21). Auf dem europäischen Kontinent sind wir vorläufig auf das von Feuerpolizisten argwöhnisch beobachtete Experiment bei den verschiedenen Bürohochhäusern angewiesen, das bis jetzt noch keine Schlüsse über Brauchbarkeit, Kosten usw. zuläßt.

15/16 Section and various plans of the Gothenburg block, 1 in 200
17/18 Block ot flats at Kallebäck, Gothenburg, Sweden. Architect Erik Friberger

15/16 Schnitt und verschiedene Grundrisse des Göteborger Hauses, 1:200
17/18 Haus in Göteborg-Kallebäck, Schweden. Architekt Erik Friberger

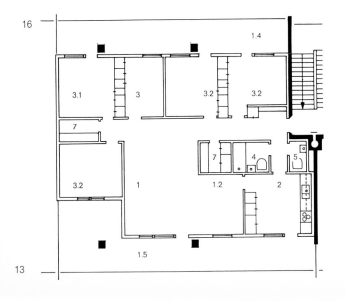

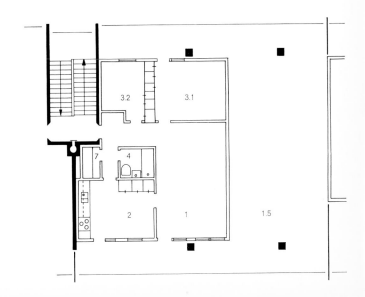

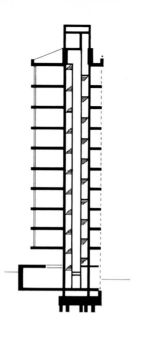

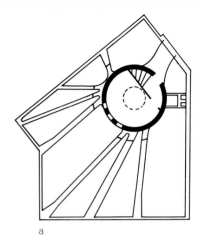

a

19 Unfinished structure of "suspended" building in Montevideo. Architect Luis Garcia Pardo
20 Section, 1 in 500
21 a Roof plan, b Floor plan, c Ground floor plan, 1 in 200
22 Structural design for "suspended" block of flats in steel construction, 1930, architect Heinz Rasch (cf. Fig. 5)

19 Der Rohbau des Hängehauses in Montevideo, Architekt Luis Garcia Pardo
20 Schnitt, 1:500
21 a Dachaufsicht, b Geschoßgrundriß, c Erdgeschoßgrundriß, 1:200
22 Konstruktionsschema eines Hängehauses in Stahlkonstruktion, 1930, Architekt Heinz Rasch (siehe Bild 5)

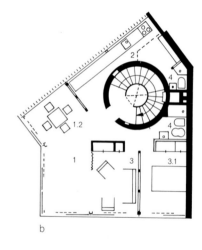

b

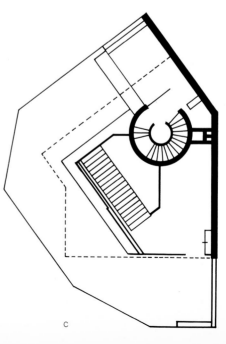

c

23 Tower block at Nytorp, Malmö. The architects, Fritz Jaenecke and Sten Samuelson, have rationalised the construction work by using pre-fabricated formwork. In doing so, they make use of the old rule that different products can be produced economically by using standardised tools. The provision of access galleries and terraces on both sides permits the use of lightweight panels for the outer walls, partly with fixed glazing which can be easily cleaned from outside. The galleries also serve as emergency exits
24 Pre-fabrication of concrete units at the factory enables a number of building operatives to work in weather-protected, permanently installed premises with better amenities. Pre-fabrication is no new invention. Any half-timbered house pre-assembled at the carpenter's shop is pre-fabricated, every brick is a handy prefabricated unit. Meanwhile, the hoisting function has been transferred from the hand to the crane. Columns, wall panels or floor slabs extending over one or two storeys and over the whole width of the room therefore represent the bricks of our time

23 Wohnhochhaus in Malmö-Nytorp. Die Architekten Fritz Jaenecke und Sten Samuelson erreichen eine Rationalisierung der Bauarbeiten durch Verwendung vorgefertigter Schalungsteile. Sie knüpfen an alte Erfahrungen an: Mit einheitlichen Werkzeugen können verschiedenartige Erzeugnisse rationell hergestellt werden. Die Anordnung von Laubengängen und Terrassen auf beiden Längsseiten ermöglicht den Einbau leichter Fassadenteile, deren zum Teil fest verglaste Flächen von außen ohne Schwierigkeiten zu reinigen sind. Zugleich ergeben sich Fluchtwege im Falle eines Brandes
24 Vorfertigung von Betonelementen in der Fabrik sichert einem Teil der Bauarbeiter einen wettergeschützten, ortsfesten Arbeitsplatz mit höheren sozialen Leistungen. Vorfertigung ist keine neue Erfindung. Jedes auf dem Zimmerplatz abgebundene Fachwerkhaus ist »vorgefertigt«, jeder Ziegelstein ist ein »handlicher« vorfabrizierter Bauteil. Inzwischen hat der Kran die Hand abgelöst. Stützen, Wand- oder Deckenplatten in einfacher oder doppelter Stockwerkshöhe und Zimmerbreite sind demgemäß die heutigen »Ziegelsteine«

25 The endeavour to obtain, with heavy pre-fabricated concrete units, the same degree of precision as with steelwork is opposed by a young Paris architect. He protests against the nondescript smoothness of the concrete elevations and attempts to enliven their surface texture by inserting pieces of natural stone. A $^3/_4''$ tolerance margin ensures that the precast panels can be fitted in (cf. Figs. 36–40)

25 Der Tendenz, mit der Vorfabrikation schwerer Betonteile eine dem Metallbau ähnliche Maßgenauigkeit zu erzielen, stellt sich ein junger Architekt in Paris entgegen. Er protestiert gegen die nichtssagende Glätte der Betonfassaden und versucht durch Einarbeiten von Natursteinbrocken die Textur der Oberflächen zu beleben. Ein Spielraum von etwa 2 cm soll die Toleranzen der trocken montierten Teile auffangen (siehe Bild 36–40)

Prefabrication

The subjects of the 'prefabricated house' and 'prefabrication' have received such a wealth of publicity that we must first look for the rather modest substance behind it.

Size and weight of the building components depend on the handling capacity of the hoisting gear, used for the erection. The traditional brick is gradually being replaced by components weighing several tons, handled by a crane. This development would appear to be so obvious that it must not be mistaken for a general industrialisation of building construction which, except for a few hardly noticed trials, has not yet come to pass. The designs of these mechanically handled wall components continue to be the subject of further experiments. It may be typical of the inertia of human thought that the British, to whom multi-storey housing came later, were at once able to obtain useful results with prefabricated units which, on the Continent, were not at first successful (Figs. 26–30). In the German Federal Republic, the subject did not begin to attract general interest until the shortage of labour made it difficult to adhere to the fashionable insistence on individualistic design. The reaction to the previous prejudice against multi-family housing and, especially, multi-storey housing gave rise to a sudden impulse for importing French and Danish ideas. In France, private research work carried out during the post-war inflation period permitted the adoption of a large-scale housing programme at the time when the New Franc was established. But, in France as well as in Germany, this development was not matched by equally progressive town planning although there was, at least, no discontinuity in technical progress. This gave rise to vast experimental building sites, designed to demonstrate prefabrication systems of the highest possible precision and dexterity. The method used by Bossard for his housing scheme at Créteil near Paris may be regarded as a protest against such mathematically exact sobriety: – By inserting an irregular sequence of boulders into the roughly levelled moulds, the colour, texture and plastic effect of the elevations have been enlivened (Figs. 25, 36–40). He thus deliberately created those irregular traits which, with the more primitive methods used in Eastern Europe, appear spontaneously as a result of technical shortcomings without however offering the residents the same degree of individual freedom as in France. A compromise between exaggerated mechanical perfection and complete disregard of any rules has been adopted by Erskine at Vaxjö, Sweden. Here, the external walls have a ribbed natural concrete surface, and the building corners are rounded off. With this slight rounding, the building becomes an integrated body, and the flat and featureless prefabricated slab acquires a third dimension. The balconies of these flats, shown in detail on page 60, are exemplary for a prefabrication method, logically derived from functional considerations. The architect's skill becomes apparent if the close-up is compared with the overall picture. If the latter shows integral buildings of given proportions, the detail reveals the clear distinctions between adjacent wall slabs. This is reminiscent of the artistic effect of old brick buildings. The architect's art does not manifest itself in the invention of sensational or fashionable designs but in the application of contemporary production methods.

Heavy building materials must be conveyed to the site – whether as raw materials or finished products is immaterial to the transport requirements. In view of the considerable breakage losses incurred with heavy and bulky components, a standardisation of tools is often more economic than the production of the components in a workshop which requires expensive equipment (Figs. 23, 41–51). In this way, it may even be possible to obtain a wider range of variation in the finished product, i.e. the dwelling.

The purpose of prefabrication should not be seen in the removal of conventional manual work to a factory hall. The proper way is shown by the industrially produced domestic appliances which go into the building (cookers, refrigerators, sinks, electric switches, and the like). It is only after the advent, on the market, of mechanically produced building components which can be used and combined at will, that one will be able to talk of the industrialisation of the building industry. A necessary pre-requisite is a coordination of measures, a modular system similar to that used for the C.L.A.S.P. schools in Britain.

26–30 One of the first examples of modern town planning and construction methods was the Alton Estate (West), Roehampton, planned by the London County Council. The reinforced concrete structure, still exposed at ground floor level, is faced with factory-made precast concrete cladding on the upper floors

26–30 Eines der ersten Beispiele neuzeitlicher Stadtplanungs- und Baumethoden war das vom London County Council geplante Stadtviertel Alton Estate West in Roehampton. Das im Erdgeschoß noch sichtbare Stahlbetonskelett wurde mit vorgefertigten Beton-Wandelementen verkleidet

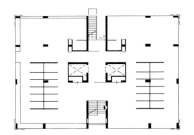

27 Ground floor and standard floor plan of a tower block, 1 in 500

27 Erdgeschoß- und Normalgeschoßgrundriß eines Hochhauses, 1:500

Vorfertigung

Um die Begriffe Fertighaus und Vorfertigung ist ein solcher Wirbel entfacht worden, daß zunächst einmal nach dem kleinen und bescheidenen Kern gesucht werden muß.

Größe und Gewicht der Bauteile sind von der Tragkraft der Hebewerkzeuge abhängig, die beim Bau Verwendung finden. Der Ziegelstein wird allmählich abgelöst von mehreren Tonnen schweren Teilen, die ein Kran versetzt. Dieser Vorgang erscheint so selbstverständlich, daß man ihn mit einer Industrialisierung des Bauens, die bisher mit Ausnahme weniger kaum beachteter Versuche ausgeblieben ist, nicht vergleichen darf. Wie nun diese von Maschinenkraft bewegten Wandteile auszusehen haben, das wird unentwegt neu erprobt. Bezeichnend für die Trägheit menschlicher Anschauungen ist, daß die Engländer sozusagen im ersten Anlauf auf dem Gebiet des bei ihnen nicht üblichen Mehrgeschoßbaus mit vorgefertigten Elementen zu brauchbaren Ergebnissen kamen, während diese auf dem Kontinent erst später erzielt werden konnten (Bild 26–30). In der Bundesrepublik Deutschland begann das Interesse sich erst allgemein zu regen, als die Arbeitskräfte für die vorher geförderte Eigenbrötelei fehlten; man fühlte sich dann um so schneller verpflichtet, in einer Augenblickswallung französische und dänische Ideenimporte hereinzulassen, als man vorher den Mehrfamilienhaus- oder gar Hochhausbau als wenig wünschenswert angesehen hatte. Die in Frankreich während der Nachkriegsinflation vorangetriebenen privaten Forschungen ermöglichten mit dem Erscheinen des Neuen Franc die Aufnahme eines großzügigen Wohnungsbauprogramms. Die städtebauliche Gesamtplanung versagte dort ebenso wie bei uns; der Prozeß technischen Fortschritts wurde aber wenigstens nicht unterbrochen. Es entstanden große Experimentierfelder mit Vorfertigungsverfahren, die ein möglichst genaues, glattes Fabrikationsergebnis zur Schau stellen wollten. Als Protest gegen diese exakte Nüchternheit ist das Verfahren aufzufassen, das Bossard bei seinen Bauten in Créteil bei Paris anwendete: In die grob geglätteten Formen wurden Felsbrocken in unregelmäßiger Folge eingelegt, um die Fassaden in Farbe, Textur und Plastik des Baukörpers zu beleben (Bild 25, 36–40). Er erreichte damit jene Unregelmäßigkeiten, die bei den primitiveren Verfahren in Osteuropa sich durch die Mängel in der Herstellung von selbst ergeben – ohne dort allerdings den gleichen Grad individueller Freiheit für die Bewohner wie in Frankreich zu bieten. Ein Mittelweg zwischen übermäßiger Maschinenvollkommenheit und regelloser Willkür ist die in Vaxjö von Erskine angewendete Methode. Die Oberfläche der Außenwandplatten und die Gebäudeecken sind gebrochen. Durch die geringfügige Rundung an den Eckplatten wird das Haus zum geschlossenen Körper; die vorgefertigte Platte verliert ihre pappartige Modellwirkung. Die Balkone an diesen Häusern, auf Seite 60 im Detail gezeigt, sind beispielhaft für eine mit allen Konsequenzen für die Baugestalt neu konzipierte Vorfertigungsmethode. Die Kunst des Architekten wird beim Vergleich der Nahaufnahme mit dem Gesamtbild offenbar. Zeigt das Situationsfoto in sich abgeschlossene, in ihren Proportionen festgelegte Bauten, so läßt das Detailfoto erkennen, wie die einzelnen Wandplatten deutlich vom Nachbarelement unterschieden sind. Damit wird an die künstlerische Wirkung alter Backsteinbauten angeknüpft. Die Kunst des Architekten manifestiert sich nicht in der Erfindung sensationeller und modischer Formen, sondern in der Anwendung zeitgemäßer Herstellungsmethoden.

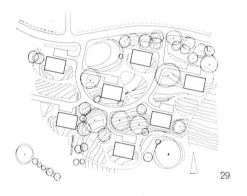

Schwere Baustoffe müssen an den Bau transportiert werden; ob als Rohmaterial oder Endprodukt ist für die Transportleistung gleichgültig. Erhebliche Bruchverluste bei schweren und großen Teilen machen eine Standardisierung der Werkzeuge oft wirtschaftlicher als die Herstellung in einem mit hohen Investitionskosten belasteten Werk (Bild 23, 41–51). Unter Umständen läßt sich so für das Endprodukt, die Wohnung, sogar eine größere Variationsbreite erzielen. Der Sinn der Vorfertigung liegt nicht im Vorverlegen der üblichen Handarbeit in eine Fabrikhalle. Das zur Ergänzung des Bauwerks gelieferte, industriell hergestellte Gerät weist den richtigen Weg (Herde, Kühlschränke, Spültische, elektrische Schalter und ähnliches). Erst wenn von Maschinen hergestellte, vielerorts verwendbare und kombinierbare Bauteile auf den Markt kommen, wird man von Industrialisierung sprechen können. Notwendige Voraussetzung dafür ist eine Maß-Koordination, ein Modulsystem ähnlich dem in England bei den C.L.A.S.P.-Schulen verwendeten.

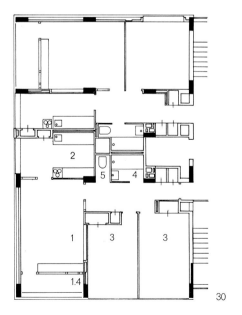

29 Site plan of multi-storey blocks, 1 in 5000
30 Enlarged part of floor plan, 1 in 200

29 Lageplan der Hochhausgruppe, 1:5000
30 Grundrißausschnitt, 1:200

31, 34/35 Views of the tower blocks of flats at Vaxjö, Sweden, architect Ralph Erskine. The external walls are of sandwich construction, with glass wool insulation between two precast concrete slabs. The earth mounds protect the footpaths against wind and snow drifts. For details of the balcony, cf. page 60

32 Top floor, standard floor and ground floor of one of the tower blocks at Vaxjö, 1 in 500. The plan module is 4 × 5 metres (13'1" × 16'5")

33 Site plan, 1 in 5000, G Garages

31, 34/35 Ansichten der Hochhäuser in Vaxjö, Schweden, Architekt Ralph Erskine. Außenwände in Sandwichkonstruktion: zwischen zwei vorfabrizierten Betonplatten eine Glaswollschicht. Die Erdhügel schützen die Fußwege gegen Wind und Schneeverwehungen. Balkondetail siehe Seite 60

32 Oberstes Geschoß, Normalgeschoß und Erdgeschoß in einem der Hochhäuser in Vaxjö, 1:500. Rastermaß der Grundrisse 4 × 5 m

33 Lageplan, 1:5000, G Garagen

  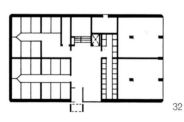

32

33

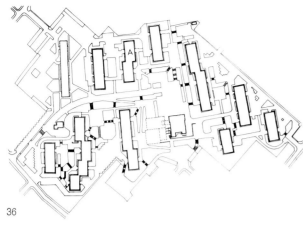

36

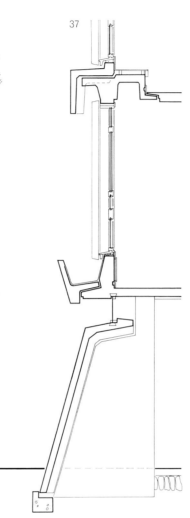

37

38

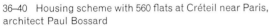

36–40 Housing scheme with 560 flats at Créteil near Paris, architect Paul Bossard
36 Site plan, 1 in 5000
37 Section of outer wall. The load-bearing concrete walls, the edge beams of the floors and the roof slabs are cast in-situ. The cranked facade units are produced in a movable factory shed on the site
38 Block A, entrance floor plan, standard floor plan and section, 1 in 500. All the flats are connected to a central air conditioning plant
39 Two types of flats, plans, 1 in 200

36–40 Siedlung mit 560 Wohnungen in Créteil bei Paris, Architekt Paul Bossard
36 Lageplan, 1:5000
37 Detailschnitt durch die Fassade. Die tragenden Wände, die Deckenrandstreifen und die Dachplatten sind an Ort betoniert. Die in einer Feldfabrik hergestellten Fassadenteile sind mit Verkröpfungen trocken montiert
38 Haus A, Eingangsgeschoß- und Normalgeschoßgrundriß sowie Schnitt, 1:500. Alle Wohnungen sind an eine zentrale Klimaanlage angeschlossen
39 Zwei Wohnungstypen, Grundrisse, 1:200

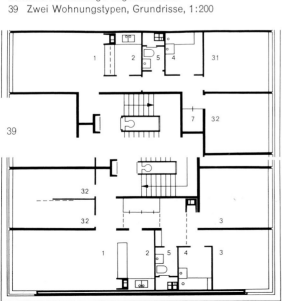

39

19

41

42

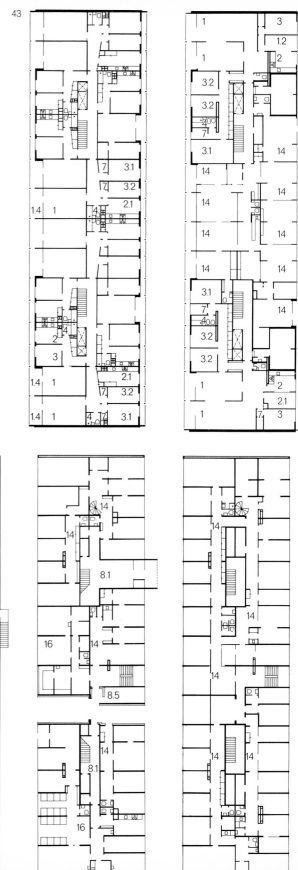
43

44

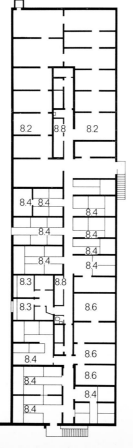

41–51 Tower block of flats in the Nytorp district of Lorensborg, Malmö, architects Fritz Jaenecke and Sten Samuelson, using the "Allbetong" construction method of Skanska Cementgjuteriet
41 View from the tower block towards east
42 The housing units are concentrated at the edge of a large open space. On the left, the tower block; in front of it the shopping centre
43 Standard floor and top floor, 1 in 500
44 Plans, 1 in 500. From left to right: Basement, ground floor, and first floor with offices
45 Erection of the wall shutters by crane
46 The wall shutters, which are provided with a working platform, are placed in position
47 The plywood shutters are coated with boat varnish and are cleaned and oiled before each casting operation
48 The electrical installation is mounted on the formwork before the concrete is cast
49 The floor shuttering, mounted on the formwork trolley which can be adjusted with great precision, has been placed by the crane. On being dismantled, the shuttering is lowered, fastened to the crane and moved out on the two rollers to be lifted to the next floor
50 The ridges between the slab joints are machine-finished. A batten nailed to the floor shuttering leaves a recess at the wall joint. Afterwards, walls and ceilings are merely trowelled and either painted or papered
51 The drainpipes for kitchens and bathrooms are placed on the floor shuttering and embedded in the concrete

41–51 Hochhaus im Quartier Nytorp in Malmö-Lorensborg, Architekten Fritz Jaenecke und Sten Samuelson. Baumethode Allbetong der Skånska Cementgjuteriet
41 Blick aus dem Hochhaus nach Osten
42 Starke Verdichtung der Wohnbebauung am Rande großer Grün- und Freiflächen. Links das Hochhaus mit dem vorgelagerten Einkaufszentrum
43 Normalgeschoß und oberstes Geschoß, 1:500
44 Grundrisse, 1:500. Von links nach rechts: Keller-, Erd- und erstes Obergeschoß mit Büroräumen
45 Kranmontage der Wandschalungsplatten
46 Die mit einer Arbeitsbühne versehenen Schalungsplatten werden eingesetzt
47 Die Sperrholz-Schalungsplatten sind mit Bootslack gestrichen und werden vor jedem Betonguß gereinigt und geölt
48 Die Elektroinstallation wird vor dem Betonieren auf der Schalung befestigt
49 Die Deckenschalung ist zusammen mit dem genau justierbaren Schalungswagen vom Kran eingefahren worden. Sie wird beim Ausschalen heruntergelassen, am Kran befestigt und auf den beiden Rollen hinausgeschoben, um ins nächste Geschoß befördert zu werden
50 Die Grate zwischen den Plattenstößen werden maschinell abgeschliffen. Eine auf der Deckenschalung angebrachte Leiste hinterläßt eine Nut am Wandanschluß. Wände und Decken werden nur noch gespachtelt und bemalt oder tapeziert
51 Die Abwasserleitungen für Küchen und Bäder werden auf die Deckenschalung gesetzt und einbetoniert

45
46

47
48

49
50

51

Environmental Considerations

Biological Necessities

Many people would like us to believe that building is a technical matter, and that a technically refined production method will automatically produce the best possible result, the good building. Their vision is limited: they do not see the roots from which the building idea springs. True, technical perfection must be a feature of a good building: but technical perfection alone is not enough and may even, if it has become a purpose in itself, lead to an absurd notion, a technical monstrosity. The building standard must be in keeping with the forces which govern all human activities; these forces may be of a sociological, political or economic kind – contrasting examples come to mind, such as the opera house in which Caruso used to sing, or the legendary city of the Brasilian rubber planters, now perished, or the inhabitants of Matera in Southern Italy who prefer to return to their old rock caves; alternatively, these forces may be of a biological or bioclimatic kind.

The assessment of these forces varies greatly. Where they have been ignored, it has generally become evident how important they are to the building and to the life which it contains. Political and sociological aspects leave unmistakable traces in housing construction. In Europe, the late feudal period coincided with the beginning of the machine age. The scant regard in which the "lower classes" were held enabled the authorities to plan and build those sinister quarters around the old cities for the rapidly growing multitudes of industrial workers (Figs. 1/2). To-day, about a hundred years later, the same process is repeated in a number of South-American countries where an uneducated population is leaving the country and flocking to the towns.

Even the application of patriarchal methods to urban conditions, particularly marked in the industrial area to the north of the Ruhr, could not provide a remedy. A town is not a manorial estate. It was as long ago as 1888 or so that Robert Koch, from his knowledge of the medical aspects of housing reminiscent of casemates, demanded "light and air for every dwelling".

It was only the politically conditioned change in sociological conditions after the First World War, from 1920 onwards, which induced the European architects, from Paris to Warsaw, to build dwellings for the broad masses, in keeping with Koch's hygienic and biological demands. Right into the nineteen-thirties, the dwelling for people in the lowest income groups was the main theme of their efforts. Sunlight in living rooms and bedrooms, suitable and hygienic equipment of kitchens and bathrooms were among the new basic demands (Figs. 4, 5, 7, 8).

The thesis that all men are equal found its expression in terrace house construction. The desire to re-admit the garden to the town from which it had been completely banished was apparent in all planning projects. 130 years after the proclamation of Equality, Central Europe began to subject this Equality to scientific research. It was calculated how much air space a human being required during his sleep, or how much water vapour was released by the body every day; the needs for ultra-violet radiation and vitamins were determined, and the work of a housewife without domestic assistance was analysed to design labour-saving equipment for the kitchen (Figs. 4/5). The notion of the minimum subsistence level was quantified. Since "living", and therefore the "living room", was regarded as paramount, all other rooms were reduced to a minimum, as in Rading's tower block layouts in Breslau (Fig. 3). This rationale recurred after the Second World War, and will recur whenever a great housing demand coincides with a period of economic weakness.

In normal times, however, it would be wrong to regard the minimum level as a target standard since any standard of permanent validity must be based on the median level of demand. It is only in times of economic weakness that one is apt to overlook the scatter range of demand on either side of the median where the demand, though less frequent, is still essential to the person concerned. A standard bed of 6 ft. length is simply too short for a person of 6′2″ height, even if it is adequate for 99.9 per cent. of all sleepers.

As long as a great part of the population must live in dwellings which are below the minimum standard, it is understandable that all efforts are, first of all, concen-

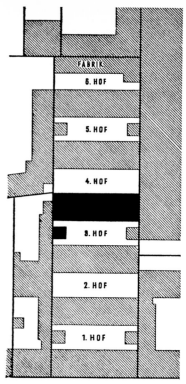

ACKERSTRASSE 132-133

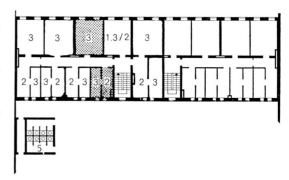

1 Excessive exploitation of the building site, still permitted by the Berlin bye-laws at the end of the 19th century: Six backyards with five- or six-storey tenement houses
2 Upper floor plan of the third backyard block at 132 Ackerstrasse, Berlin, with the lavatories in the courtyard. By placing kitchen, bedroom and sitting room along a common corridor, a minimum housing standard for working class families was, according to contemporary thought, achieved "economically"

1 Ausnutzung des Baugeländes wie sie die Polizeiverordnung Ende des 19. Jahrhunderts in Berlin gestattete: sechs Hinterhöfe mit fünf- bis sechsgeschossiger Bebauung
2 Obergeschoßgrundriß vom 3. Hinterhaus der Ackerstraße 132 in Berlin, dazu Grundriß der im Hof gelegenen Toilettenanlage. Mit Küche, Kammer und Stube am gemeinsamen Flur glaubte man das Existenzminimum an Wohnraum für Arbeiterfamilien in »wirtschaftlicher« Form gesichert zu haben

Vom Wohnungsgrundriß zum Stadtplan

Biologische Notwendigkeiten

Viele wollen uns vormachen, Bauen sei eine technische Angelegenheit und eine technisch ausgeklügelte Herstellungsmethode ergebe von selbst den größtmöglichen Effekt, »den guten Bau«. Sie sehen nur einen kleinen Ausschnitt, wollen nicht die Wurzeln erkennen, aus denen der Baugedanke keimt. Gewiß wird die technische Höchstleistung den guten Bau auszeichnen; sie genügt allein aber nicht und führt, einmal Selbstzweck geworden, zum Absurden, zum technischen Unikum. Die Bauleistung muß mit den Kräften übereinstimmen, die das Leben der Menschen bestimmen, seien sie nun soziologischer, politischer oder wirtschaftlicher Art – ich denke an Gegenbeispiele wie das Theater, in dem einst Caruso sang, in der verwunschenen, untergegangenen brasilianischen Gummipflanzerstadt, oder an die Bewohner von Matera in Süditalien, die lieber in ihre alten Erdhöhlen zurückkehren –; oder seien die Kräfte biologischer und bioklimatischer Art.
Die Wertung dieser Kräfte schwankt; erst ihre Mißachtung läßt in den meisten Fällen deutlich werden, wie wichtig sie für den Bau und das Leben darin sind. Politische und soziologische Aspekte hinterlassen im Wohnungsbau unverkennbare Spuren. In Europa fiel die Spätzeit einer Feudalherrschaft mit dem Beginn des »Maschinenzeitalters« zusammen. Die geringschätzige Wertung der »niederen Stände« ermöglichte den Behörden Planung und Bau jener finsteren Quartiere rings um die alten Städte für die rasch anwachsende Menge der Industriearbeiter (Bild 1/2). Mit einem zeitlichen Abstand von hundert Jahren wiederholt sich heute z.B. in einigen südamerikanischen Staaten der gleiche Vorgang bei einer von den Städten angelockten, noch ungebildeten Bevölkerung.
Auch die Übertragung patriarchalischer Zustände auf städtische Verhältnisse, besonders ausgeprägt im Industriegebiet nördlich der Ruhr, konnte dem Übel nicht abhelfen. Eine Stadt ist kein Gutshof. So forderte Robert Koch um 1888 aus seiner Kenntnis der medizinischen Folgen eines Daseins wie in Kasematten: »Licht und Luft für jede Wohnung.« Erst die politisch bedingte Änderung der gesellschaftlichen Verhältnisse im Nachkriegseuropa, ab 1920, gab den Architekten von Paris bis Warschau den Anstoß, Wohnungen für die »breite Masse« zu bauen, die Kochs hygienischen und biologischen Forderungen entsprachen. Die Wohnung für das Existenzminimum war bis in die dreißiger Jahre hinein das Thema ihrer Bemühungen. Sonne in Wohn- und Schlafräume, zweckmäßige und hygienische Einrichtungen der Küchen und Bäder waren einige der neuen Grundforderungen (Bild 4, 5, 7, 8). Die Idee von der Gleichwertigkeit aller Menschen fand ihren Ausdruck im Zeilenbau. Der Wunsch, das völlig aus der Stadt verbannte Grün in die Wohnviertel wieder einzubeziehen, durchdrang alle Planungen. 130 Jahre nach der Proklamation der Gleichheit begann Mitteleuropa, diese »Gleichheit« wissenschaftlich zu erforschen. Man überlegte, wieviel Luftraum ein Mensch während des Schlafs zur Verfügung haben muß; man errechnete die vom Körper täglich abgegebene Wasserdampfmenge, suchte den Bedarf an ultravioletter Strahlung und an Vitaminen festzustellen und ermittelte durch Analyse der Arbeit einer dienstbotenlosen Hausfrau eine kräftesparende Einrichtung der Küche (Bild 4/5). Das »Existenzminimum« wurde ausgelotet. Da man dem Wohnen und damit dem Wohnraum die größte Bedeutung zubilligte, wurden wie in Radings Breslauer Turmhausgrundrissen (Bild 3) alle anderen Räume auf das kleinstmögliche Maß gebracht. Dieser Gedankengang wiederholte sich nach dem zweiten Weltkrieg und wird sich immer wiederholen in Zeiten, in denen einem großen Wohnungsbedarf eine allzu geringe Wirtschaftskraft gegenübersteht.
Dennoch ist es falsch, in normalen Zeiten das Minimum zur Norm zu erheben, denn eine auf die Dauer gültige Norm liegt als Durchschnittswert im mittleren Bereich des Bedarfs. Nur wirtschaftliche Not kann darüber hinwegtäuschen, daß außer dem mittleren »normalen« Bereich stets ein Streubereich nach beiden Richtungen vorhanden ist, in dem zwar der Bedarf mit geringerer Häufigkeit auftritt, für den einzelnen Betroffenen jedoch zwingend vorhanden ist; ein Zwei-Meter-Normbett ist für einen 2,05 m langen Menschen einfach zu kurz, auch wenn es für 99,9% aller Schläfer ausreicht.

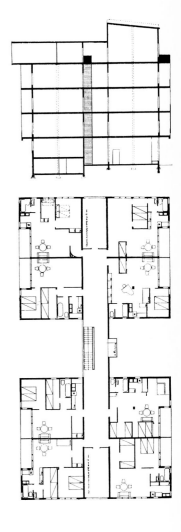

3 Plan and section of a tower block of flats in Breslau, originally planned as an eight-storey block: 1929, architect Adolf Rading, 1 in 500

3 Grundriß und Schnitt des zunächst achtgeschossig geplanten Turmhauses in Breslau 1929, Architekt Adolf Rading, 1:500

trated on securing this minimum standard for all dwellings. But, as circumstances become more normal, the minimum level is no longer sufficient.

How cautiously the standard and mean values must be assessed can be demonstrated by the example of the target room temperature of 18°C (64°F) which, for decades, was regarded as adequate during the winter. In the meantime, scientific research has shown that the feeling of comfort, engendered by adequate warmth, can only be experienced if the air temperature is in a given relation to the surface temperature of the walls. The tabulated results of the thermal research carried out at Ravensburg in 1962/63 indicate the relationships between outdoor temperature, indoor temperature, and the temperature at the inside of the outer walls (with a relative air humidity ranging from 30 to 75 per cent.). If the temperatures are lower than those quoted in columns 2 and 3, the room is felt to be cold; if they are higher than those indicated in columns 4 and 5, the room is felt to be too warm:

Admissible temperatures (°C)

Out door temperature (°C)	minimum		maximum	
	Air temperature in the room	Surface temperature on inside of outer wall	Air temperature in the room	Surface temperature on inside of outer wall
1	2	3	4	5
+ 10	17.2	15.4	21.2	18.6
± 0	18.6	14.0	22.7	17.1
— 10	20.0	12.6	24.2	15.6
— 20	21.3	11.2	25.5	14.2

The position is similar as regards window area requirements. The large Dutch window and the comparatively small windows encountered in Upper Bavarian houses are conditioned by the fact that daylight intensity shows a drastic decrease towards northern latitudes so that, to create equivalent working conditions, the same volume of light can only be obtained by window openings of different sizes (Fig. 6). Since, in the meantime, living conditions and habits have changed and become more variegated, the old recipes are no longer sufficient, regrettable as this may be from a superficial aesthetic point of view. If, for instance, a smallholder in the Black Forest, working outdoors all day, is able to make do with small windows, the city dweller who spends most of the day in an artificial climate, in artificial surroundings and often even with artificial light, needs compensation by means of a much larger window offering a distant view or the sight of a garden or at least a tree.

In our European climate, it is the stimulating effect of the contrast between summer and winter, with the long transition periods in the spring and autumn, that has enabled us to attain those achievements in all spheres of science which gave rise to the highest technical standards. But, if this climate is moderate, any attempt to level out all differences by technical means and to procure an average climate calculated on a scientific basis would, like any artificial uniformity, be doomed to failure. Similar contrasts and transitions are encountered during the course of the day. Logical as it may appear, a differentiated control of heat input, lighting, air exchange in accordance with a given rhythm is by no means taken for granted. Though glaring effects are gradually eliminated, the cold shock experienced by a person leaving a room with a temperature of 68°F or more for an outdoor temperature of, say, 14°F is still regarded as unavoidable.

We have thus developed a maximum of technical skill without, at the same time, investigating the natural conditions by which the human being is governed. This has given rise to the contrast between nature and technology, incomprehensible to the Asiatic, which must now again be reduced. An Asiatic will no doubt find it easier to make use of Western technology than a European to understand the mentality of Asia which leaves full rein to Man and his activities. It is at this point that fundamental research on housing construction and town planning should commence,

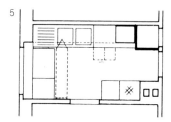

4/5 Frankfurt prototype kitchen, designed by architect Grete Lihotzky, 1931; plan, 1 in 100. The functionally most favourable combination of sink, working top and cooker has not yet been realised; but the cooker is provided with a ventilation hood

6 Daylight intensity depends on the geographical position. Daylight obstruction by different forms of balconies; white: suitable for writing desk; hatched: suitable for kitchenette; black: working space no longer adequately lit

7/8 Flat conforming to a minimum housing standard, Siemensstadt, Berlin, 1929/30; plans, 1 in 200. 7. Architect Walter Gropius, 8. Architect Otto Bartning

4/5 Die Frankfurter Küche der Architektin Grete Lihotzky, 1931; Grundriß, 1:100. Die für den Arbeitsablauf günstige Kombination Spültisch, Arbeitsfläche, Herd ist noch nicht verwirklicht. Immerhin hat der Herd bereits eine entlüftete Dunsthaube

6 Die Intensität des Tageslichts ist von der geografischen Lage abhängig. Verschattung eines Raumes durch verschiedene Balkonformen; weiß: Schreibplatz möglich; schraffiert: Arbeitsplatz in Kleinküche möglich; schwarz: Arbeitsplatz nicht mehr ausreichend beleuchtet

7/8 Die Wohnung für das »Existenzminimum«, Berlin-Siemensstadt 1929/30, Grundrisse, 1:200; 7 Architekt Walter Gropius, 8 Architekt Otto Bartning

Solange ein großer Teil der Bevölkerung in Wohnungen leben muß, die unter dem Existenzminimum liegen, ist das Bestreben verständlich, zunächst dieses Minimum für alle Wohnungen zu sichern. Mit zunehmender Normalisierung genügt das Minimum nicht mehr.

Wie vorsichtig Norm- und Durchschnittswerte beurteilt werden müssen, kann am Beispiel der jahrzehntelang im Winter als ausreichend angesehenen Raumluft-Temperaturen von 18°C gezeigt werden. Inzwischen wurde wissenschaftlich nachgewiesen, daß sich ein Gefühl der Behaglichkeit, also ausreichender Wärme nur einstellt, wenn Luft- und Oberflächentemperaturen der Wände in einem bestimmten Verhältnis zueinander stehen. Die Zahlentafel der wärmetechnischen Untersuchungen 1962/63 in Ravensburg gibt Aufschluß über den Zusammenhang zwischen den Temperaturen im Freien, im Innenraum und an den inneren Wandoberflächen der Außenwände (die relative Luftfeuchtigkeit lag im Bereich von 30 bis 75%). Bei tieferen Temperaturen als nach Spalte 2 und 3 wird der Raum als kalt empfunden, bei höheren als nach Spalte 4 und 5 als zu warm:

Zulässige Temperatur in °C (+)

Temperatur im Freien in °C	mindestens		höchstens	
	Raumluft	Innere Wand-oberfläche	Raumluft	Innere Wand-oberfläche
1	2	3	4	5
+ 10	17,2	15,4	21,2	18,6
± 0	18,6	14,0	22,7	17,1
− 10	20,0	12,6	24,2	15,6
− 20	21,3	11,2	25,5	14,2

Ähnlich steht es mit den Aussagen über die notwendige Fensterfläche. Das große holländische Fenster und die verhältnismäßig kleine Lichtöffnung in oberbayerischen Häusern haben sich herausgebildet, weil die Strahlungsintensität nach Norden zu drastisch abnimmt und für gleiche Arbeitsbedingungen in den beiden Landschaften die gleiche Lichtmenge nur mit unterschiedlich großen Lichtöffnungen zu beschaffen war (Bild 6). Da sich inzwischen die Lebensbedingungen und Gewohnheiten differenziert und gewandelt haben, genügen die alten Rezepte nicht mehr, so sehr das bei einer oberflächlich ästhetischen Betrachtungsweise auch bedauert werden mag. Kommt beispielsweise der tagsüber im Freien arbeitende Schwarzwaldbauer mit kleinen Fenstern aus, so braucht der Großstadtmensch, der den größten Teil des Tages in künstlichem Klima, künstlicher Umgebung und häufig auch unter künstlichem Licht zubringt, als befreienden Ausgleich den Blick in die Ferne oder ins Grüne – zumindest auf einen Baum – durch ein wesentlich größeres Fenster.

In unserer Klimazone hat die stimulierende Wirkung des Sommer-Winter-Gegensatzes unter Einschaltung langer Übergangszeiten im Frühjahr und Herbst jene Leistungen auf allen Wissensgebieten möglich gemacht, die den technischen Höchststand herbeiführten. Ist dieses Klima insgesamt auch ausgeglichen, »gemäßigt«, der Versuch, mit technischen Mitteln alle Differenzierungen abzuschleifen und uns in ein wissenschaftlich errechnetes Durchschnittsklima zu versetzen, müßte sich wie jede Einseitigkeit rächen. Im Tageslauf sind ähnliche Gegensätze und Übergänge zu beobachten. In einem bestimmten Rhythmus unterschiedliche Regulierung der Wärmezufuhr, der Beleuchtung, des Luftaustausches ist, so logisch das klingen mag, beileibe nicht selbstverständlich. Blendeffekte werden zwar allmählich vermieden, der Kälteschock zum Beispiel beim Verlassen eines auf + 20°C oder mehr temperierten Raumes bei − 10°C Außentemperatur wird noch als unvermeidlich angesehen.

Wir haben also ein Höchstmaß an technischen Fertigkeiten entwickelt, ohne gleichzeitig die natürlichen Abhängigkeiten des Menschen zu erforschen. So konnte sich der dem Asiaten unverständliche Gegensatz zwischen Natur und Technik bilden, den es jetzt wieder abzubauen gilt. Dem Menschen in Asien fällt es sicherlich leichter, sich der europäisch-amerikanischen Technik zu bedienen, als dem Euro-

BALKONFORM FORM OF BALCONY	MASSE/DIMENSIONS	FENSTERFORM FORM OF WINDOW	MASSE/DIMENSIONS	GEOGRAPHISCHE BREITE GEOGRAPHICAL LATITUDE								
				BERN 47°	FREIBURG I.B. 48°	KARLSRUHE 49°	FRANKFURT A.M. 50°	KÖLN 51°	BIELEFELD 52°	BREMEN 53°	LÜBECK 54°	FLENSBURG 55°
	4,0 / 4,0		112,5 / 137,5									
			112,5 / 212,5									
			175,0 / 137,5									
			212,5 / 137,5									
	4,0 / 4,0		112,5 / 137,5									
			112,5 / 212,5									
			175,0 / 137,5									
			212,5 / 137,5									
	4,0 / 4,0		112,5 / 137,5									
			112,5 / 212,5									
			175,0 / 137,5									
			212,5 / 137,5									
	0,6		112,5 / 137,5									
			112,5 / 212,5									
			175,0 / 137,5									
	3,0 / 4,0		212,5 / 137,5									
	0,9		112,5 / 137,5									
			112,5 / 212,5									
			175,0 / 137,5									
	3,0 / 4,0		212,5 / 137,5									
	1,5		112,5 / 137,5									
			112,5 / 212,5									
			175,0 / 137,5									
	3,0 / 4,0		212,5 / 137,5									
	1,5		112,5 / 137,5									
			112,5 / 212,5									
			175,0 / 137,5									
	3,0 / 4,0		212,5 / 137,5									

6

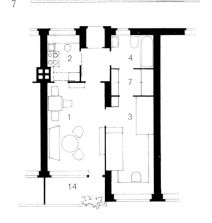

7

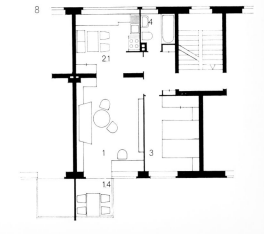

8

and not with the comparatively trivial question as to the cross-sectional area of a flue required for oil heating.

Once in a while, it is useful to go back to the roots of developments – in other words, to adopt a radical approach. In the history of mankind, the hellenic era marks the development of Man's self-consciousness. Having lived in fear of deities and forces of nature, Man discovers his own Ego and thus his relationship to the elements, "earth", "water", "air" and "fire". To-day, after two-and-a-half millenia of human endeavour, these elements have been brought under control, with nuclear fission as the latest province of "fire", just conquered. Just as with colonisation, the limits are gradually apparent; the spheres of the different elements cannot be expanded at will.

All human activities are affected by changes. In keeping with present-day means of locomotion, modern conurbations extending over distances of 60 miles and more grow up in the United States and in Europe, in defiance of any historic boundaries, as inescapable results of the process of industrialisation (Fig. 119). In these areas of intense concentration, there is a shortage of "earth" as represented by the parcelled land; "water" and "air" are polluted, toxic and unfit for human consumption; the use of "fire" in any form – right up to the atomic reactor – must be subjected to strict controls to avoid the destruction of vegetable, animal or human life.

Every human dwelling, and particularly the urban dwelling sandwiched in layers, demands its share of the four ancient elements. If one of them is missing or cannot be regenerated in a biologically compatible composition, life and living become impossible, and investment in housing is wasted.

In this way, all the disciplines of science affect the work of the architect and help to decide whether it is good or bad.

The standards of water supply, drainage, sunlight access, availability of shade, ventilation, heating are part-aspects of biological necessities which can not be discussed here in detail but which are possibly more important than all the technical, structural or aesthetic refinements conceived by an architect or engineer. The technical expert may be content with his particular sphere; but the universal "archi-technician" must be, at one and the same time, an engineer, moralist, sociologist, biologist and a person of integrity if he does not want to be just a drawing board craftsman, an estate agent, or a builder of monuments.

"If, during the nineteen-twenties and -thirties, i.e. during the so-called New Building Era, the problem of housing construction mainly presented itself from the functional and biological aspects, to-day's aim must be to tackle the sociologically orientated problems derived from the basic research of that period. The demand for integrated town planning reflects to-day's recognition that there is no such thing as an ideal type of dwelling. Housing construction must be perceived as an element of town planning at large. If, in modern town planning, civic amenities are closely related to the individual sphere of the dwelling, there must be an equally close relationship between the different types of dwellings in multi-storey and low-height housing". Otto Senn, 1962

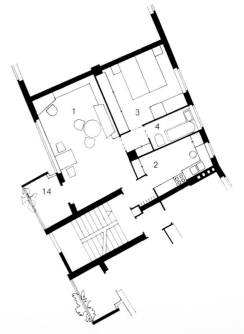

9/10   Siemensstadt, Berlin, 1930; architect Hans Scharoun; elevation and plan, 1 in 200

9/10   Berlin-Siemensstadt 1930, Architekt Hans Scharoun; Ansicht und Grundriß, 1:200

päer, sich in die Geisteswelt Asiens einzufühlen, die den Menschen und sein Tun
verstehen läßt. An diesem Punkt hätte die Grundlagenforschung für den Woh-
nungs- und Städtebau eher einzusetzen als bei der vergleichsweise banalen Frage,
welche Kaminquerschnitte bei Ölheizung erforderlich sind.

Hin und wieder ist es gut, den Ablauf des Geschehens bis zur Wurzel zurückzuver-
folgen, »radikal« zu sein. In der Geschichte der Menschheit nimmt die Epoche des
Griechentums eine dem Entstehen des Selbstbewußtseins entsprechende Stellung
ein. Der in Furcht vor Göttern und Naturgewalten dahindämmernde Mensch entdeckt mit dem Ich die Abhängigkeit und die Distanz von den Elementen Erde,
Wasser, Luft und Feuer. Heute, nach zweieinhalbtausendjährigem Bemühen, werden diese Elemente, mit der Kernspaltung als jüngster, soeben eroberter Provinz
des »Feuers«, beherrscht. Wie einst bei der Landnahme werden allmählich Grenzen
spürbar: die Elemente lassen sich in ihren vorhandenen Anteilen nicht beliebig
vermehren.

Alle Lebensbereiche werden von Veränderungen ergriffen. Den heutigen Fort-
bewegungsmöglichkeiten entsprechen die Siedlungsgebilde von hundert und mehr
Kilometern Länge, die ungeachtet aller historischen Grenzen zur Zeit in den USA
und in Europa zwangsläufig im Gefolge der Industrialisierung entstehen (Bild 119).
In diesen Konzentrationsgebieten ist die Erde, der kartierte Boden, knapp, sind
Wasser und Luft krank, giftig und ungenießbar, muß die Verwendung von »Feuer« in
jeglicher Form – bis zum Atomreaktor – strengen Kontrollen unterworfen werden,
um nicht pflanzliches, tierisches oder menschliches Leben zu vernichten.

Jedes Wohnhaus, besonders das städtische, in mehreren Wohnebenen übereinander geschichtete, fordert seinen Anteil an den alten vier Elementen. Fehlt eines
der Elemente, oder läßt es sich in biologisch verträglicher Zusammensetzung nicht
zurückgewinnen, dann ist Leben und Wohnen unmöglich, der Bau des Hauses eine
verlorene Investition. – So wirken sämtliche Wissenschaften auf das Werk des Architekten ein und entscheiden mit, ob es gut oder schlecht ist.

Qualitäten der Bewässerung, Entwässerung, Besonnung, Beschattung, Belüftung,
Beheizung sind Teilaspekte biologischer Notwendigkeiten, die hier nicht alle ein-
gehend erörtert werden können, jedoch möglicherweise wichtiger sind als die
technisch-konstruktiven oder ästhetischen Raffinessen, die einem Ingenieur oder
Architekten einfallen. Dem Techniker mag sein Teilgebiet genügen, der »Arche-
Techniker« ist Ingenieur, Moralist, Soziologe, Biologe und ungespaltener Mensch
in einer Person, oder er ist Reißbretthandwerker, Grundstücksmakler, Denkmal-
bauer.

*Wenn sich das Problem des Wohnbaus in den zwanziger und dreißiger Jahren, das
heißt in der Epoche des Neuen Bauens, wesentlich unter dem funktionellen und biologischen Aspekt präsentierte, so gilt es heute, auf der damals erarbeiteten Grundlage die soziologisch orientierte Problemstellung zu bewältigen. Die Forderung nach
dem »integrierten Städtebau« ist Ausdruck der heutigen Erkenntnis, daß es keine an
sich ideale Wohnform gibt. Es geht darum, den Wohnbau als Element des umfassenden städtebaulichen Verbandes zu verstehen: Wenn bei der heutigen Stadtplanung
die Einrichtungen der Allgemeinheit in enger Wechselbeziehung zum individuellen
Bereich der Wohnung stehen, so auch die verschiedenen Wohnformen des mehrgeschossigen und des flachen Wohnbaus unter sich.* Otto Senn, 1962

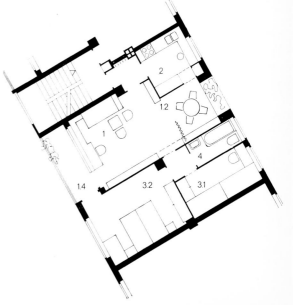

11/12 Siemensstadt, Berlin, 1930; architect Hans Scharoun;
entrance to the ring-shaped housing estate
13 Plan, 1 in 200, of the block visible in Fig. 11, right

11/12 Berlin-Siemensstadt 1930, Architekt Hans Scharoun.
Der Eingang zur Ring-Siedlung
13 Grundriß, 1:200, des Hauses, das in Bild 11 rechts zu
sehen ist

Historical Development

What is "dwelling"? The room in which the Scottish poet Robert Burns was born (in 1759) was typical for the original all-purpose living room: – The fireplace serves, at the same time, as kitchen and resting place, near the minute window is a workplace, next to it a linen cupboard which, together with table, chair and timepiece, represents the only furniture. The sleeping recess can be curtained off (Fig. 14). Thick walls protect against a generally hostile nature which is not invited into the house since most of the day must, in any case, be spent in outdoor work.

In many respects, modern small houses and flatlets reflect similar tendencies even though the domination over the elements achieved with the aid of the natural sciences has given rise to a less fearful attitude towards the surrounding nature.

A second line of descent can be traced back through the bourgeois dwelling of the nineteenth century to the manorial palace rather than to the medieval houses of the citizen or craftsman. The representative function was regarded as the most important of all. The failure of the newly arrived bourgeois classes – and indifference must, in this connection, also be regarded as failure – to solve the housing problems of the population at large in the towns of the nineteenth and early twentieth century induced the reformers to condemn the pompous bourgeois forms of dwellings just as much as the unhygienic habitations of the poor. Purism was raised to the status of dwelling culture. Today, we regard such purism as a necessary purge; but we also know that it cannot be regarded as a permanent condition suitable for all. Comfortable as a hot bath may be, who would wish to spend all his days in the bath tub?

The plans from Breslau (1929) and from Siemensstadt, Berlin (1930) are milestones on the path from legalised housing misery to a dignified abode for all town dwellers (Figs. 3, 7, 8, 10, 13, 15). Hugo Häring's type, for instance (Fig. 15), a twin unit with a floor area of 620 sq.ft. and a balcony area of 64 sq.ft. designed for four occupants, already offers considerable advantages within a minimum space: – access from the hall to all the rooms; kitchen next to the entrance with a hatch to the sitting room; a proper living room with a balcony of adequate size (6 ft. at its widest point) facing the afternoon sun; balconies of adjacent flats separated from each other; kitchen windows protected against excessive sunlight; main bedroom which, though of much reduced size, still leaves sufficient space for a cot; nursery with accommodation for two beds; bathroom next to the bedrooms; short distance between kitchen and bathroom. Scharoun's site plan ensured a quiet position of the blocks along a purely residential road. To-day, we might criticize the lack of a spare room and built-in cupboards; we might prefer a separation of the W.C. from the bathroom and might welcome a special dining recess and a larger nursery; but this does not detract from the achievements of 1930. It is in the nature of milestones to indicate that the road continues. These buildings made it clear that housing is a moral obligation; the attitude to the building task has become the key to planning.

The New Architecture was regarded as a concrete manifestation of the school of thought which visualized Man climbing another high plateau of his existence. Le Corbusier, Gropius and Mies van der Rohe had worked under Peter Behrens, the past master who had made his way from painter to designer and architect. Ludwig Mies van der Rohe and Hugo Häring later worked in the same drawing office, wall to wall as it were, whilst the bulk of the buildings erected at that time were still confined to conventional, academic designs. To-day, when a broad phalanx of experts has reached the level of the reformers of 1920, Mies and Häring are regarded as antipodes. Conservative forces have taken control of the simple formal language of Mies van der Rohe which is capable of mathematical formulation. Häring's inclination to regard chaos as the origin of all life is suspect to all those who aim at orderliness, classification and regimentation.

Between then and now lies the come-back of the outstripped epoch of the past which came to power not only in the German "Heimatstil" but also in the bourgeois fin-de-siècle style of the Stalin period. The restorative mentality which made a Second World War possible asphyxiated the tender germs of a new building and housing culture so that, after 1945, a new beginning had to be made even in technical respects. Standardisation and prefabrication had already been tried out at the co-

14 All-purpose room in the rural cottage where the Scottish poet Robert Burns was born in 1759

14 Geburtsraum von Robert Burns, bäuerlicher »Allraum« 1759 in Schottland

15 Excellent design of a flat conforming to a minimum housing standard, Siemensstadt, Berlin, 1930, architect Hugo Häring, plan, 1 in 200

15 Hervorragende Lösung für eine Wohnung, die das »Existenzminimum« bietet. Berlin-Siemensstadt 1930, Architekt Hugo Häring, Grundriß, 1:200

Geschichtliche Entwicklung

Was heißt wohnen? Der Geburtsraum des schottischen Balladendichters Robert Burns (1759) bezeichnet einen Ausgangspunkt: den »Allraum«; am Kamin ist zugleich der Koch- und Ruheplatz, am winzigen Fenster ein Arbeitsplatz, daneben ein Wäscheschrank, außer Tisch, Stuhl und Standuhr einziges Mobiliar; die Bettnische ist durch Vorhänge abzuschließen (Bild 14). Dicke Mauern schützen gegen eine meist feindliche Natur, die man nicht ins Haus hineinzieht, da man ohnehin den Tag über im Freien arbeiten muß.

In vieler Hinsicht tendieren neue Einfamilienhäuser und Einraumwohnungen in ähnliche Richtung, wenn auch die mit Hilfe der Naturwissenschaften erreichte Herrschaft über die Elemente eine andere, von Furcht befreite Einstellung zur umgebenden Natur bewirkt hat.

Die zweite Abstammungslinie führt über die bürgerliche Wohnung des 19. Jahrhunderts mehr auf das Adelspalais als auf die Handwerker- und Bürgerhäuser des Mittelalters zurück; Repräsentation wurde als wichtigste Wohnfunktion aufgefaßt. Das Versagen der arrivierten bürgerlichen Schicht – auch Gleichgültigkeit zählt hier als Versagen – gegenüber den Wohnproblemen der Gesamtbürgerschaft in den Städten des 19. und beginnenden 20. Jahrhunderts bewog die Neuerer, pomphafte »bürgerliche« Wohnformen ebenso zu verdammen wie die unhygienischen Wohnlöcher der Armen. Purismus galt als Wohnkultur. Heute erkennen wir diesen Purismus als notwendigen Reinigungsakt, wissen jedoch, daß er kein Dauerzustand für jedermann sein kann. So wohltätig ein warmes Bad sein kann, wer wollte seine Tage nur in der Badewanne zubringen?

Die Grundrisse aus Breslau (1929) und Berlin-Siemensstadt (1930) sind Meilensteine auf dem Wege aus einer polizeilich erlaubten Wohnsklaverei zu einer menschenwürdigen Unterkunft für jeden Stadtbewohner (Bilder 3, 7, 8, 10, 13, 15). Hugo Härings Typ beispielsweise (Bild 15), ein Zweispänner mit 58 m² Wohnfläche und 6 m² Balkon, für vier Betten, bietet auf kleinstem Raum bereits beachtliche Vorzüge: Zugang vom Flur zu sämtlichen Räumen der Wohnung, Küche neben dem Eingang mit Durchreiche zum Wohnraum, Wohnraum und ausreichend großer Balkon (1,80 m an der breitesten Stelle) an der Feierabendseite, Trennung der Balkone benachbarter Wohnungen, Abschirmung des Küchenfensters gegen übermäßige Sonneneinstrahlung, knapp bemessenes Elternschlafzimmer, das dennoch Platz läßt für ein Kleinkinderbett, Kinderzimmer, das die Aufstellung von zwei Betten ermöglicht, Zuordnung des Bades zu den Schlafräumen, günstige Verbindungswege Küche-Bad. Scharouns Lageplan sicherte den Wohnzeilen die ruhige Lage am Wohnweg. Wir würden heute den in der Wohnung fehlenden Abstellraum und Garderobenschrank bemängeln und eine Trennung von WC und Bad anstreben, ein besonderer Eßplatz wäre willkommen und das Kinderzimmer könnte größer sein; das schmälert nicht die Leistungen des Jahres 1930. Meilensteine zeigen an, daß der Weg weitergeht. Mit diesen Bauten wurde klargestellt: Bauen ist eine moralische Angelegenheit, die »Einstellung zur Bauaufgabe« ist zum Schlüssel der Planung geworden.

Das Neue Bauen wurde aufgefaßt als eine Verfestigung des Gedankengebäudes, das den Menschen schlechthin eine neue Stufe seines Daseins erklimmen sah. Le Corbusier, Gropius und Mies van der Rohe hatten bei Peter Behrens, dem vom Maler zum »Designer« und Architekten aufgestiegenen Altmeister, gearbeitet; Mies van der Rohe und Hugo Häring zeichneten später in einer Büroetage, sozusagen Wand an Wand, während die Masse der Bauten dieser Zeit weiterhin in akademischen, konventionellen Formen entstand. Heute, da eine breite Front von Fachleuten den Stand der Neuerer von 1920 erreicht hat, werden Mies und Häring als Antipoden empfunden. Die konservativen Kräfte haben sich der einfachen, in Formeln zu fassenden Mies'schen Formensprache bemächtigt. Der dem Chaotischen als Ursprung allen Lebens zuneigende Anspruch Härings gilt dem nach Ordnung, Klassifizierung und Reglementierung begehrenden Teil der Menschheit als suspekt.

Zwischen damals und heute liegt die Zeit des Aufbegehrens der überrundeten Epoche der Vergangenheit, die im »Heimatstil«, der nicht nur Deutschland erfaßte, ebenso wie im bürgerlichen Fin-de-siècle-Stil der Stalinzeit »an die Macht kam«. Das restaurative Denken, das einen zweiten Weltkrieg möglich machte, er-

16 Flats at Botnang, Stuttgart, 1930, architect Heinz Rasch

16 Haus in Stuttgart-Botnang 1930, Architekt Heinz Rasch

"The architecture of the nineteen-twenties, permeated by the idea of fundamental solutions of eternal validity, envisaged the space as a geometrical structure consisting of identical cubic components as shown by Malewitsch's sculpture. The flat-roofed blocks without cornice have neither beginning nor end. The party walls emphasize the random character of the cadence, the classic proportions of height and width are superseded by the infinite horizontal. If, previously, the load bearing parts of a building consisted of vertical brickwork into which the floors were then inserted, it was now the continuous horizontal concrete floor slab which was then sub-divided by party walls, merely serving as secondary space partitions. In principle, it was possible to remove the party walls without affecting the building as a whole."
Heinz Rasch, 1959

Die Architektur der zwanziger Jahre, durchdrungen von der Idee prinzipieller, d.h. letzter gültiger Lösungen, sah im Raum ein geometrisches Gebilde, aus lauter gleichen Teilen von würfelförmiger Gestalt zusammengesetzt, wie es die Plastik von Malewitsch zeigt. Die Häuser mit gesimslosen flachen Dächern haben keinen Anfang und kein Ende. Ihre Brandmauern betonen die Zufälligkeit der Unterbrechung, an die Stelle der klassischen Proportionen von Höhe und Breite ist die unendliche Horizontale getreten. Bestanden früher die tragenden Teile des Hauses aus dem vertikalen Ziegelmauerwerk, in das die Decken nachträglich eingefädelt wurden, so waren es jetzt umgekehrt die durchlaufenden horizontalen Betondecken, die durch die Zwischenwände, welche nur der Trennung sekundärer räumlicher Beziehungen dienten, nachträglich unterteilt wurden. Man konnte die Zwischenwände im Prinzip fortnehmen und versetzen, ohne daß sich am Baukörper etwas änderte.
Heinz Rasch, 1959

operative housing schemes at Stuttgart, Breslau, Vienna and Zurich as well as in the housing estates in Frankfurt-on-Main, Warsaw and Prague. But the technical successes and failures were largely forgotten; the experiments had to be repeated. Some of the best examples of the latest post-war period show how laborious was the new beginning, the revival of the New Architecture.

In the opinion of the first Minister for Reconstruction of the German Federal Republic, balconies of low-rent housing had to be regarded as a luxury which could not be economically justified. The prototype estate at Crailsheim, built in 1950 and sponsored by the Building and Housing Research Association, Stuttgart, still had bathrooms in the basement, shared by several families (Fig. 22). The provision of cupboard rooms, spare rooms and built-in kitchens, albeit of the simplest kind, and the connection of the small rooms by sliding doors to gain a certain measure of width were notable progressive features in the houses designed by Heinrich Lauterbach for families of two or three. Later on, these flats were occupied by families of five or six so that the original intentions were frustrated since any overcrowding is the beginning of the slum.

The different sections of the great housing scheme at Spandauer Damm, West Berlin, specifically planned for the housing requirements of a large city, and completed during the period from 1953 to 1960, reflect the gradual change in attitude. In the earliest parts, the strict limitation of the floor area and the need to make do with individual heating can only be overcome by such gimmicks as the built-in bedroom, already encountered in Rading's tower block plans of 1929 (Fig. 25).

In the later sections, the balcony zone is more strongly featured, e.g. by staggering the building volumes (Fig. 24). It had meanwhile become apparent that, from a social-economic point of view, even low-rent housing calls for the provision of central heating. To-day, no more than 5 per cent. of all the dwellings in West Berlin are still built with individual heating.

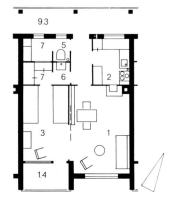

In common with the countries devasttead by the war, Israel was forced to create, at short notice, housing accommodation for numerous immigrants which differs from European housing by being adapted to a completely different climate. With its relatively large bedrooms, permitting flexible use, its separation of bathroom and W.C. and, mainly its skilful juxtaposition of hall, dining space, living room and a large and therefore really habitable balcony, this plan from Tel-Aviv may also be regarded as exemplary for different latitudes (Figs. 26–28).

Poland, with her shortage not only of housing accommodation but also of skilled labour is forced to rely on industrialised housing construction. Here, French influence is noticeable. In contrast to Russia or Poland's Western neighbours, the standardisation of plans has been avoided and prefabricated units are used for the construction of a great variety of dwellings so that, despite drastic limitations in size, flexible use becomes possible. The desire to avoid monotony is underlined by a sculptural and colourful treatment of the facades. Admittedly, however, the desired precision of workmanship has only been attained in certain interiors (Figs. 29–33).

As in all other spheres, Russia has to catch up with an enormous demand so that quantity is the principal watchword. The industrial production of large and heavy components calls for such a concentration of efforts that layout design and town planning are decades behind the times. A relatively progressive example (Fig. 34), where the fatal four-unit type layout is replaced by a three-unit type, may illustrate the present position better than any description can do.

It is presumably no coincidence that, both in Russia and in the centrally controlled French housing effort, production techniques have received strong impulses, and a wide pool of experience has been gathered on ultra-large "economic" building sites. The planning projects insist on an adequate number of large dwellings, in keeping with the government policy of furthering large families (Fig. 41). In the juxtaposition of the straight building blocks and in the composition of the "Grand Ensembles", the influence of a formal aesthetic tradition continues to prevail, and to radiate into Central Europe as in the times of the last Bourbon kings (Fig. 40).

stickte die zarten Keime einer neuen Bau- und Wohnkultur, so daß nach 1945 auch in technischer Hinsicht alles noch einmal neu begonnen werden mußte. Standardisierung und Vorfertigung waren bereits in den Werkbund-Siedlungen in Stuttgart, Breslau, Wien und Zürich ebenso wie in den Siedlungen in Frankfurt am Main, Warschau und Prag erprobt worden. Die technischen Erfolge und Mißerfolge waren jedoch zum großen Teil vergessen, die Experimente mußten wiederholt werden. Einige der besten Beispiele der jüngsten Nachkriegszeit lassen erkennen, wie mühsam der neue Anfang, das Wiederaufleben des Gedankens »Neues Bauen« war.

Der erste Wiederaufbau-Minister der Bundesrepublik hielt Balkone für einen im Sozialen Wohnungsbau wirtschaftlich nicht vertretbaren Luxus. In der Crailsheimer Mustersiedlung von 1950, betreut durch die Forschungsgemeinschaft Bauen und Wohnen in Stuttgart, haben die Wohnungen noch ein gemeinsames Bad im Keller (Bild 22). Kleiderkammer, Abstellräume und eingebaute Küchen, wenn auch in einfachster Art, und die Verbindung der kleinen Räume durch eine Schiebetür, um ein gewisses Maß an Weite zu erhalten, waren in den von Heinrich Lauterbach geplanten Häusern beachtliche Fortschritte für einen Zwei- bis Drei-Personen-Haushalt. Später wurden diese Wohnungen mit fünf- und sechsköpfigen Familien belegt; dadurch mußten die ursprünglichen Absichten zunichte werden, denn jede Überbelegung ist der Beginn des Slums.

Die im großstädtischen Rahmen geplante Siedlung am Spandauer Damm im Westen Berlins, deren Bau in den Zeitraum von 1953 bis 1960 fällt, läßt in ihren einzelnen Abschnitten den langsamen Wandel der Auffassungen hervortreten. Die Beschränkung der Wohnfläche und der Zwang, sich mit Einzelofenheizung zu begnügen, können nur mit Raffinessen überspielt werden wie etwa dem eingebauten Schlafzimmer (Bild 25), das schon in Radings Turmhaus-Grundrissen von 1929 auftauchte.

In späteren Teilen der Siedlung ist die Gruppierung um den Balkon herum stärker herausgearbeitet, so zum Beispiel in den gestaffelten Hauskörpern (Bild 24). Man hatte eingesehen, daß auch der Soziale Wohnungsbau im volkswirtschaftlichen Sinne »wirtschaftlich« nur mit Zentralheizungen betrieben werden kann; in Berlin (West) werden heute nur noch 5% der Wohnungen mit Einzelofenheizung gebaut.

Wie in den vom Krieg verwüsteten Ländern mußten auch in Israel für zahlreiche Einwanderer in kürzester Frist Wohnungen geschaffen werden, die sich in der Anpassung an ein völlig anderes Klima von den europäischen unterscheiden. Relativ große Schlafräume, die dadurch in der Nutzung variabel werden, die Aufteilung der sanitären Räume und die geschickte Aneinanderreihung von Eingangsdiele, Eßplatz, Wohnraum und großem, damit wirklich bewohnbaren Balkon, lassen dieses Beispiel aus Tel Aviv auch für andere Breitengrade vorbildlich erscheinen (Bild 26–28).

In Polen, dem es an Wohnungen wie auch an ausgebildeten Handwerkern mangelt und das schon deshalb gezwungen ist, sich auf die industrialisierte Herstellung von Wohnhäusern zu stützen, ist die Anlehnung an die französische Lebensart zu spüren. Man hat es vermieden, wie in Rußland oder bei dem westlichen Nachbarn Wohnungsgrundrisse zu typisieren, und zieht es vor, aus vorfabrizierten Teilen die verschiedensten Wohnungen zu bauen, damit trotz einschneidender Größenbeschränkung unterschiedliche Nutzung möglich wird. Fassadengliederung und Fassadenbemalung unterstreichen den Wunsch, jeder Monotonie zu entgehen. Die gewünschte Exaktheit der Ausführung ist allerdings nur in einzelnen Innenräumen erreicht (Bild 29–33).

Rußland hat wie auf allen Gebieten einen ungeheuren Nachholbedarf, so daß Quantität die Maxime ist. Die industrielle Herstellung großer, schwerer Bauteile nimmt alle Kräfte so in Anspruch, daß Grundrisse und Stadtpläne um Jahrzehnte hinter der allgemeinen Entwicklung zurückbleiben. Ein relativ fortschrittliches Beispiel (Bild 34), bei dem die fatalen Vierspänner-Grundrisse von einem Dreispänner abgelöst sind, zeigt den Stand der Überlegungen besser als jede Beschreibung. Vermutlich ist es kein Zufall, daß ebenso wie in Rußland im zentralistisch dirigierten französischen Wohnungsbau die Fabrikationstechnik starke Impulse erhielt und in »wirtschaftlichen« Großbaustellen ein reicher Erfahrungsschatz angesammelt werden konnte. Bei den Planungen wird immerhin auf eine ausreichende Anzahl großer Wohnungen – für den staatlich geförderten Kinderreichtum – geachtet (Bild 41). In den äußeren Beziehungen der Wohnzeilen zueinander, der »Komposition« der *grands ensembles*, überwiegt der Einfluß einer formal-ästhetischen Tradition, der wie zu Zeiten der letzten gekrönten Ludwige nach Mitteleuropa ausstrahlt (Bild 40).

17/22 Experimental housing estate at Crailsheim, erected by the Building and Housing Research Association, Stuttgart, 1949/50, architect Heinrich Lauterbach
17 View of the two-storey blocks
18 Plan of top floor flat, 1 in 200
19/20 Sitting room and bedroom are connected by a sliding wall
21 Access gallery
22 Basement, ground floor and top floor of another block, 1 in 500

17–22 Versuchssiedlung der Forschungsgemeinschaft Bauen und Wohnen, Stuttgart, in Crailsheim 1949/50, Architekt Heinrich Lauterbach
17 Ansicht der zweigeschossigen Miethäuser
18 Grundriß der Obergeschoßwohnung, 1:200
19/20 Wohn- und Schlafraum sind durch eine Schiebewand verbunden
21 Der Laubengang
22 Kellergeschoß, Erdgeschoß und Obergeschoß einer weiteren Hauszeile, 1:500

23

24

26

27

23–25 Low-rent housing, Spandauer Damm, Berlin, 1953 to 1960, architect Klaus Ernst
23/25 Views and plan of the first blocks, 1 in 200
24 View of the blocks built in 1960

23–25 Sozialer Wohnungsbau, Berlin-Spandauer Damm 1953–60, Architekt Klaus Ernst
23/25 Ansicht und Grundriß der ersten Hauszeilen, 1:200
24 Ansicht der 1960 gebauten Häuser

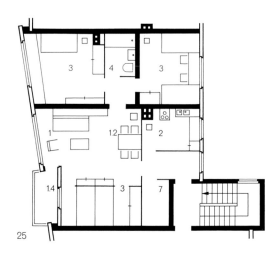

25

26–28 Housing scheme near Tel-Aviv, architects Rechter, Zarhy, Rechter. Elevation, interior of sitting room, and plan, 1 in 200

26–28 Siedlung bei Tel Aviv, Architekten Rechter, Zarhy und Rechter. Ansicht, Blick in den Wohnraum und Grundriß, 1:200

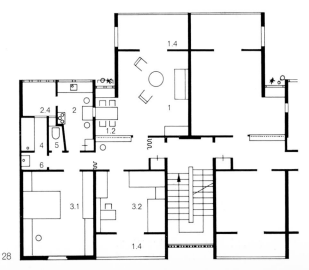

28

32

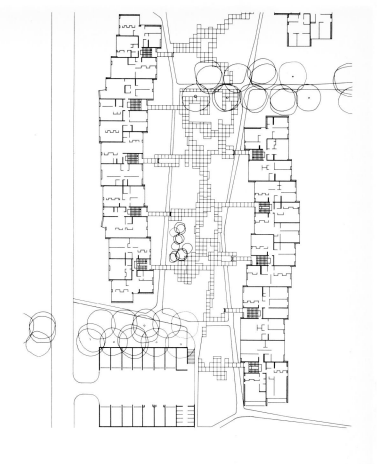

29–33 Housing scheme at Rakowiec, Warsaw, 1959, architects Oskar Hansen, Zofia Hansen, Zastaw Malicki, Marion Szymanowski
32/33 Part of site plan, 1 in 2000, and ground floor plan, 1 in 200

29–33 Siedlung in Warschau-Rakowiec 1959, Architekten Oskar Hansen, Zofia Hansen, Zastaw Malicki, Marion Szymanowski
32/33 Ausschnitt aus dem Lageplan, 1:2000, und Erdgeschoßgrundriß, 1:200

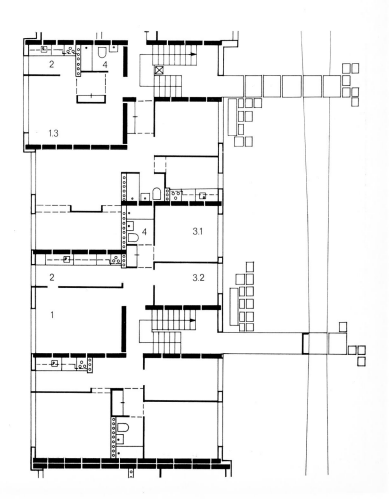

"But, in going in for functional building construction – which is generally still the ideal of contemporary architects – or in analysing technical functions, are we really doing justice to housing? Could it not be that, by a thoughtless rationalisation of building construction, and by turning from spacious multi-purpose dwellings to relatively small if technically perfected single-purpose dwellings, we neglect those imponderables which, though wholly or partly defying strict rationalisation, nevertheless have a considerable influence on Man's satisfaction or dissatisfaction with his habitation, and which may even make all the difference-even if the occupants may not be conscious of it – between the humanity or inhumanity of the dwelling?"

Dietrich Goldschmidt, 1959

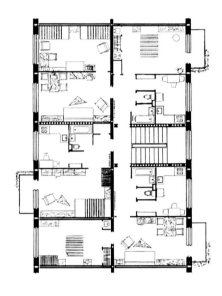

35

37

36

38

34 Russian standard plan with a 3.2 metres (10'6") facade module, 1 in 200

34 Russischer Grundriß mit 3,20 m Achsmaß der Fassadenteile, 1:200

35–38 Temperament, mentality and other national peculiarities mark the appearance of the buildings just as much as that of the people
35 Flats in England, London, architect Lasdun
36 Flats in Japan: Haruni Apartment House, architect Mayekawa
37 Flats in Germany, (Berlin), occupying a position between derelict sites
38 Flats in Poland, built by pre-fabrication methods

35–38 Temperament, Eigenart und sonstige nationale Bindungen prägen das Antlitz der Häuser ebenso wie das Antlitz der Menschen
35 Haus in Großbritannien, London, Architekt Lasdun
36 Haus in Japan, Haruni-Apartment, Architekt Mayekawa
37 Haus in Deutschland, Berlin – Baulückensituation
38 Haus in Polen, Montagebauweise

Werden wir aber mit funktionsgerechtem Bauen, das auch unseren heutigen Architek-
ten im allgemeinen als Ideal vorschwebt, beziehungsweise werden wir mit der Analyse
technischer Funktionen dem Wohnen wirklich gerecht? Kann es nicht sein, daß mit
gedankenloser Rationalisierung des Bauens, mit Übergang vom geräumigen Mehr-
zweck- zu relativ kleinen, technisierten Wenigzweckwohnungen jene Imponderabilien
des Wohnens vernachlässigt werden, die sich einer strengen Rationalisierung zwar
teilweise oder ganz entziehen, die jedoch die Zufriedenheit oder Unzufriedenheit der
Menschen mit ihren Wohnungen wesentlich mitbestimmen, ja die die eigentliche
Menschlichkeit oder Unmenschlichkeit des Wohnens – den Bewohnern möglicher-
weise unbewußt – zu einem hohen Grade ausmachen mögen?

Dietrich Goldschmidt, 1959

39 Housing scheme in Germany: Wellingsdorf near Kiel,
architect H. W. Nitsche, Technical Director of the Schleswig-Holstein Housing Association, Kiel, 1952

39 Siedlung in Deutschland, Kiel-Wellingsdorf, Architekt
H. W. Nitsche, technischer Direktor der Wohnungsbaugesellschaft Schleswig-Holstein GmbH in Kiel, 1952

40 Housing scheme in France: Chatenay-Malabry, architects Pierre Sonrel and Jean Duthilleul
41 Housing scheme at Chatenay-Malabry, part of floor
plan, 1 in 200

40 Siedlung in Frankreich, Chatenay-Malabry, Architekten
Pierre Sonrel und Jean Duthilleul
41 Chatenay-Malabry, Grundrißausschnitt, 1:200

41

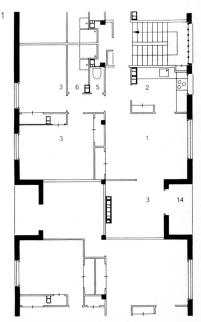

40

Extraneous Conditions and Regional Differences

"Each room thus has its own theme. But each theme, in its turn, also has its own place in the regions of this earth. There is a correlation between a landscape and the theme imposed on the peoples of this landscape. This is why the Gothic was unable to penetrate to the South, and this also the reason why the aims of the Werkbund movement have not found acceptance outside the sphere of the nordic peoples: this, too, is the reason why the objectives of "Neues Bauen" differ from those of "Architecture Moderne". This might also conflict with the thesis that a creative effort is merely the work of an individual. For, the effect is commanded by the theme with which the person is confronted. In this sense, the individual is merely the tool of the spirit concealed in the mysticism of the form".

Hugo Häring

42 Sketches by Ralph Erskine, illustrating the principles on which the planning of houses in the polar region should be based

42 Skizzen von Ralph Erskine, die darlegen, nach welchen Prinzipien in der Polarregion Häuser zu planen sind

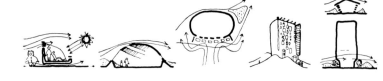

From minor nuances and differences it is very difficult to detect the restraints imposed on architects and their clients by geographical, or indeed local, conditions which are often overlaid by extraneous features. The differences are more clearly recognisable from the extreme case, and it is the essence of the mental effort of every creative builder to try to find, among the possible alternatives, the one best suited to his particular case.

Among the basic influencing factors, landscape and climate are first and paramount. Recognition is made more difficult by the multiplicity of new building materials and by the many novel designs made possible by them. From an analysis of traditional building forms – from the roots of their origin as it were – the structural principle appropriate to our time can be derived. Erskine follows this approach with his buildings in the polar region. Examples are the tower blocks at Vaxjö, discussed in the Chapter on Prefabrication (pages 16f.). If, in the polar region, it is appropriate to adopt the enclosed form of building which takes into account wind, sun, snowdrifts and mosquitos (Fig. 42), the solution appropriate to the hot and moist coastal forests under the tropical sun is the dissolution of the house into different, well ventilated and sun-protected levels (Fig. 45). The stanchion-supported flats in Mozambique would be just as much out of place at Vaxjö as would be the transplantation of either building to any other climatic zone, e.g. Central Europe or England. Whilst such transplantation of European types of flat to other climatic zones was still widely practised during the last century, to-day's Europeans are more inclined towards a thoughtless adoption of architectural forms which are appropriate to different climatic conditions. The rain-proof flat roof, however, is not among these sins; this was simply a feature which it would have been impracticable to achieve in earlier times when straw, reed or imbricated roofing tiles were the only building materials available.

The Portuguese architect Guedes has attempted an integration of native (African) and modern art in a building which he regards as a masterwork of plastics but which is still governed by conventional plans. He is unable to free himself from the shackles of convention because the society for whom he builds is not yet ripe for this step (Figs. 43–46).

Equal in strength to landscape and climate among the forces affecting the design of a building are society and national origin. In Mediterranean Romanesque, for instance, even the villages are small towns. The vitality springing up after the summer mid-day heat is not confined in the dwellings but fills the "living room" of the town – the piazza or street, the recognized rendezvous where the social status of each individual is probed every day afresh. That, to-day, this rendezvous has been made a witches' cauldron by that modern status symbol, the motor car, is easy to understand. Even so, the Romanesque example is copied again and again by sun-

43

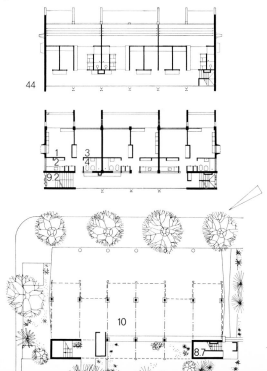
44

Bindungen und regionale Unterschiede

Jeder raum hat also sein eigenes thema. Jedes thema hat aber auch seinen eigenen ort in den gebieten dieser erde. Es besteht ein zusammenhang zwischen der gestalt einer landschaft und dem thema, das den völkern dieser landschaft zu bearbeiten auferlegt ist. Dies war der grund, warum die gotik nicht nach dem süden vordringen konnte, und dies ist auch der grund, warum die gestaltziele, die die ziele der werkbundbewegung sind, den raum der nordischen völker nicht überschritten haben, und auch der grund, warum die ziele des »neuen bauens« anders sind als die ziele der »architecture moderne«. Auch möchte dies der meinung entgegenstehen, daß ein gestaltwerk nur das werk eines individuums ist. Denn es entsteht aus dem auftrag eines themas, das vor einem menschen auftaucht. Das individuum ist demgegenüber nur das organ des geistes, den das geheimnis der gestalt umhüllt. Hugo Häring

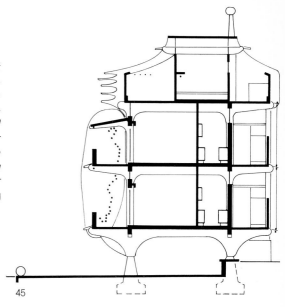

45

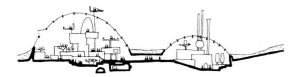

Von kleinen Abstufungen und Unterscheidungen her ist es ungemein schwer, die Bindungen zu erkennen, die Bauherrn und Architekten auferlegt sind. Äußerlichkeiten treten oft mehr ins Blickfeld als die für den jeweiligen, nicht nur geographischen, Ort gemeingültigen Festlegungen. Am Extremfall sind die Unterschiede deutlicher ablesbar und es ist die »geistige Schwerarbeit« jedes Bauenden, von den für jede Entscheidung möglichen Gegensatzpaaren die Abstufungen zu dem für ihn gültigen Punkt zu finden.

Landschaft und Klima sind erste und wichtigste Gegebenheiten. Die Vielzahl neuer Baumaterialien und die damit möglichen neuen Bauformen erschweren das Erkennen. Aus der Analyse der traditionellen Bauformen läßt sich, sozusagen von der Wurzel ihrer Herkunft her, das für den gegenwärtigen Zeitpunkt richtige Konstruktionsprinzip ableiten. Erskine geht diesen Weg bei seinen Bauten in der Polarregion. Als Beispiel sind die Wohntürme von Vaxjö im Abschnitt Vorfertigung (Seite 17f.) und im Abschnitt Balkone (Seite 57) dargestellt. Ist im Polargebiet die Wind, Sonne, Schneewehen und Moskitos berücksichtigende, geschlossene Form richtig (Bild 42), so ist im feuchtwarmen Küstenwaldgürtel unter tropischer Sonne die Auflösung des Hauskörpers in durchlüftete und gegen Sonneneinstrahlung geschützte Ebenen »richtig« (Bild 45). Der auf Stützen gestellte Bau in Mosambik wäre in Vaxjö ebenso falsch wie die Verpflanzung beider Bauten in irgendein andersartiges Klimagebiet, beispielsweise nach Mitteleuropa oder England. War noch im vergangenen Jahrhundert die Übertragung europäischer Hausformen in andere Klimazonen üblich, so neigen heutzutage die Europäer eher zur unbedachten Übernahme der Architekturformen, die unter anderen klimatischen Voraussetzungen richtig sind. Das regensichere Flachdach zählt jedoch nicht zu derartigen Sünden; wie hätte man es früher aus Stroh, Schilf oder schuppenartigen Tonziegeln auch herstellen sollen.

Der Portugiese Guedes versucht eine Integration der einheimischen (afrikanischen) und modernen Künste an einem Bauwerk, das er als große Plastik auffaßt, dessen Wohnungsgrundrisse dennoch das übliche Schema nicht verlassen. Er kann den Schritt zu einer Befreiung aus den Fesseln der Konvention nicht tun, weil die Gesellschaft, für die er baut, für diesen Schritt noch nicht reif ist (Bild 43–46).

Gesellschaft und nationale Herkunft sind in gleicher Stärke wie Klima und Landschaft auf den Bauentwurf einwirkende Prägekräfte, sind doch zum Beispiel in der romanischen Mittelmeerkultur selbst die Dörfer kleine Städte. Die nach der sommerlichen Mittagshitze aufbrechende Lebendigkeit bleibt nicht in den Wohnungen gefangen, sondern erfüllt die »Wohnstube« der Stadt, den Platz oder die Straße, die als ausgemachter Treffpunkt gelten, wo die Rangordnung jedes einzelnen täglich neu ausgelotet wird. Daß heute das Auto als Rangsymbol aus diesem »Treff« einen Hexenkessel macht, ist leicht verständlich. Dennoch findet das romanische Vorbild

43–46 Flats in a tropical climate, Mozambique, East Africa, architect A. d'Alpoim Guedes
44 Ground floor, first floor, second floor and top floor of the house in Mozambique, 1 in 500
45 Section, 1 in 200; air circulation and sun protection

43–46 Haus im tropischen Klima, Mosambik, Ostafrika, Architekt A. d'Alpoim Guedes
44 Erdgeschoß, 1. und 2. Obergeschoß, Dachgeschoß des Hauses in Mosambik, 1:500
45 Schnitt, 1:200; Luftzirkulation und Sonnenschutz

46

starved Central and Northern Europeans, as exemplified in recent years by the town centre of Cumbernauld where the Italian hill-top town has been transplanted to a windswept Scottish brae. And yet, the habits of the island race are almost diametrically opposed to this mode of living. Withdrawal into a closely guarded privacy of the dwelling (or into the armchair of the club) reflects a mentality which avoids undesired contacts and can never produce a genuine Italian street life. In this context, the differences in size, layout and equipment of different peoples' habitations, and especially of the living room, become understandable. If, in Italy and parts of France, some of the functions of the home are assumed by the street, the cafeteria, the bistro, the Englishman requires his living room with fireplace and a separate dining room which survives at least in the form of a "dining area" (page 102, Fig. 2).

French housing plans indicate that the living room does not assume the same importance as in Britain, Sweden or Germany (Fig. 51). The "sejour" is smaller and often used as a passage; table and chairs occupy the dominating position. (More recently, as a result of motorisation which has reduced the value of the street as a living space, a tendency towards a better equipped living room has become apparent.)

As in politics, French housing construction suffers from a serious historic handicap, viz. the centralisation of all activities in Paris. A feature which, three hundred years ago, was instrumental in establishing French hegemony – the geographical concentration of all leading personalities in the intellectual, cultural and technical spheres and the intensification of their efforts through continual contact – now tends to impede the healthy development of the entire country.

Centralistic thinking gives rise to planning projects which reflect a centralistic mode of life. Typical of this mentality is Le Corbusier's "Ideal City" of 1922 (Fig. 118). Central axes, monumental avenues, dominant vistas and a propensity for decorative elevations are the means of expressing such basically anachronistic associations of ideas. In housing construction, however, no principle has been more fatal than the Man-enslaving absolutism of the "l'Etat-c'est-Moi" kind, be it practised by Louis XIV, Hitler, Stalin, or other autocratic rulers.

The small-house tradition in countries such as Britain or Japan does not arise from technical reasons; it stems from political or religious causes. On the Continent of Europe, however, where technical conditions were basically the same, the long-standing system of manor houses and farm labourers' cottages was bound to end in a tenement house tradition. To appreciate the makings of the Modern City, it is highly revealing to observe how this single-family housing tradition has been transformed into urban types of dwellings (Figs. 50, 52). In contrast to Europe where similar attempts had few repercussions (Mies van der Rohe, Weissenhof Estate, Stuttgart, 1927, Fig. 42; William Olsson, Järnbrott, Gothenburg, experimental building, 1952; Gottwald, Hansa District, Berlin, 1957), the flexible use of rooms is traditional practice in Japan. Kikutake has been able to adhere to the principle of the traditional Japanese house by placing kitchen, bathroom and lavatory in a separate unit which remains outside the mat partition system (Figs. 53–57). The interior (Fig. 55) comes close to the non-realisable dream of a whole generation of young European architects: the puritanically simple coherent rooms with wholly glazed outer walls, governed by standard modules and variable in many ways by means of sliding doors. What has been possible in Japan as a result of a development over centuries, marked by over-population, religious outlook and earthquakes, and by the acceptance of severe limitations on personal freedom, cannot be transferred to European conditions. It can only serve as a ferment, instigating similar developments elsewhere without accepting the limitations to individual freedom customary in ancient Japan.

Even the London example of a differentiated housing programme is not a recipe for low-rent housing; its relationship to the latter may rather be likened to that between a racing car and a mass-produced car: Without trying out technical innovations which, during racing, are exposed to the greatest strains, it is not possible to develop the inexpensive mass-produced car. The transition from single-family to multi-storey housing similarly calls for preliminary experiments: experiments with luxury-type flats, examination of the results obtained with prototype dwellings, and a steady development of new types of single-family houses.

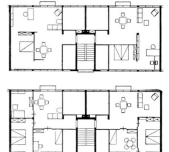

47/48 Block of flats at the Weissenhof estate, Stuttgart, 1927, architect Ludwig Mies van der Rohe. Plans, 1 in 500, with open and closed room partitioning
49 Removable party walls in Mies van der Rohe's block of flats

47/48 Haus in der Weißenhofsiedlung in Stuttgart 1927, Architekt Ludwig Mies van der Rohe. Grundrisse, 1:500, mit offener und geschlossener Zimmereinteilung
49 Demontable Trennwände im Mies-van-der-Rohe-Haus

immer wieder Nachahmer unter den sonnenhungrigen Mittel- und Nordeuropäern, wie in jüngster Zeit das als italienisches Bergnest auf eine windgepeitschte schottische Hügelkuppe verpflanzte Zentrum von Cumbernauld beweist. Dabei sind die englischen Gewohnheiten dieser Lebensart etwa genau entgegengesetzt. Das Zurückziehen in den streng gehüteten Privatbereich der Wohnung (oder in den Sessel im Klub) ist Ausdruck einer Lebensauffassung, die unerwünschte Kontakte meidet und ein echt italienisches Straßenleben niemals hervorbringen kann. Aus dieser Sicht werden die Unterschiede in Größe, Anordnung und Einrichtung der Wohnung in den einzelnen Ländern, insbesondere des Wohnraums, verständlich. Übernimmt in Italien und einem Teil Frankreichs die Straße, die Cafeteria, das Bistro Teile der Wohnfunktionen, so braucht der Engländer die mit einer Wärmequelle ausgestattete »Wohnhalle« und den besonderen »Dining-room«, der zumindest als Eßplatz erhalten bleibt (Seite 102, Bild 2).

An französischen Grundrissen ist abzulesen, daß dem Wohnraum nicht die gleiche Bedeutung zugemessen wird wie in England, Schweden oder Deutschland (Bild 51). Das Zimmer ist kleiner, die Tischgruppe steht beherrschend in dem oft als Durchgangsraum benutzten »séjour«. – Die Motorisierung mit ihren Nebenerscheinungen, zum Beispiel der Entwertung der Straße als Aufenthaltsraum, bewirkt neuerdings eine Tendenz zum besser ausgestatteten Wohnraum hin.

Wie auf politischem Gebiet lastet auch auf dem Wohnungsbau in Frankreich eine schwere historische Hypothek: die Zentralisierung in Paris. Was vor 300 Jahren Frankreichs führende Stellung begründete, die Versammlung aller geistig, kulturell oder in der Technik führenden Köpfe und die Potenzierung ihrer Leistung durch die ständig möglichen Kontakte, das wird heute zum Hemmschuh für eine gesunde Entwicklung des ganzen Landes.

Die zentralistische Denkweise zeugt zentralistischem Lebensgefühl entsprechende Pläne; typisch ist Le Corbusiers Idealplan von 1922 (Bild 118). Mittelachsen, Prachtstraßen, Blickpunkte und die Freude an dekorativen Fassadenmustern sind Ausdrucksweise derartiger, im Grunde anachronistischer Denkspiele. Für den Wohnungsbau jedoch war kein Prinzip verhängnisvoller, infolge seiner den Menschen zum Sklaven erniedrigenden Denkweise, als das des Absolutismus, »L'état c'est moi«, mögen es nun Ludwig XIV., Hitler, Stalin oder andere autokratisch regierende Herrscher zu verwirklichen getrachtet haben.

Die Einfamilienhaustradition in Ländern wie Großbritannien oder Japan hat nicht technische, sondern politische oder religiöse Grundlagen. – Die »Leute«-Häuser und »Kavaliers«-Häuser des europäischen Festlandes, bei denen an sich gleichgelagerte technische Fragen auftraten, mündeten dagegen zwangsläufig in Mietskasernentraditionen. – Für das Bild der Neuen Stadt ist die Beobachtung, wie diese Einfamilienhaustraditionen in großstädtische Bebauungsformen überführt werden, äußerst aufschlußreich (Bild 50, 52). Anders als in Europa, wo ähnliche Versuche wenig Resonanz fanden (Mies van der Rohe, Stuttgart, Weißenhofsiedlung 1927 [Bild 47]; William-Olsson, Göteborg-Järnbrott, Experimenthaus 1953; Gottwald, Berlin, Hansaviertel 1957), ist in Japan die flexible Raumnutzung Tradition. Die Einfügung des Einfamilienhausschemas gelingt Kikutake unter Festlegung eines Installationskernes, der außerhalb der Mattenaufteilung bleibt (Bild 53–57). Das Innenraumbild (55) enthüllt den nicht erfüllbaren Traum einer ganzen jungen europäischen Architektengeneration: die puritanisch einfachen, durch genormte Grundmaße bestimmten und durch Schiebetüren vielfältig variierbaren ineinanderfließenden Räume mit völlig verglasten Außenwänden. Was sich in Japan als Folge der Übervölkerung, der Religion und der Erdbeben seit Jahrhunderten unter größter Einschränkung der persönlichen Freiheit ausbilden konnte, ist nicht übertragbar auf europäische Verhältnisse. Es kann nur Ferment sein zur Auslösung ähnlichen Verhaltens, ohne die Einschränkung des Individuums, die im alten Japan üblich war, zu übernehmen.

Auch das Londoner Beispiel eines räumlich differenzierten Wohnprogramms ist nicht ein Rezept für den Volkswohnbau, sondern steht dazu etwa im gleichen Verhältnis wie ein Rennwagen zu einem Serienmodell: Ohne die Erprobung technischer Neuerungen, die beim Autorennen härtester Beanspruchung ausgesetzt werden, kann das in der Serie billigere Automobil nicht gefunden werden. – Der Übergang vom Einfamilienhaus zum mehrgeschossigen Wohnhaus erfordert ebenfalls zunächst Experimente – Experimente mit »Luxus-Appartementhäusern«, Überprüfung

50 Flats in Japan, architect Kikutake (cf. Figs. 53–57)
51 Flats at d'Orly, Paris, architects P. Badani and P. Roux Dorlut. Plan of a three-storey block, 1 in 500
52 Flats in London, architect Lasdun (cf. Figs. 58–62)

50 Haus in Japan, Architekt Kikutake (siehe Bild 53–57)
51 Haus in Paris-d'Orly, Architekten P. Badani und P. Roux Dorlut. Grundriß eines dreigeschossigen Hauses, 1:500
52 Haus in London, Architekt Lasdun (siehe Bild 58–62)

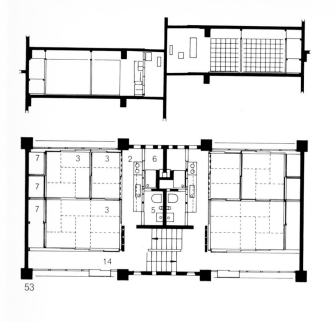

53

56

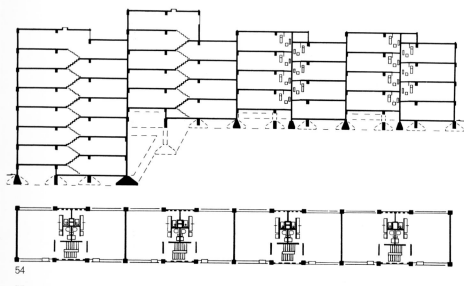

54

55

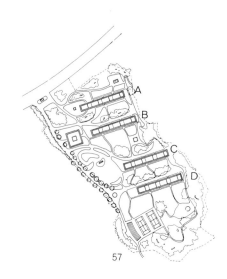

57

53–57 Flats between Tokyo and Yokohama, imaginatively adapted to the landscape in spite of wholly identical plans. Architect Kiyonori Kikutake, assisted by Makoto Kuji, Shokan Endo, Koichi Sasaki

53 Section and plan of two apartments, 1 in 200. Entrance through the verandah; shoe box in the balustrade

54 Section and plan, Block A, 1 in 1000

55 Interior; the traditional pattern of the Japanese family house is implanted on the concrete platform. Kitchen, bathroom and lavatory remain outside the mat partition system

57 Layout plan, 1 in 5000. Blocks B, C and D are planned

58–62 Flats in St. James's Place, London
Architect Denys Lasdun

58 Penthouse plan, 1 in 500

59 Section, 1 in 500

60 Three split-level floor plans, 1 in 500

61 The park front of the flats

62 Living room on ''c'' level

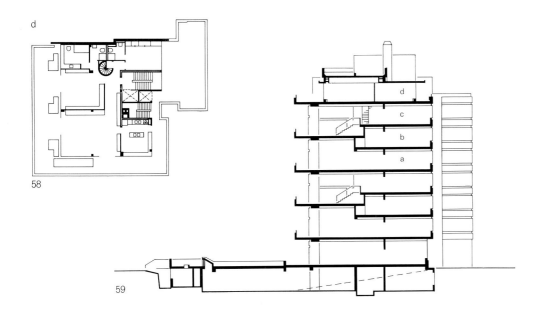

d

58

59

c

b

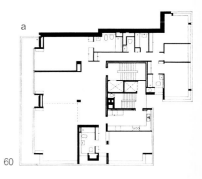

a

60

53–57 Trotz völlig gleichartiger Grundrisse phantasievoll der Landschaft angepaßtes Appartementhaus zwischen Tokio und Yokohama, Architekt Kiyonori Kikutake, Mitarbeiter Makato Kuji, Shokan Endo, Koichi Sasaki

53 Schnitt und Grundriß zweier Wohnungen, 1:200. Eingang über die Veranda; Schuhschrank in der Brüstung

54 Schnitt und Grundriß Block A, 1:1000

55 Innenansicht; das traditionelle Einfamilienhausgefüge ist auf der Betonplattform aufgebaut. Die Installationsräume bleiben außerhalb der Mattenaufteilung

57 Lageplan, 1:5000. Block B, C und D geplant

58–62 Appartementhaus am St. James's Platz in London, Architekt Denys Lasdun

58 Dachgeschoßgrundriß, 1:500

59 Schnitt, 1:500

60 Drei Grundrißebenen mit Variation der Wohnraumhöhe, 1:500

61 Die Parkseite des Hauses

62 Wohnraum der Grundrißebene c

61

62

Lasdun, with his building in St. James's Place (Figs. 58–62), reintroduced the one-and-a-half storey living room into multi-storey housing, thus breaking with the idea that multi-storey housing must necessarily take the form of flats. He also provides an example of how to fit a new building into a traditional urban environment merely by adapting the scale, yet without conforming to pseudo-historic styles.

Financing

Whilst the effects on housing construction of technical knowledge and of regional or national characteristics are obvious, the effects of the financing system are often under rated, unless the architect acts as his own estate agent. But even the intrusion of financial activities and property deals into the architect's sphere in post-war Germany has not improved the standard of modern building construction as it was generally accompanied by a lowering of architectural quality. "He who pays invests", as a German proverb has it. It is only in exceptional cases that the building is financed by the developer himself; mortgagees, however, always insist on having a say in the matter, be they private bankers, or administrators of government funds or subsidies. The Cooperative Building Society, a type of organisation widely encountered in Germany, is no exception. Monetary transactions, keeping a precarious balance between speculation and bona-fide investment, tend to favour conservative ideas. Conditions attached to loans may retard the necessary reorientation by decades. That is why the problems of industrialised building construction which, in Central Europe, had already been solved in the years following the First World War, must now be taken up again, and why American slum clearance schemes have not yet reached the level of know how obtained in Berlin, Warsaw and Prague as early as 1930.

According to investigations carried out by the German Research Association in 1930, a lowering to 3½ per cent. of the interest rate of 4½ per cent. then prevailing would have permitted an increase in the floor area of a dwelling by 40 per cent. since the cost of the expensive installations is not greatly increased. Such a progression would far exceed any savings made possible by technical improvements. In the Netherlands and in Switzerland, the comparatively low rate of interest, ranging from 3½ to 4¼ per cent., has permitted a great increase in building activities. It was Switzerland among all European countries which, in 1962, built the greatest number of dwellings per 1000 inhabitants.

The larger dwelling is relatively cheaper than the smaller dwelling. The fact that the rent is calculated, in general, per square metre of habitable surface means, therefore, that the large families, which are often economically weak, are made to pay for part of the cost of the dwellings for small households. It would be advisable to make provision for a corrective.
(International Federation for Housing, Town Planning and Regional Planning, Standing Committee for Rents and Family Income, 1960)

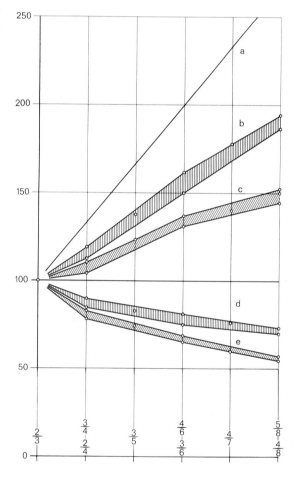

63 Progression of the flat costs in the Federal Republic of Germany, according to the Activity report by Standing Committee "Rent and Family Income" of the *International Federation For Housing and Planning*, in 1960
a Persons / Dwelling Unit, b Surface, c Price / Dwelling Unit, d Surface / Person, e Price / Person. The number of the rooms and beds is to be found under the graph

63 Progressivität der Kosten im Geschoßwohnungsbau in der Bundesrepublik Deutschland, nach einem Bericht des »Ständigen Ausschusses für Miete und Familieneinkommen« im Internationalen Verband für Wohnungswesen, Städtebau und Raumplanung, 1960
a Personen pro Wohnung, b Fläche, c Kosten der Wohnungseinheit, d Fläche pro Person, e Kosten pro Person. Untere Spalte: Zimmer- und Bettenzahl

der Ergebnisse in den sogenannten Nullserien und die stetige Weiterentwicklung der neuen Wohnformen im Einfamilienhausbau.

Lasdun führt mit dem Haus am St.-James's-Platz (Bild 58–62) den 1½-geschossigen Wohnraum wieder in den Mehrgeschoßbau ein und bricht mit der Anschauung, daß die Wohnungen ohne Höhendifferenzierung geschichtet sein müßten. Er gibt weiterhin ein Muster der Einpassung eines neuen Hauses in das Bild einer alten Stadt ohne Übernahme historisierender Stilformen, lediglich durch die Ausgewogenheit des Maßstabs.

Finanzierung

Während die Auswirkungen technischen Könnens und regionaler oder nationaler Eigenarten auf den Wohnungsbau offensichtlich sind, werden die vom System der Finanzierung ausstrahlenden Wirkungen oft unterschätzt, es sei denn, der Architekt sei gleichzeitig als Makler tätig. Doch auch der Einbruch der Geldgeschäfte und des Grundstückhandels in das Tätigkeitsfeld der Architekten im Nachkriegsdeutschland hat, da er meist mit einem Absinken der architektonischen Qualität erkauft wurde, für ein Neues Bauen keine Vorteile gebracht. »Wer zahlt, schafft an«, sagt ein Sprichwort. Gebaut wird nur im Ausnahmefall mit dem Eigenkapital des Bauherrn; Hypothekengläubiger aber fordern stets ein Mitspracherecht. Sind es im Falle der Privatwirtschaft Banken und ihre Direktoren, so sind es im anderen Fall die Verwalter staatlicher Mittel und Subventionen. Die besonders in Deutschland ausgeprägte Form der Gemeinnützigen Wohnungsgesellschaften bildet keine Ausnahme. Geldgeschäfte fördern als Balanceakt zwischen Spekulation und seriöser Geldanlage konservative Anschauungen. Beleihungsmaßstäbe können die notwendige Neuorientierung um Jahrzehnte hinauszögern. So kommt es, daß die in den Jahren nach dem ersten Weltkrieg in Mitteleuropa gelösten Fragen der Industrialisierung des Bauwesens heute erneut aufgeworfen werden müssen und amerikanische Sanierungsprojekte noch nicht den 1930 in Berlin, Warschau und Prag vorhandenen Erkenntnisstand erreichen.

Nach Untersuchungen der Reichsforschungsgesellschaft aus dem Jahr 1930 kann durch eine Herabsetzung des damaligen Zinssatzes von 4½ auf 3½% die Wohnfläche einer Wohnung um 40% vergrößert werden, da die Kosten für die teuren Installationen sich nicht wesentlich erhöhen. Das ist eine Relation, die weit über alle durch technische Verbesserungen möglichen Einsparungen hinausgeht. In den Niederlanden und der Schweiz konnte durch den vergleichsweise niedrigen Zinsfuß von 3½ bis 4¼% das Bauvolumen sehr gesteigert werden. in der Schweiz wurden im Vergleich zur Bevölkerungszahl im Jahr 1962 die meisten Wohnungen in Europa gebaut!

Die größere Wohnung ist relativ billiger als die kleinere. Die direkte Berechnung des Mietpreises nach m² Wohnfläche, die vielfach üblich ist, muß daher als soziale Ungerechtigkeit betrachtet werden, da auf diese Weise den größeren, und damit wirtschaftlich schwächeren Familien ein Teil der Lasten der kleineren, bessergestellten Familien aufgebürdet wird. Es müßte also hier bei der Mietpreisberechnung ein Korrektivum eingefügt werden.

(Internationaler Verband für Wohnungswesen, Städtebau und Raumordnung, Ständiger Ausschuß Miete und Familieneinkommen, 1960)

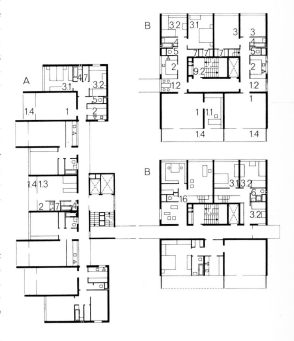

64 Plans, 1 in 500, and perspective view of the Fasan tower block of flats, Stuttgart, 1964, architects Otto Jäger and Werner Müller
The larger flats (A), which are intended for sale, are cheaper in construction and general equipment than the smaller flats (B) which are designed for letting in accordance with the low-rent housing regulations

64 Grundrisse, 1:500, und Perspektive des Hochhauses Fasan in Stuttgart 1964, Architekten Otto Jäger und Werner Müller
Die größeren Wohnungen (A), als Eigentumswohnungen geplant, sind sowohl im Rohbau als in der Gesamtausstattung billiger als die kleineren (B), die als Mietwohnungen nach den Bestimmungen des Sozialen Wohnungsbaus geplant wurden

A New Approach

Basic Layout

The qualities of a dwelling can best be appreciated from its layout plan, though this must often be interpreted with the aid of a section. The examples shown in this book are classified by plan criteria. By adopting, as far as possible, a uniform mode of presentation and standard scales (1 in 200 and 1 in 500), comparisons are possible. Where certain features are not intelligible from the plans (environments, transport facilities, social aspects, etc.), the attempt has been made to describe them textually.

One of the foremost teachers of a whole generation of architects, Hans Poelzig, was well aware of the complications involved in working out the layout plan of a dwelling. He made his students design theatres, department stores and other large buildings before asking them to deal with housing. The ancient watchmakers' rule was confirmed: the smaller the mechanism and its components, the more difficult is the work, and the more sensitive and precious the product. Even to-day, the design of a highly automated factory is a fairly easy job compared with a good design for a housing scheme and its layout plans. Any gross over-simplifications in this field are courting failure. Branches of science like sociology and biology must be consulted. Even they will not have their answers ready, and many questions will first have to be put to them during the next few years. Their first research object must be the town dweller, i.e. the person prevented by his environment from giving free play to all his capabilities. But since Man is able to adapt himself to his surroundings and to preserve the necessary freedom of action even under unfavourable conditions, it is possible, even to-day, to draw certain conclusions from experience in old towns of large or metropolitan size. Age and job distribution, the geographical distribution of workplaces, the juxtaposition of homes and workplaces, are capable of statistical analysis. Even the changes in these relationships caused by deliberate direction of building activities are open to statistical scrutiny. This is not to say that such investigations, which should be an indispensible basis of any planning project, are in fact always available.

Nature has taught us that small particles of a large organism often are an image of the whole; this may also serve as a guide to housing construction. An urban district must offer the same variety as the city or region as a whole. One of the gravest criticisms that can be directed against post-war housing construction stems from the fact that these conditions of urban life have been too often ignored, and have led to mono-cultures reserved for certain groups: – persons in the same income group, employees of one company, refugees, large size families and the like. All these are conditions which are liable to change and should therefore never be the sole basis for such extensive long-term investments. The partitioning of a town into working class districts, villa quarters, civil service districts, millionaire suburbs, refugee settlements etc. lies at the root of the desease of our conurbations. This thesis is corroborated by facts such as the high criminality experienced in the bungalow paradise of Los Angeles and, on the other hand, the decrease in criminality in those former working class districts of Berlin (Wedding, Neukölln) where, after the war, a mixture of all income groups took place. Planners and local authorities should regard it as an alarm signal if this fusion of all job and income groups in certain urban districts is no longer possible so that the residents move away from each other and retire to their own villages. For, in that case, there is something wrong with certain living conditions in these areas, and the wealthy or otherwise privileged inhabitants are the first to look for healthier places after the failure of these environmental conditions. That their judgement may sometimes be at fault is proved by the apartment house boom in the United States, caused by the return of suburbanites to the central areas: – Living in open surroundings had been bought at too high a price in terms of journey-to-work and lack of urban amenities.

Work on the layout plan of a dwelling should therefore be governed by the desire to provide as many groups of persons as possible with a dwelling appropriate to them. It is not enough to find a single type of dwelling which may be appropriate to, say, half the population and which, built by the hundreds with but small variations, will attract just one group of town dwellers. It is only now that sociologists have begun to investigate the results of such lack of balance. Among the pioneers were

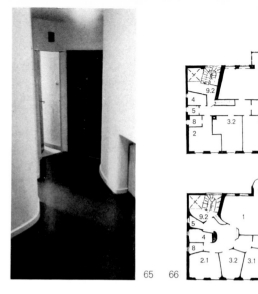

65   66

65   Corridor of the flat shown at the bottom of Fig. 66
66   Plan of a flat, 1 in 500, designed to provide the shortest indoor walking distances. Architect Heinz Rasch

65   Flur der Wohnung in Bild 66, unten
66   Grundriß eines Wohnhauses, 1:500, der in ein Baugefüge umgewandelt wurde, das den Spuren der Wege innerhalb einer Wohnung entspricht. Architekt Heinz Rasch

67/68   Casa Milà, Barcelona, 1935/36, architect Antoni Gaudí, plans 1 in 500 (approx.). The building, erected on an awkwardly cut corner site, is conceived as an entity with organically composed – not just additive – parts

67/68   Casa Milà in Barcelona 1905–10, Architekt Antoni Gaudí, Grundrisse, etwa 1:500. Der auf einem ungünstigen Eckgrundstück entstandene Bau ist aufgefaßt als eine Gesamtgestalt, deren Teile sich nicht additiv sondern organisch zusammenfügen

67

Auf neuen Wegen

Der Grundriß

Den besten Aufschluß über die Wohnqualitäten einer Behausung kann der Grundriß geben; meist ist er durch den Schnitt zu interpretieren. Die Beispiele dieses Buches sind nach Grundrißmerkmalen geordnet. Möglichst einheitliche Darstellung und Maßstäbe (1:200 und 1:500) lassen Vergleiche zu. Was aus den Grundrissen selbst nicht ablesbar ist (Außenraum, Verkehrsverbindungen, soziale Gliederungen usw.), wurde durch die Objektbeschreibung zu ergänzen versucht.

Einer der bedeutendsten Lehrer einer ganzen Architektengeneration, Hans Poelzig, hatte erkannt, wie kompliziert die Arbeit am Wohnungsgrundriß ist. Er ließ seine Studenten zunächst Theater, Kaufhäuser und andere »große« Bauten entwerfen, bevor er ihnen die Beschäftigung mit einem Wohnhaus zumutete. – Die alte Uhrmacherregel bestätigte sich: Je kleiner das Werk und seine Einzelteile, desto komplizierter die Arbeit, desto empfindlicher und kostbarer das Erzeugnis. Auch heute ist der Entwurf einer weitgehend automatisierten Fabrik eine vergleichsweise leichte Arbeit gegenüber dem guten Entwurf eines Wohnviertels und seiner Grundrisse. Alle groben Vereinfachungen führen hier zu Fehlschlägen. Wissenschaftsdisziplinen wie Soziologie und Biologie müssen zu Rate gezogen werden. Auch sie haben die Antworten nicht bereit liegen, ihnen werden viele Fragen in den nächsten Jahren erst noch gestellt werden müssen. Ihr Untersuchungsobjekt ist zunächst der Stadtbewohner, das heißt der Mensch in einer Umgebung, die eine freie Entfaltung aller seiner Fähigkeiten nur sehr bedingt zuläßt. Die Anpassungsfähigkeit des Menschen, der sich auch unter ungünstigen Verhältnissen den nötigen Spielraum freizuhalten weiß, läßt in den alten Groß- und Weltstädten schon heute gewisse Rückschlüsse zu. Der Altersaufbau, die Mischung der Beschäftigten, die Verteilung der Arbeitsplätze, die Trennung oder Kombination von Wohnen und Arbeiten lassen sich statistisch untersuchen. Auch die Veränderungen in diesen Zusammenhängen, durch Eingriffe in die bauliche Substanz hervorgerufen, können statistisch erfaßt werden. Damit ist nicht gesagt, daß derartige Untersuchungen, die notwendige Grundlage jeglicher Planung, immer vorliegen.

Die auf dem Gebiet der Natur erkannte Tatsache, daß die Teile im kleinen die Organisationsform des Großen wiederholen, weist auch dem Wohnungsbau die Richtung. Ein städtisches Siedlungsgebiet muß die gleiche Vielfalt bieten, wie sie sich im Stadtganzen oder der Region herausgebildet hat. Einer der schwersten Vorwürfe ist gegen den Nachkriegswohnungsbau deswegen zu richten, weil er diese Voraussetzungen städtischen Lebens zu häufig mißachtet hat und zu »Monokulturen« führte, sortiert nach Einkommen, Arbeitgeber, Flüchtlingseigenschaft, Kinderzahl usw. All dies sind Voraussetzungen, die einem Wandel unterworfen sein können und daher niemals alleinige Grundlage derart umfangreicher und langlebiger Investitionen sein dürften. Die Aufteilung der Stadt in »Arbeiterviertel«, »Landhausgegenden«, »Beamtenviertel«, »Millionärsvororte«, »Flüchtlingssiedlungen« und so fort ist Ursache der Krankheit des Stadtkörpers. Diese These wird einerseits bestätigt durch die hohe Zahl der Verbrechen im Bungalow-Paradies Los Angeles, andererseits durch die Abnahme der Kriminalität in jenen Berliner Arbeitervierteln (Wedding, Neukölln), in denen sich nach dem Krieg alle Berufsgruppen mischten. Es sollte für die Planer und Kommunalpolitiker ein Alarmzeichen sein, wenn diese Verschmelzung aller Berufs- und Einkommensschichten in einzelnen Bereichen der Stadt nicht mehr möglich ist, wenn die Bewohner auseinanderrücken und sich auf ihre »Dörfer« zurückziehen. Denn dann sind in diesen Gebieten bestimmte Voraussetzungen des Lebens nicht mehr gegeben und die Begüterten oder sonstwie Privilegierten sind die ersten, die das Fehlen dieser Umweltbedingungen veranlaßt, gesündere Plätze zu suchen. Daß sie unter Umständen einer Fehleinschätzung erliegen, beweist der Apartment-House-Boom in den USA, den die in die Innenstädte zurückströmenden »Suburbia«-Bewohner auslösten: das Wohnen im Grünen wurde mit zu weiten Wegen zur Arbeit und dem Mangel an städtischer Atmosphäre erkauft.

Die Arbeit am Wohnungsgrundriß muß also unter dem Gesichtspunkt beginnen, möglichst vielen Personengruppen zu einer ihnen gemäßen Unterkunft zu verhelfen; und nicht mit dem Versuch, einen einzigen Wohnungstyp zu finden, der vielleicht für die Hälfte der Bevölkerung zu gebrauchen ist und, mit geringen Variatio-

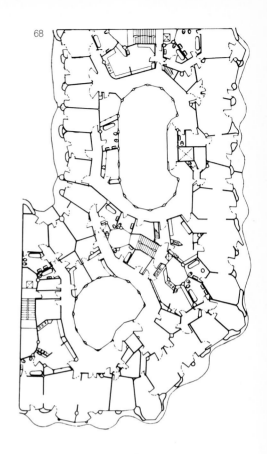

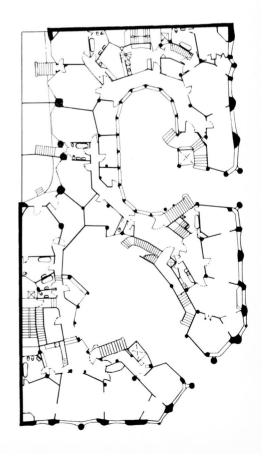

the planners of the London County Council and the Institute for Town Planning of Berlin Technical University, then under the direction of Hans Scharoun, who had already in the nineteen-fifties begun to include the sociological necessities in their planning efforts (cf. pages 204 ff.). Unfortunately, a more general adoption and scientific treatment of these relationships have been impeded by the great housing shortage, since even in badly planned estates, the dwellings were eagerly taken up. The price mechanism must fail if all the goods are sub-standard, and if even these are in short supply.

Design and layout of the individual rooms of a dwelling are governed by their functions. Since everybody must eat, sleep and wash, it would seem to be a simple matter to ascertain and allocate the necessary space. But even a first attempt to lay down certain rules for the requirements of families of different sizes (Fig. 78) already reveals the difficulties in laying down such standards even where the family size is the only variable. Yet even the family itself is at present, as a result of changes in technology and industry, in the throes of a structural change which affects the living habits. If the rooms of a dwelling are to reflect these living habits, they too must differ from the standards valid about 30 or 40 years ago.

Whilst the early post-war efforts in small-house and multi-storey housing construction were still based on the experience of the nineteen-thirties, this basis was soon found to be too narrow. True, the simplifications adopted under emergency conditions made it possible to give every person a roof over his head; but family life calls for further differentiation. The small dwellings are too confined and not flexible enough for large families. Even a merely "optical" expansion can help to burst the confines of the cell-like dwellings (Fig. 70). Every-day life in Finland is reflected in the living room solution proposed by Aalto at the Hansa District, Berlin, where a so-called all-purpose living room branches out in all directions into the bedrooms and ancillary rooms (Fig. 69). Many of the Berliners occupying these dwellings have preferred to segregate from this all-purpose room, at least optically, a small corridor in order to screen the path from kitchen or entrance to bathroom and bedrooms. In many cases, they have also segregated a dining area with access to the loggia or balcony. Surveys conducted in Britain, Sweden, Germany and Switzerland brought the, at first glance, surprising result that about half of all families eat in the kitchen, even where the latter is designed as a working kitchen only. The dining table which architects have, for a long time, regarded as a matter-of-course ingredient of the living room was thus found to be of little practical value in about half the number of all dwellings because the distances from the kitchen, even where a hatch is provided, are too long. Swedish proposals aim at reducing the size of the living room and relieving it from activities closely related to the housewife's work in the kitchen such as eating, ironing, sewing, children's work and hobbies, etc., – all of them activities not sufficiently considered in the standard layouts (Fig. 74). Altogether, the normal standard type dwellings are much too exclusively designed for families with one or two children. A "symbiotic" type, such as the one proposed by Scharoun in 1960 for some dwellings in the Siemensstadt district of Berlin, was not realisable. These dwellings were designed to enable a lone relative to live with the family, while occupying a self-contained part of the dwelling (Fig. 71).

Among the creatures overlooked in normal multi-storey housing are the children. It may be objected that this is not true; the children have sand boxes, playgrounds, schools, sportsgrounds and even their own bedrooms; we live, after all, in the "century of the child". But what are the cages like, which, in most standard layouts, must serve as nurseries!

That all children can grow up in single-family houses is inconceivable; this is thwarted by the high cost of building construction, the inadequacy of land use regulations or the shortage, well-nigh insuperable in metropolitan cities, of inexpensive houses, especially those available for letting.

Most modern dwellings are still designed to the pattern of a patriarchal family where the children, in the evening, gather around the father of the house reading the Bible to them until they go to bed in their little chambers. Perhaps all that has changed is that the tired father has been superseded by the television screen. How can a teenager live, and develop, in a small room with cupboard, bed, chair and possibly a desk, without tyrannizing the family! The so-called half-size rooms so frequently encountered in German low-rent housing are an emergency solution,

69 Block of flats in the Hansa District, Berlin, 1957, architect Alvar Aalto. The living room is the hub from which the paths lead to all the other rooms, 1 in 500

69 Haus im Hansaviertel in Berlin, 1957, Architekt Alvar Aalto. Aus dem Wohnraum verzweigen sich die Wege in alle übrigen Räume, 1:500

70 Block of flats at Linköping, Sweden, architect Gustav Kaunitz. Ground floor, first floor and second floor, 1 in 500. Minor deviations from the rectangular pattern can offer shorter walking distances and provide a better integration of indoor and outdoor space

70 Haus in Linköping, Schweden, Architekt Gustav Kaunitz. Erdgeschoß, 1. und 2. Obergeschoß, 1:500. Geringe Abweichungen vom rechtwinkligen Schema bieten bessere Wegeführungen und öffnen den Innenraum zur Umgebung

71 "Symbiotic" type of flat (not built), designed by Hans Scharoun for the Siemensstadt housing scheme, Berlin, 1958, plan, 1 in 500; providing optionally self-contained accommodation for a lone relative

71 Nicht gebauter »Symbiosetyp«, von Hans Scharoun für die Siedlung Berlin-Siemensstadt 1958 geplant, Grundriß, 1:500. Möglichkeit zur Absonderung oder Einbeziehung in den Familienverband für einen alleinstehenden Verwandten

nen hundertfach gebaut, automatisch nur einen bestimmten Interessentenkreis aus der Stadtbevölkerung heraussiebt. Die Folgen derartiger Einseitigkeiten beginnen die Soziologen eben erst zu untersuchen. Die Planer des London County Council und das Städtebau-Institut der Technischen Universität Berlin, solange es von Hans Scharoun geleitet wurde, begannen bereits in den fünfziger Jahren, die soziologischen Notwendigkeiten in ihre Planungen einzubeziehen (siehe Seite 204ff.). Der große Wohnungsmangel verhinderte leider die Weiterverbreitung und weitere Erforschung dieser Zusammenhänge, da die Wohnungen auch noch so schlecht geplanter Siedlungen den Bauträgern jederzeit abgenommen wurden. Das Marktprinzip kann nicht regulierend wirken, wenn nur mangelhafte Waren angeboten werden, und diese auch noch in zu geringer Menge.

Die einzelnen Räume der Wohnung werden ihren Funktionen entsprechend festgelegt und gruppiert. Da alle Menschen essen, schlafen und sich waschen müssen, erscheint die Ableitung und Zuordnung der Raumbedürfnisse recht einfach. Der Versuch, gewisse Regeln für den Bedarf verschieden großer Familien aufzustellen (Bild 78) beweist bereits, wie schwierig es bei nur einer Variante, der Familiengröße, ist, Festlegungen zu treffen. Die Familie selbst ist jedoch als Folge der Veränderungen im Bereich der Technik und Industrie gegenwärtig in einem Strukturwandel begriffen, der die Lebensgewohnheiten verändert. Wenn die Räume der Wohnung eine Funktion der Lebensgewohnheiten darstellen, müssen sie ebenfalls Veränderungen gegenüber dem vor dreißig oder vierzig Jahren üblichen Schema aufweisen.

Während nach dem Zweiten Weltkrieg zunächst angeknüpft wurde an die in den dreißiger Jahren gewonnenen Erkenntnisse für den Kleinwohnungs- und Hochhausbau, zeigte sich bald, daß diese Basis zu schmal ist. Die Vereinfachungen der Notzeiten verschafften zwar jedem ein Dach über dem Kopf, das Leben der Familie erfordert jedoch weitere Differenzierungen. Für größere Familien sind die Kleinwohnungen zu eng und nicht variabel genug. Eine optische Ausweitung kann viel dazu beitragen, die Beengtheit der zellenartigen Wohnungen zu sprengen (Bild 70). Finnischem Alltag entspricht die von Aalto im Berliner Hansaviertel vorgeschlagene Wohnraumlösung, als Allraum bezeichnet, der sich nach allen Seiten in die Schlaf- und Nebenräume verzweigt (Bild 69). Viele Bewohner haben sich in Berlin wenigstens optisch einen Flur vom All-Wohnraum abgetrennt, um den Weg von der Küche und vom Eingang zu Bad und Schlafräumen abzuschirmen. Häufig wird ein Eßplatz vom Wohnraum ausgesondert, der zur Loggia oder dem Balkon Zugang hat. Befragungen in England, Schweden, Deutschland und der Schweiz brachten das zunächst erstaunliche Ergebnis, daß in oft der Hälfte aller Haushalte in der Küche gegessen wird, auch wenn diese als reine Arbeitsküche geplant ist. Der lange Zeit hindurch ganz selbstverständlich von den Architekten in den Wohnraum eingezeichnete Eßtisch erweist sich also bei der Realisierung der Pläne in der Hälfte aller Fälle als unpraktisch, weil die Wege aus der Küche – auch beim Einbau einer Durchreiche – zu weit sind. Schwedische Vorschläge zielen auf eine Verkleinerung des Wohnzimmers und Entlastung dieses Raumes von Tätigkeiten, die zum Arbeitsbereich der Frau in der Küche in enger Beziehung stehen wie Essen, Bügeln, Nähen, Arbeiten oder Basteln der Kinder usw., Nutzungen also, an die in den Standardgrundrissen nicht ausreichend gedacht ist (Bild 74). Überhaupt sind die normalen Wohnungstypen viel zu einseitig auf die Familie mit ein bis zwei Kindern abgestellt. Ein Symbiosetyp, den zum Beispiel Scharoun 1960 in einigen Fällen für die Siedlung in Siemensstadt vorschlug, konnte nicht gebaut werden. Alleinstehende Verwandte sollten dort mit der Familie zusammen wohnen und dennoch ihren unabhängigen Wohnteil haben (Bild 71).

Zu den vergessenen Geschöpfen gehören im normalen Mietwohnungsbau die Kinder. Man wird entgegnen, das sei nicht wahr, denn für die Kinder werden Sandkästen, Spielplätze, Schulen, Sportfelder und sogar Schlafzimmer gebaut; man lebe im Jahrhundert des Kindes. Aber wie sehen denn die Käfige aus, die in den meisten Grundrissen als Kinderzimmer fungieren!

An ein Aufwachsen aller Kinder in Einfamilienhäusern ist nicht zu denken, das verhindern die Baukosten, die fehlende Bodenordnung oder das, in der Großstadt gar nicht zu schaffende, mangelnde Angebot an billigen – und auch an vermietbaren – Einfamilienhäusern.

Die meisten neuen Wohnungen sind noch auf das Modell der patriarchalischen Familie zugeschnitten, in der die Kinder sich abends um den etwa aus der Haus-

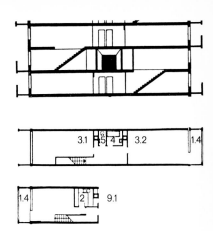

72 Section and plans of a dwelling unit in Le Corbusier's tower block in Berlin, 1956, 1 in 500. The attempt to design a family dwelling like a monastery cell with a wide vista on the landscape is doomed to failure because of the contrast, unbearable to the eye, between the bright and glaring, but narrow, glass fronts and the dark room in the depth of the dwelling. Ultimately, the rigid and narrow side walls cause a feeling of claustrophobia. The quality of the plans is not in keeping with the high standard of the logically conceived three-dimensional treatment of the block

72 Schnitt und Grundrisse einer Wohneinheit in Le Corbusiers Berliner Wohnhochhaus 1956, 1: 500. Der Versuch, die Idee einer Klosterzelle mit weitem Blick in die Landschaft auf die Wohnung einer mehrköpfigen Familie zu übertragen, scheitert an der für das Auge unerträglichen Differenz zwischen den hellen, blendenden Glaswänden an den Schmalseiten und dem dunklen Raum in der Tiefe der Wohnung. Die starren und engen Seitenwände rufen auf die Dauer ein Gefühl der Beklemmung hervor. Die Qualität der Wohnungsgrundrisse steht nicht im Einklang mit der hohen Qualität der rational durchdachten plastischen Gesamtform des Hauses

73 Tower block at Gladbeck, 1964, architect Werner Ruhnau, floor plan, 1 in 500

73 Wohnhochhaus in Gladbeck 1964, Architekt Werner Ruhnau, Geschoßgrundriß, 1:500

and not an example to be followed. The Swedish directives insist that each room must have accommodation for at least two beds. This may well be regarded as a reasonable minimum provision. In the normal case, each room in which a person must live, including a nursery, should have a clear space of 13 to 15 ft. at least in one direction. Nurseries must be flexible; but flexibility calls for more space not earmarked for a specific purpose. This also applies to any experiments with flexible space partition, e.g. by party walls. Such demands are unfortunately incompatible with the concept of the so-called economic calculations which aim at consolidating a momentary condition. 60 years ago, an old-fashioned privy on the intermediate landing was regarded as the most economic solution for four to six dwellings; who would dare to provide such facilities for tenement houses to-day?

Flexibility implies adaptability to change. The dwelling must be adaptable to the changing requirements of the family. Such adaptability can be attained in many different ways. In normal times, a change in space demand can be satisfied by moving to another dwelling in the district. A survey at the Neubühl estate, Zürich, showed that this system of flexibility has worked very well in the time from 1930 to 1960. The individual dwelling can be adapted to the demand. The system permits the complete utilisation of the dwelling space.

A second possibility is offered by the provision of sufficiently large rooms with independent entrance from a neutral zone, a hall or corridor. Many old-fashioned flats are built in this way and prove their advantages especially where a removal would be dependent on planning permission, and expensive. In this way, a large room may be used, for instance, as a nursery with sufficiently large playing space, whilst a smaller room is often sufficient as a sitting room or parents' bedroom (Fig. 76). This possibility of varying the user of rooms of fixed size is likewise a form of flexibility; but it calls for certain space reserves.

A third possibility is given by modifying the partitions within a dwelling (Fig. 77). This, too, calls for a space reserve which can be optionally added to the different zones of dwellings. As the partitions are generally light and access may be restricted to jointly used rooms, this method will, however, in general be confined to cases where the living requirements of the family do not change greatly. With this type of flexibility, outsiders such as relatives forming part of the household, guests or visitors are apt to cause considerable disturbances.

A fourth variety of flexibility is offered by a "space grid system" variable at will. The utopian projects of one Yona Friedman and one Eckard Schulze Fielitz appear to solve, by launching out into the "free air space", all those problems which, on earth, are hopelessly entangled in a labyrinth of regulations and restraints. What is no longer possible on the densely populated soil, is to be moved "up there" whilst the blighted buildings of the past are left to decay slowly and to make room for roads, car parks and open spaces. In the space grid, everyone will be able to satisfy his increased space demand by just fitting in a few more panels into the grid structure and thus enlarging his living space – a pioneering situation akin to that experienced when the Europeans gained a foothold in America and Africa.

But this ideal is removed from reality. The space grid would very soon be parcelled out, zoned and subjected to manifold regulations in just the same way as the land. In a talk, Yona Friedman admitted that his flexible system could just as well be established on the ground. It is merely the restraints placed on the utilisation of the ground by centuries-old easements which prevent the realisation of such an experiment. In fact, the existing towns and buildings are, in a sense, no more than a timespace grid which has merely been consolidated to such an extent that it has, in many respects, become unsuitable for present-day needs. Too many of the space cells have died since their original functions have ceased and their dead mass is an obstruction to any functional change. The idea of a space system adaptable to changes in demand should be separated from the structural principle of a suspended town, and investigations should be made into the limits to which the desired flexibility can usefully go. It would, for instance, be pointless to design a space structure in such a way that it could be used, equally well, for dwellings, heavy industry, and insurance offices.

Flexibility considerations must also be applied to certain individual rooms such as the kitchen. Departing from the Frankfurt prototype kitchen (Figs. 4/5), all the efforts were aimed at obtaining a concentration of activities comparable to a dining car

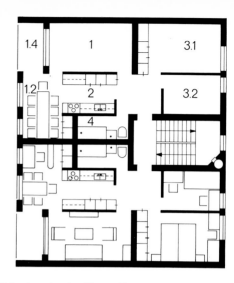

74 Swedish plans for dwelling units, 1960, 1 in 200. Proposal for a novel way of grouping the kitchen, dining and working area, sitting room and balcony

74 Schwedische Wohnungsgrundrisse 1960, 1:200. Vorschlag einer neuen Gruppierung von Küche, Eß- und Arbeitsplatz, Wohnraum und Balkon

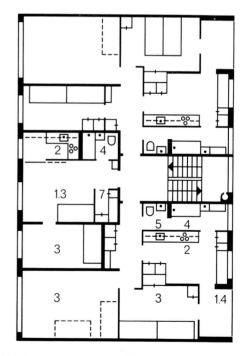

75 Markbacken housing scheme, Örebro, Sweden, architects Alm, Falk, White (see page 84), part of plan, 1 in 200. Mixture of dwellings of different sizes with flexibly used rooms

75 Siedlung Örebro-Markbacken, Architekten Alm, Falk, White (siehe Seite 84), Grundrißausschnitt, 1:200. Mischung verschieden großer Wohnungen, deren Räume unterschiedlich genutzt werden können

postille vorlesenden Hausvater scharen, bis sie sich im kleinen Kämmerchen zur Ruhe legen. Allenfalls nimmt der Bildschirm den Platz des müde gewordenen Hausvaters ein. Wie soll ein Jugendlicher zwischen 10 und 20 Jahren in einer Koje, die Schrank, Bett, Stuhl und zur Not einen Schreibplatz faßt, wohnen und sein Eigenleben entfalten, ohne die Familie zu tyrannisieren? Die sogenannten »halben« Zimmer des deutschen Sozialen Wohnungsbaus sind eine Notlösung, kein Vorbild. Nach den schwedischen Förderungsrichtlinien muß in jedem Raum die Aufstellung von zwei Betten möglich sein. Damit ist das vernünftige Minimum abgesteckt. Als Normalfall sollte in jedem Raum, der zum Wohnen dient – auch im Kinderzimmer –, in einer Richtung eine Distanz von 4,5 bis 5 m zwischen den Abschlußwänden erreicht werden. Kinderzimmer müssen sich verändern lassen; aber das erfordert mehr Raum ohne festgelegte Zweckbestimmung. Das gilt ebenso für alle Versuche mit einer variierbaren Raumaufteilung, zum Beispiel durch Montagewände. Derartige Forderungen passen leider nicht ins Konzept der sogenannten Wirtschaftlichkeitsberechnungen, die einen momentanen Zustand fixieren wollen. – Vor sechzig Jahren glaubte man mit dem Trockenabort auf halber Treppe für 4–6 Wohnungen als »wirtschaftlichster« Lösung auszukommen; wer würde heute wagen, Wohnhäuser derart auszustatten?

Flexibel bedeutet biegsam, wandlungsfähig. Die Wohnung soll also einem veränderten Bedarf der Familie angepaßt werden können. Diese Wandlungsfähigkeit läßt sich auf sehr verschiedene Art erreichen. Bei normalem Wohnungsbestand kann ein veränderter Raumbedarf durch Umzug in eine andere Wohnung des Wohnquartiers befriedigt werden. Wie aus einer Untersuchung über die Siedlung Neubühl in Zürich hervorgeht, hat sich dieses System der Flexibilität dort von 1930 bis 1960 ausgezeichnet eingespielt. Die einzelne Wohnung kann auf den jeweiligen Bedarf passend zugeschnitten sein. Das Verfahren erlaubt die volle Ausnutzung des gebauten Raumes.

Die zweite Möglichkeit bietet der Bau ausreichend großer Zimmer, die über eine neutrale Zone – einen Flur oder eine Diele – unabhängig voneinander zu erreichen sind. Viele Altbauwohnungen sind nach diesem Prinzip gebaut und beweisen ihre Vorteile besonders dann, wenn ein Wohnungswechsel mit behördlichen Genehmigungen und mit hohen Kosten belastet wäre. Ein großer Raum kann dann beispielsweise als Kinderzimmer mit genügend großer Spielfläche genutzt werden, ein kleinerer reicht oft als Wohnraum und als Elternschlafzimmer aus (Bild 76). Diese Möglichkeit, die Zweckbestimmung fest umgrenzter Räume zu verändern, ist auch Flexibilität, erfordert aber gewisse Raumreserven.

Die dritte Möglichkeit wird mit der Veränderung der Raumgrenzen innerhalb einer Wohnung geboten (Bild 77). Auch sie erfordert eine Platzreserve, die den einzelnen Teilen des Wohnbereichs nach Bedarf zugeschlagen wird. Sie funktioniert im allgemeinen wegen der meist leichten Trennwände und des Zugangs durch gemeinsam benutzte Räume nur, wenn die Wohnbedürfnisse der Familie nicht sehr differieren. Fremde, seien es in der Wohngemeinschaft lebende Verwandte, Gäste oder Besucher, können bei dieser Art Flexibilität erhebliche Störungen verursachen.

Die vierte Variante der Flexibilität bietet sich mit einem beliebig variierbaren Raumgitternetz. Die utopischen Projekte eines Yona Friedman und eines Eckard Schulze-Fielitz scheinen mit dem Griff in den »freien Luftraum« alle Probleme zu lösen, die auf dem Erdboden hoffnungslos in ein Gewirr von Vorschriften und Bindungen eingefangen sind. Was auf den dichtbevölkerten Gebieten des Erdbodens nicht mehr möglich ist, soll sich »dort oben« vollziehen, während die darunterliegende Altbebauung langsam verrottet und Straßen, Parkplätzen und grünen Wiesen Platz macht: Jeder soll im Raumgitterwerk die Möglichkeit erhalten, bei vermehrtem Raumbedarf sich einige Felder des Gestänges mit Platten zu füllen und das Wohnungsvolumen zu vergrößern; eine Pioniersituation wie sie sich beim Auftauchen der Europäer in Amerika und Afrika ergab.

Dennoch liegt diesen Gedanken ein Ausweichen vor der Wirklichkeit zugrunde. Der Raum im Gitterwerk würde in kurzer Zeit ebenso kartiert, eingezont und durch mannigfache Vorschriften festgelegt sein wie bisher die Erdoberfläche. Yona Friedman räumte im Gespräch selber ein, daß sein flexibles System ebenso gut auf diesem Erdboden etabliert werden könnte. Nur die Bindung des Bodens an zum Teil jahrhundertealte Rechte läßt ihm für die Erprobung keinen Raum. Dabei sind die vorhandenen Städte und Bauten ebenfalls ein räumlich-zeitliches Gitterwerk,

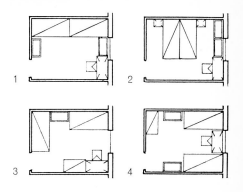

76 Danish proposal for the design of rooms which can be furnished in many different ways, 1 in 200

76 Dänischer Vorschlag zum Bau von Zimmern, die auf verschiedenerlei Weise möbliert werden können, 1:200

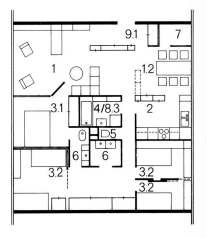

77 System of flats designed for flexible utilisation, 1 in 200. Proposal by the ''Syndicat des Architectes de la Seine'', Paris 1960. The plan, with a floor area of about 880 sq. ft., is primarily intended to demonstrate the method. There is adequate cupboard accommodation in the entrance zone and in the nursery

77 System einer veränderlichen Wohnungsaufteilung, 1:200, Vorschlag des »Syndicat des Architectes de la Seine«, Paris 1960. Der Grundriß mit 82 m² Fläche soll in erster Linie die Methode zeigen. Für genügend Schrankraum im Eingangsbereich und im Kinderzimmer ist gesorgt

kitchen. In the meantime, just as the industrial worker is gradually being freed from heavy physical labour, the kitchen fatigue of the housewife is being reduced by the increasing use of mechanical aids. These aids require space which is not available in small kitchens where every cubic foot of space has already been assigned to a specific purpose. If to-day, cooker, sink, built-in cupboards and refrigerator are regarded as part of the standard equipment, this may well, in a few years, also apply to the dishwasher, deep-freeze cabinet and other kitchen utensils. The only way of preventing kitchens from becoming out of date is to provide space which must, at the moment, be regarded as useless. In this respect, the German Standards (DIN 18022) are out of date. It must be hoped that the revised version, at present in preparation, will not again become a source of grave errors.

Sound Protection and Building Technology

Surveys conducted among tenants of new blocks of flats in Berlin have confirmed that inadequate sound protection between flats is among the shortcomings most criticized by the occupiers. Neither the previous German Standards nor the standards applied by the architects were sufficient to satisfy the tenants. Initially, in the endeavour to adopt structural systems which require little material and can be fully utilized for load-bearing purposes, acoustic considerations tended to be ignored since sound transmission was not so much of a problem in the heavier buildings of the past. At the same time, there was a great increase in potential sources of noise: loudspeakers, record players, tape recorders and television sets, so that sound transmission, often right across intermediate dwellings, became an intolerable intrusion into the privacy of the dwelling. The town dweller, already worn down by street noises, has become particularly sensitive to this kind of nuisance. Sound transmission is facilitated by homogeneous or light-weight building materials with good thermal insulating properties. Little noticed by-pass channels and pipes installed in wall recesses become a frequent source of trouble (Figs. 79–83). With the ever-increasing demands to protect the intimacy of the dwelling, a much higher standard of acoustic protection will, in future, have to be regarded as normal equipment. The urban amenity of "accessibility" is bought at too high a price of the restrictions imposed on the use of one's own dwelling far exceed an acceptable measure so that the town dwelling is brought into disrepute. Why should it not be possible, in the present state of technology, to listen to one's radio or to have a bath in the small hours of the morning without disturbing a neighbour – or perhaps even eight of them? If the town is required to provide a maximum of communication facilities, the dwelling must offer the possibility of escaping from these communications. In Scandinavia, the double doors usually provided for the entrance to the flat afford an effective protection.

It is almost only in new residential districts that the noise intruding into the dwelling from the street and from the surroundings can be reduced by reasonable planning measures. Traffic noise, which has a loudness range of 60 to 100 phons, can be damped by earth mounds, by placing the roads and railways in cuttings, or by planting. If, in the open air, a noise is reduced by 5 to 6 phons whenever the distance is doubled, planting is able to bring about a further reduction by 0.1 to 0.25 phons per metre, i.e. by as much as 10 to 25 phons over a distance of 100 metres (330 ft), though it is rather less effective where the foliage is high above the ground. A comparison of loudness values, expressed in German Standard "DIN-phons", is given in the table, Fig. 79. Green wedges with variegated plantation must have a width of, say 250 to 500 ft. – the wind may cause differences up to 10 DIN-phons – if a reasonable protection against traffic noise is to be provided. To create such conditions is not within the power of the person responsible for an individual building. Yet they have a greater influence on dwelling amenities than any sound-damping windows which merely protect the interior. Dwelling amenities also include the undisturbed use of a balcony or terrace and the right to sleep with open windows.

It is difficult to prove that noise has a detrimental effect on the human being. Medically, the only known disability caused by noise is the deafness experienced by, e.g., boiler makers or gunners. Research work carried out in 1961 by Professor Lehmann and Dr. Jansen at the Max Planck Institute for Work Physiology, Dortmund, succeeded in clarifying the influence on the blood circulation of sounds and noises of different frequency and duration. Measurements of the finger pulse amplitudes

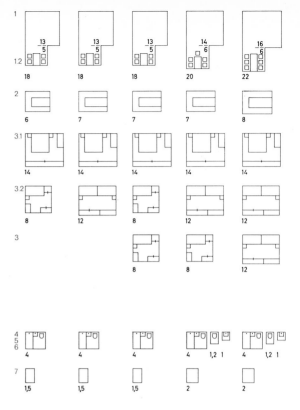

78 Minimum habitable surfaces as a function of the size of the family: Cologne Resolutions
The Committee for Family Housing of the *International Union of Family Organizations* and the Standing Committee "Rent and Family Income" of the *International Federation For Housing and Planning* in joint session at Cologne on April 11th 1957 voted unanimously that the housing surfaces envisaged below are the absolute minima required for the families of the sizes stated; and urge public authorities to see to it by all the means at their disposal that these absolute minima are observed

das sich lediglich so verfestigt hat, daß es für den heutigen Gebrauch in vieler Hinsicht ungeeignet geworden ist. Zu viele »Raumzellen« sind abgestorben, da ihre ursprünglichen Funktionen erloschen sind und die nun tote Masse sich einer Funktionswandlung widersetzt. Man sollte den Gedanken an ein räumliches System, das sich den Bedarfsänderungen anpassen läßt, von dem Konstruktionsprinzip der »schwebenden Stadt« trennen und die Abgrenzungen der Frage untersuchen, wie weit die erstrebte Flexibilität gehen kann und sinnvoll ist. Zum Beispiel wäre es unsinnig, eine räumliche Struktur so anzulegen, daß sie gleichermaßen für Wohnungen, Schwerindustrie und Versicherungsbüros brauchbar ist.

Überlegungen zur Flexibilität betreffen auch einzelne Räume wie die Küche. Ausgehend von der Frankfurter Küche (Bild 4/5) zielten die Bestrebungen dahin, eine der D-Zug-Küche entsprechende Konzentration aller Arbeitsvorgänge zu erreichen. Inzwischen geht wie im industriellen Bereich die Befreiung des Arbeiters von schwerer Muskelarbeit auch die Befreiung der Hausfrau von der Küchenfron durch die Einschaltung mechanischer Arbeitshilfen weiter. Diese Maschinen brauchen Platz, der in ausgetüftelt kleinen Küchen fehlt. Gehört neben Herd, Spülbecken und Einbauschränken der Kühlschrank heute zur Normalausstattung, so können in wenigen Jahren Geschirrspülautomat, Tiefkühltruhe und andere Küchenmaschinen dazugekommen sein. Nur »unnützer«, weil im Augenblick nicht zweckgebundener Raum kann die heute gebauten Küchenräume vor dem Veralten schützen. Die deutsche Norm 18022 ist in dieser Hinsicht veraltet. Hoffentlich wird die in Arbeit befindliche Neufassung nicht wieder zu einer schweren Fehlerquelle.

Schallschutz und Haustechnik

Mieterbefragungen über den Wohnwert von Berliner Neubauten haben bestätigt, daß mangelnder Schallschutz zwischen den Wohnungen zu den Fehlern zählt, die von den Bewohnern mehrgeschossiger Häuser am unangenehmsten empfunden werden. Weder die bisherigen deutschen Normen noch die Kenntnisse der Architekten genügten den Forderungen der Mieter. – Auf dem Wege zu materialsparenden, statisch voll ausnutzbaren Konstruktionen ließ man zunächst die schalltechnischen Gesichtspunkte außer acht, denn beim schweren Massivbau trat das Problem der Schallübertragung nicht in gleichem Maße auf. Gleichzeitig vervielfachten sich die Möglichkeiten der mechanischen Lärmerzeugung durch Lautsprecher, Plattenspieler, Tonband- und Fernsehgeräte, so daß die Schallübertragung, oft über dazwischenliegende Wohnungen hinweg, in unzumutbarer Weise in die Privatsphäre der Wohnungen einbrach. Der vom Außenlärm strapazierte Stadtbewohner ist gegenüber diesen Störungen besonders empfindlich geworden. Homogene oder leichte, besonders gut wärmedämmende Baumaterialien erleichtern die Schallübertragung. Wenig beachtete Nebenwege und in Mauerschlitzen verlegte Installationsleitungen wurden zu häufigen Fehlerquellen (Bild 79–83). Da die Ansprüche an den Schutz der Intimsphäre der Wohnung zunehmend steigen, muß in Zukunft ein besonders guter Schallschutz als »Normalfall« vorgesehen werden. So nützlich Kommunikation sein kann, die Beeinträchtigung der Freiheit, die eigene Wohnung nach Belieben zu nutzen, geht weit über das erträgliche Maß hinaus und hat dazu beigetragen, die Stadtwohnung in Verruf zu bringen. Warum sollte es beim heutigen Stand der Technik nicht möglich gemacht werden, daß man in seinen Räumen nachts um 2 Uhr Radio hören oder in die Wanne steigen kann, ohne einen Nachbarn – wenn nicht gar acht Nachbarn – zu stören? Ist von der Stadt ein Höchstmaß an Kommunikationsmöglichkeiten zu fordern, so muß die Wohnung die Möglichkeit bieten, sich dieser Kommunikation auch zu entziehen. – In Skandinavien schirmen die am Wohnungseingang üblichen Doppeltüren gegen eine Störungsquelle weitgehend ab.

Der von der Straße und der Umgebung in die Wohnung dringende Lärm kann fast nur in Neubaugebieten durch vernünftige Planung eingedämmt werden. Erdwälle, Straßen und Bahnen im Einschnitt sowie Bepflanzungen können den 60–100 phon lauten Verkehrslärm dämpfen. Nimmt in freier Luft ein Geräusch bei Abstandsverdopplung um 5–6 phon ab, so kann Bodenbewachsung eine weitere Verminderung um 0,1–0,25 phon/m bringen, bei 100 m sind das immerhin 10–25 phon. Bei großem Bodenabstand des Laubwerks sind die Werte geringer. Einen Vergleich verschiedener DIN-phon-Werte gibt die Tabelle Bild 79. Unterschiedlich bepflanzte Grünstreifen müssen etwa 80 bis 150 m breit sein – der Wind kann dabei Unterschiede bis zu 10 DIN-phon hervorrufen –, um einigermaßen gegen starken Verkehrs-

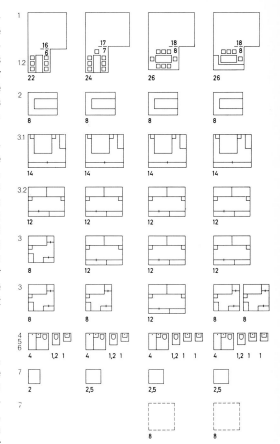

78 Mindestwohnflächen in Abhängigkeit von der Familiengröße: Kölner Empfehlungen.

»Die Wohnungskommission der ›Internationalen Union der Familienorganisationen‹ und der ›Ständige Ausschuß Miete und Familieneinkommen‹ des ›Internationalen Verbandes für Wohnungswesen, Städtebau und Raumplanung‹ haben am 11. April 1957 in einer gemeinsamen Sitzung in Köln einstimmig erklärt, daß die hier angegebenen Wohnflächen für die jeweilige Familiengröße den absoluten Mindestbedürfnissen entsprechen. – Sie empfehlen den zuständigen Behörden nachdrücklich, mit allen ihnen zur Verfügung stehenden Mitteln dafür zu sorgen, daß diese Mindestmaße unter allen Umständen eingehalten werden.«

clearly indicated a narrowing of the blood vessels. A single sound at a frequency of 3200 c/s, which is generally felt to be unpleasant, causes a relatively small discontinuity in the curve (Fig. 80) which increases with the band width and becomes widest and longest as a result of a broad-band noise comprising sounds from the entire audio-frequency range. Subjectively, such broad-band noise is regarded as much less disagreeable than the isolated sound at a frequency of 3200 c/s. The subjective sensation is therefore not in keeping with the objectively measured influence on the vegetative nerve system, but intensifies in the opposite direction. In the course of long-term tests, the drop in the finger pulse amplitude was found to be always the same; in other words, one does not get used to the noise.

In the course of sleeping tests, measurements were taken of the brain current curve and pulse amplitude. A noise of 50 DIN-phons which, according to Fig. 79, still permits highly concentrated brain work in daytime and does not wake the sleeper from a deep sleep, nevertheless reduces the depth of the sleep. There is a clearly recognisable reduction in the peripheral blood circulation even if the noise lasts no longer than a fraction of a second. This investigation, too, proves that the reaction of our vegetative nerve system to disturbances differs from our conscious reaction. Questioning about noise nuisances can therefore not result in an objective judgement of possible damage to health and is apt to lead to completely fallacious conclusions. Countless further investigations will be required in order to assess the different influences of noise on the healthy and the ill, on children and aged people. During the last decades, the sanitary installations and other domestic appliances have undergone considerable changes so that too firm an adherence to the present standards would entail the risk that the designs may already be out-dated in ten years or so.

In small-house construction, there is a widespread tendency to include the kitchen functions, by now freed from their nuisance effects, in the living zone. In keeping with the development of the consumer goods industry, the first and most widespread examples are to be found in the United States where this tendency coincides with a traditional romantic trait of recalling the pioneering period. How little it is possible

79 Comparison of the loudness of known noises with those noise levels which, according to W. Bobran, should not be exceeded for certain activities:

Work	Maximum degree of loudness in DIN-phons, measured at the working place
A Work calling for high mental concentration	40 to 50
B Office work	60 to 70
C Other work	80 to 90

Sources of noise nuisance	Maximum degree of loudness in DIN-phons, 1'8" in front of the open window	
	By day	By night
D/E Industrial areas	65	50
F/G Predominantly residential areas	60	45
H/I Purely residential areas	50	35
Sources of noise inside the building	35/44	25/30

79 Vergleich der Lautstärke bekannter Geräusche mit den Lautstärken, die nach H. W. Bobran bei verschiedenen Tätigkeiten nicht überschritten werden sollen:

Arbeit	DIN-phon maximal (am Arbeitsplatz gemessen)
A Arbeiten mit hoher geistiger Konzentration	40–50
B Büroarbeit	60–70
C sonstige Arbeit	80–90

Störungsquellen	DIN-phon maximal (0,5 m vor dem offenen Zimmerfenster)
D/E in Industriegebieten	tagsüber 65/nachts 50
F/G vorwiegend Wohngebiet	tagsüber 60/nachts 45
H/I reines Wohngebiet	tagsüber 50/nachts 35
Schallquellen im Haus	tagsüber 35–45/nachts 25–30

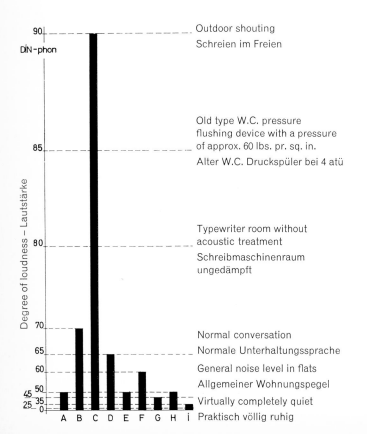

Outdoor shouting
Schreien im Freien

Old type W.C. pressure flushing device with a pressure of approx. 60 lbs. pr. sq. in.
Alter W.C. Druckspüler bei 4 atü

Typewriter room without acoustic treatment
Schreibmaschinenraum ungedämpft

Normal conversation
Normale Unterhaltungssprache

General noise level in flats
Allgemeiner Wohnungspegel

Virtually completely quiet
Praktisch völlig ruhig

lärm zu schützen. Diese Voraussetzungen zu schaffen liegt nicht in der Macht des für ein Einzelbauwerk Zuständigen. Sie sind für ein ruhiges Wohnen wichtiger als alle schallschützenden Fensterkonstruktionen, die nur den geschlossenen Innenraum betreffen. Zum Wohnen gehört auch der ungestörte Aufenthalt auf Balkon oder Terrasse und das »Menschenrecht, bei offenem Fenster zu schlafen«.

Eine Schädigung des Menschen durch den Lärm läßt sich nur schwer feststellen. Als Krankheit ist nur die Lärmschwerhörigkeit z. B. bei Kesselschmieden und Kanonieren bekannt. Forschungen von Professor Lehmann und Dr. Jansen im Max-Planck-Institut für Arbeitsphysiologie in Dortmund klärten 1961 den Einfluß verschieden hoher und verschieden lang auftretender Töne und Geräusche auf den Blutkreislauf. Die Messungen an den Fingerpulsamplituden zeigten deutlich Gefäßverengungen an. Der einzelne Ton in einer allgemein als unangenehm empfundenen Höhe von 3200 Hz verursacht in der Kurve einen relativ geringen Einschnitt (Bild 80), der bei größerer Bandbreite zunimmt und beim Breitbandgeräusch, das Töne aus dem gesamten hörbaren Wellenbereich umfaßt, am stärksten und längsten in Erscheinung tritt. Dieses Breitbandgeräusch wird subjektiv gegenüber dem 3200-Hz-Einzelton als viel weniger unangenehm empfunden. Die subjektive Belästigung und der objektiv gemessene Einfluß auf das vegetative Nervensystem entsprechen sich also nicht, sondern steigern sich in einander entgegengesetzter Richtung. Bei über längere Zeit hinweg fortgesetzten Versuchen zeigte sich jedesmal der gleiche Abfall der Fingerpulsamplitude; eine Gewöhnung an den Lärm tritt also nicht ein.

Bei Schlafversuchen wurden Hirnstromkurve und Pulsamplitude gemessen. Ein Geräusch von 50 DIN-phon, das nach Bild 79 am Tage noch Arbeiten mit hoher geistiger Konzentration zuläßt und das den Schläfer nicht aus dem Tiefschlaf weckt, vermindert dennoch die Tiefe des Schlafs. Die periphere Durchblutung wird deutlich erkennbar gedrosselt, selbst wenn das Geräusch nur Bruchteile einer Sekunde andauert. Auch diese Untersuchung liefert den Beweis, daß unser vegetatives Nervensystem anders auf Störungen reagiert als unser Bewußtsein. Befragungen über auftretende Lärmbelästigungen können daher kein objektives Urteil über mögliche Schädigungen herbeiführen; sie verleiten zu völlig falschen Schlüs-

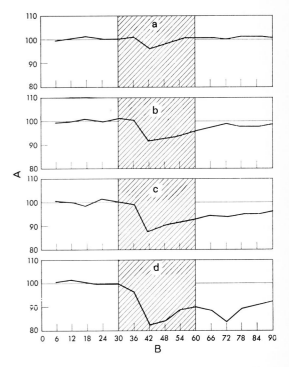

80 Influence of noises of certain frequencies on the blood circulation of a person, measured as finger pulse amplitude (according to Jansen, "Stahl und Eisen" No. 81/1961)
A Finger pulse amplitude in percent, B Time in seconds,
a Sound, 3200 c/s, b Third, 3200 c/s (mean value),
c Octave, 3200 c/s (mean value), d Broad-band noise

80 Einfluß von Geräuschen bestimmter Tonhöhen auf die Durchblutung eines Menschen, als Fingerpulsamplitude gemessen (nach Jansen, »Stahl und Eisen«, Heft 81/1961).
A Fingerpulsamplitude in %, B Zeit in Sekunden,
a Ton 3200 Hz, b Terz 3200 Hz (Mittelwert), c Oktave 3200 Hz (Mittelwert), d Breitbandgeräusch

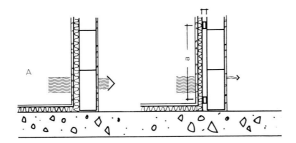

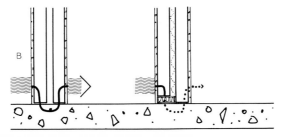

81 Sound insulation of light-weight party walls:
A The insulating boards should be mounted, with an air gap, on battens having a minimum distance of 1′8″ (a); B If the wall consists of two thin panels, one of them should be insulated against the floor

81 Schalldämmung leichter Zwischenwände:
A die Vorsatzschale aus Isolierplatten muß mit Luftzwischenraum auf einem mit mindestens 50 cm Abstand (a) angebrachten Lattenrost montiert werden; B bei einer Wand aus zwei dünnen Schalen muß eine Schale gegen die Decke isoliert werden

for domestic technology to lay down rules for the equipment of the rooms is well demonstrated by the example of the washing machine. With the advent of modern, close-at-hand Launderettes, laundering has been completely eliminated from the living zone. If the installation of a washing machine in the dwelling becomes necessary, the question of the best location (kitchen, bathroom, utility-room) can only be decided on the merits of each case. Two years ago, a corner space measuring 2′8″ by 2′8″ was still sufficient. In the meantime, many manufactures have gone over to new models with separate washing and spin-drying facilities which require a space of about 3′4 × 1′10″. Where in low-rent housing is such a space available, with the necessary water supply and a power supply of at least 3 kW?

In any case, the power supply grids have not kept pace with the development of the appliances. In older districts, the increase in electrical appliances has given rise to a much higher power consumption than the old distribution networks are capable of supplying. In 1962, the power requirements for an all-electric German dwelling were found to be as follows: – minimum standard 1.2 to 2.2 kW; improved standard 7 to 9 kW; good standard 18 to 37 kW; exceptionally high standard 40 to 48 kW. Flexibility calls for the provision of adequate reserves as the exceptionally high standard of to-day may well become the minimum standard of to-morrow. Suffice to recall some perfectly normal modernisation trends: – electric cooker 6 kW; washing machine 3 kW; dishwasher 3 kW; heating fan 2 kW; spin-dryer 1.8 kW – to demonstrate the inadequacy of the present minimum standard supply of 2 kW, even allowing for the fact that these appliances are not all used simultaneously. Whether such exclusive reliance on electric power, still economic to-day, will still be advisable to-morrow will greatly depend on the integration of the gas supply with the natural gas network or on the detoxication of the town gas (as in Basle).

Nor is it possible to provide a generally valid answer to the question of the most favourable heating system. Individual heating is obviously out-dated, at least as far as town dwellings are concerned. In view of the inescapable further coalescence of the communities into large conurbations, the question of air pollution by flue gases which, in most Western countries, is still left to the house-owner's discretion, will call for a joint solution of the heating problem, akin to the solutions conventionally adopted for water supply and refuse collection.

In future, district heating plants and electricity supply companies will compete with each other; the outcome will depend on the speed and efficiency with which they can adapt their distribution systems to the demand. The choice of fuel or energy will pass from the flat-owner to the power or heat supplier. In any case, it will be advantageous to provide a better thermal insulation of the outer walls than that prescribed by the present German Standards, DIN 4108. The additional capital costs incurred for this purpose are either immediately compensated by the lower costs of the heating installation or recovered within a few years by savings in heating. Excellent experience has been gathered with the floor heating system of the type used in the Swedish House, designed by Jaenecke and Samuelson, in the Hansa District of Berlin; in accordance with Swedish practice, the windows were equipped with triple-glazing.

In multi-storey housing, the most ideal form of heating is undoubtedly electric heating. There are no waste gases except at the power station; the charges are in exact relation to the demand; there is no need for carting fuel to the residential districts; the temperature can be controlled at will in each individual room. So far, however, it is only a country such as Norway, with her ample water-power resources, which can offer the current so cheaply that electric heating is cheaper than coal or oil firing. Wall panels heated by day-time current are widely used and provide an agreeable, even warmth.

In Oslo, the price per unit, payable in addition to a normal basic charge, amounts to 2.5 ⌀ re, i.e. 0.3d (cf. page 138). In other European countries, the electricity supply undertakings are not in a position to generate sufficient low-cost day-time current. It is only at night when industrial consumption is lower, that there is a margin of production capacity for low-cost night-time current which is increasingly used in Britain, Belgium, Austria and the German Federal Republic for the operation of storage heating plants. The widely used heating fans, however, are still of greatly variegated quality as regards noise nuisance and service life.

Any economic calculations intended to serve as a basis for the choice of a given

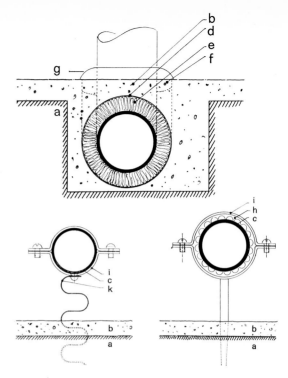

82 Possible sound insulation methods for water pipes, according to Hans Werner Bobran
a Brick wall, b Plaster, c Pipe, d Bituminous paper or plastic foil, e Mineral fibre felt or equivalent material, f Elastic sealing, g Rosette, h Ribbed rubber DVM 80, i Pipe clip, k Steel spring
83 Sound insulating method of mounting sanitary equipment on a floating floor
a Concrete floor, b Insulating layer, c Floating floor, d Mortar bed, e Tiles, f Plastic pointing

82 Mögliche Schallisolierung von Wasserleitungen nach H. W. Bobran
a Mauerwerk, b Putz, c Rohrleitung, d Bitumenpapier oder Kunststoff-Folie, e Mineralfaserfilz oder Gleichwertiges, f elastische Dichtung, g Rosette, h Rippengummi DVM 80, i Rohrschelle, k Stahlfeder
83 Geräuschisolierende Befestigung sanitärer Objekte auf einem schwimmenden Estrich
a Betondecke, b Dämmschicht, c Estrich, d Mörtelbett, e Fliesen, f plastische Fugenvergußmasse

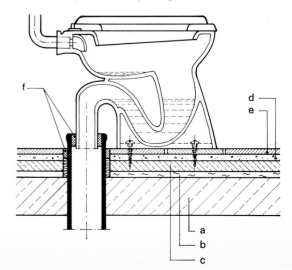

sen. Unzählige weitere Untersuchungen werden notwendig sein, um den unterschiedlichen Einfluß des Lärms auf Gesunde und Kranke, auf Kinder und Alte zu erforschen.

Die sanitären und haustechnischen Geräte und Installationen unterlagen in den letzten Jahrzehnten derart starken Wandlungen, daß eine Fixierung auf den gegenwärtigen Stand bedeuten würde, vielleicht schon in 10 Jahren von der Weiterentwicklung überrollt zu werden.

Vielfach zeigt sich in Einfamilienhäusern die Tendenz, die störungsfrei gemachten Küchenfunktionen in den Wohnbereich einzubeziehen – entsprechend dem Stand der Konsumgüterindustrie sind in den USA die ersten und meisten Beispiele zu finden –, wobei diese Tendenz mit einem traditionellen romantischen Zug zusammenfällt, sich der Pionierzeit zu erinnern. Wie wenig es besonders bei der Haustechnik möglich ist, Rezepte zur Einrichtung der Räume zu geben, beweist das Beispiel der Waschmaschinenaufstellung. In der Nähe eingerichtete, mit modernen Automaten ausgestattete Waschküchen sondern das Wäschewaschen ganz aus dem Wohnungsbereich aus. Ist die Aufstellung einer Waschmaschine in der Wohnung notwendig, so kann die Frage nach dem besten Aufstellungsort (Küche, Bad, Hauswirtschaftsraum) nur im Einzelfall entschieden werden. Vor zwei Jahren reichte eine 80 × 80 cm große Ecke, inzwischen sind sehr viele Hersteller zu neuen Typen mit getrenntem Wasch- und Schleudergang übergegangen, die etwa 1,0 × 0,55 m Platz benötigen. Wo findet sich im Sozialen Wohnungsbau diese Stellfläche mit Wasser- und mindestens 3-kW-Stromanschluß?

Die Auslegung der Energienetze hat mit der Entwicklung der Geräte ohnehin nicht Schritt gehalten. In Altbaugebieten erfordert die Zunahme elektrischer Geräte erheblich höhere Stromlieferungen, als sie die alten Ortsnetze leisten können. 1962 wurden in Deutschland für die (einschienige) Wohnungsausstattung folgende kW-Werte ermittelt: »Mindestausstattung« 1,2–2,2 kW, bessere Ausstattung 7–9 kW, gute Ausstattung 18–37 kW, sehr gute Ausstattung 40–48 kW. »Flexibilität« erfordert die Einplanung ausreichender Reserven, denn die »sehr gute« Ausstattung ist schon in Kürze der Normalfall, also »Mindestausstattung«. Man braucht nur ganz normale Modernisierungswünsche aufzuzählen: Elektroherd 6 kW, Waschautomat 3 kW, Geschirrspülautomat 3 kW, Heizlüfter 2 kW, Wäschetrockengerät 1,8 kW, um auch bei Berücksichtigung des Gleichzeitigkeitsfaktors zu merken, wie rückständig die »Normalausstattung« der Wohnung mit 2 kW ist. Ob die heute noch günstigere sogenannte einschienige Versorgung mit Energie morgen noch zu empfehlen ist, hängt weitgehend vom Anschluß der Gasversorgung an das Erdgasnetz oder von der Entgiftung des Stadtgases (Basel!) ab.

Auch die Frage nach der günstigsten Beheizung kann nicht pauschal beantwortet werden. Einzelofenheizung ist jedenfalls für die Stadtwohnung widersinnig. Die Luftverschmutzung durch Abgase, in den meisten westlichen Ländern heute noch ins Belieben der Hauseigentümer gestellt, wird mit dem unausweichlichen Zusammenwachsen der Gemeinden zu großen Agglomerationen ebenso gemeinsame Regelungen der Beheizung erfordern wie sie für die Wasserversorgung und die Müllabfuhr üblich sind.

Fernheizwerke und Elektrizitätswerke werden in Zukunft die Konkurrenten sein, je nachdem, wie rasch und anpassungsfähig sie ihre Verteilernetze aufbauen. Die Entscheidung über Brennstoffwahl oder Energiebezug wird vom Hauseigentümer auf den Energie- bzw. Wärmelieferanten übergehen. In jedem Fall wird eine bessere Wärmedämmung der Außenwände, als sie nach der deutschen DIN 4108 zulässig ist, vorteilhaft sein. Den dafür erforderlichen Aufwand gleichen die geringeren Anlagekosten der Heizung zum Teil sofort aus, zum anderen Teil amortisiert er sich innerhalb weniger Jahre durch geringere Heizungskosten. Ausgezeichnete Erfahrungen liegen mit Fußbodenheizung aus dem »Schwedenhaus« von Jaenecke und Samuelson im Berliner Hansaviertel vor; nach schwedischen Vorbildern wurden die Fenster dreifach verglast. Die idealste Form der Heizung im mehrgeschossigen Wohnungsbau ist zweifelsohne die elektrische Heizung: Abgase entstehen nur beim Elektrizitätswerk, die Heizkosten werden individuell nach dem Verbrauch berechnet, es sind keine Brennstofftransporte in den Wohnhäusern erforderlich, die Temperatur kann in jedem Raum nach Belieben geregelt werden. Nur das an Wasserkraftwerken reiche Norwegen bietet bisher den Strom so billig an, daß er für Beheizung wirtschaftlicher ist als Kohle- oder Ölfeuerung. Mit Tagstrom be-

84 Dining recess in the corridor of low-rent flats, Charlottenburg, Berlin, 1961, architect Hans Hoffmann
85 The "Building-Heart", a bathroom-cum-W.C.-cum-kitchen unit with oil heating, manufactured by a Swedish company. One precision method for the prefabrication of complicated technical installations, which does, however, in multi-storey housing, call for high-capacity hoisting gear

84 Erweiterung des Flures zu einer Eßdiele in Wohnungen des Sozialen Wohnungsbaus, Berlin-Charlottenburg 1961, Architekt Hans Hoffmann
85 Das »Bauherz«, eine von einer schwedischen Zementfirma herausgebrachte Bad-WC-Raumzelle mit angebauter Küche und Ölheizung. Ein Weg zur präzisen Vorfertigung der technisch komplizierten Installationsräume, der allerdings im Mehrgeschoßbau schwere Hebewerkzeuge voraussetzt

type of heating are of merely momentary validity, as long as the situation is liable to be affected by day-to-day changes in tariffs, taxes, market position or technical innovations.

Dwelling and Outdoor Space

In earlier ages, the town offered protection against the forces of nature. The gradually gained precinctual peace of the fortified town also encouraged the citizens to break the seclusion of the dwelling and to open up the house frontages by more elaborate window arrangements as, e.g., in medieval Brunswick or Ghent. From the safety of their habitation, they wanted to participate in the urban life pulsating in the streets. The towns were still so small that the lack of open space was not felt; the distance from the house to the open fields outside the town was short and the backgarden was the rule rather than the exception in many places. It was only when the built-up areas began to spread and the garden space was used for sheds, store rooms, workshops and finally factories that the lack of open space was felt. The historic city centres, surrounded by newer residential districts, are cut off from the open space, so necessary as a compensation; they deteriorate hygienically and decay into slums. Any person conscious of his status moves to the villa in the outskirts and, in doing so, accelerates the decaying process of the city centres which are literally deprived of air. The authorities responsible for urban expansion only become aware of the inter-relations between town size, building density and open space when the population deprived of air, light, sun and vegetation begins to revolt and the irresponsible stupidity of old time planning is exposed (Figs 1, 2, page 22). Just as any shortage of a commodity normally in good supply gives rise to an overvaluation, the mighty development of the Garden City movement can be attributed to the disregard of the inter-relations between built-up area and open space. The town dweller, threatened in his health, is attracted to the open country; his ideal is a vista of the countryside as offered in the example from Copenhagen (Fig. 87). A position such as that at Blackheath, London (Fig. 88) is still accepted as tolerable. To the population of a metropolitan city, however, such advantages cannot be offered. The high building density calls for different means of linking the dwelling with the environment. Rarely have the planners shown as much understanding for the needs of children and young people as in those Swedish housing schemes where the preservation, within the residential area, of a piece of wilderness offers playing facilities not rivalled by any skilfully contrived playground placed between forbidden lawns (Fig. 86). But if, as in Stockholm, every other family spends the three months of the summer school holidays in a summer cottage or on a boat, it is of course possible to accept a higher degree of building density in town: The open space allocated to each dwelling can be smaller, being replaced by the regular change of residence. In the cities of other industrial countries in Europe, the longing for the open countryside cannot be satisfied by the summer cottage to the same extent; in any case, the space available for weekend and summer cottages in the environs of the cities is almost exhausted.

Balconies and Roof Terraces

One demand has become general: every dwelling should have some outdoor space – a terrace, loggia or balcony to enable the occupiers to sit or stay outside the enclosed living space. Even if the balcony can only be used for a few days or weeks of the year, it enables the town dweller, deprived of his association with the open countryside, to escape even in a block of flats from the artificial climate of his dwelling – albeit, as in winter, for a moment only. To the practical usefulness of the balcony during the favourable season must be added the psychological advantage that the town dweller does not feel completely debarred from the natural rhythm of the seasons. An interesting example is provided by Mayekawa's Haruni Apartment House where the attempt has been made to reconcile the traditional Japanese house layout, here arranged in cells one above the other which, for climatic reasons, must permit full opening on either side, with the possibilities of concrete design (Fig. 89). The airing of the dwelling and its contents – here conspicuous from the bedding aired on the balconies – is for Japan a hygienic necessity. The wide balconies are therefore not an architect's whim but a consequence of the hot and moist climate. The outdoor galleries of the African apartment house, likewise con-

86 "Natural" playground in the central area of the Baronbackarna housing estate, Örebro (cf. pages 80 ff.)
87 View from a sitting room in a housing estate near Copenhagen (cf. page 77)
88 Garden zone of a housing estate at Blackheath (cf. pages 102 f.)

86 Natürliches Spielgelände im Innenbereich der Siedlung in Örebro-Baronbackarna (siehe Seite 80 ff.)
87 Blick aus dem Wohnraum einer Siedlung bei Kopenhagen (siehe Seite 77)
88 Gartenbereich der Siedlung in Blackheath (siehe Seite 102 f.)

heizte Wandplatten sind üblich und verbreiten eine angenehme, gleichmäßige Wärme. Zusätzlich zu einem Grundpreis, der sich im üblichen Rahmen hält, werden in Oslo für die kWh 2,5 Öre bezahlt, das sind etwa 1,4 DPfennige (siehe Seite 138). In anderen europäischen Ländern sind die Elektrizitätswerke nicht in der Lage, genügend Tagstrom mit geringen Kosten zu erzeugen. Sie haben nur nachts, wenn die Industrie weniger Strom abnimmt, Überkapazitäten und geben dann Nachtstrom verbilligt ab, der in England, Belgien, Österreich und der Bundesrepublik Deutschland in steigendem Maß zum Betrieb von Speicherheizungen verwendet wird. Die vielfach eingebauten Lüfter sind im Hinblick auf Geräuschbelästigung und Lebensdauer allerdings noch von sehr unterschiedlicher Qualität.

Alle Wirtschaftlichkeits-Berechnungen, die als Grundlage für die Wahl einer bestimmten Heizungsart dienen sollen, gelten nur für den Augenblick, solange Tarifänderungen, Besteuerungen, Veränderungen der Marktlage oder technische Neuerungen die Situation von heute auf morgen ändern können.

Wohnung und Außenraum

In früherer Zeit befreite die Stadt ihre Bewohner von der Furcht vor den Naturgewalten. Der allmählich gewonnene Stadtfriede ermunterte außerdem die Bürger, die Abgeschlossenheit der Wohnung zu durchbrechen, die Hausfronten wie zum Beispiel im mittelalterlichen Braunschweig oder Gent in Glasfronten aufzulösen. Sie wollten von der Geborgenheit ihrer Wohnung aus teilnehmen am städtischen Leben, das in den Straßen pulsierte. Die Städte waren so klein, daß man einen Mangel an »Grünraum« nicht empfand; die Wege vom Haus bis zum freien Feld vor der Stadt waren kurz, Gärten hinter den Häusern vielerorts die Regel. Erst die Ausweitung der bebauten Flächen und die Überbauung der Gärten mit Remisen, Lagerhäusern und Werkstätten – schließlich Fabriken – läßt den Mangel spürbar werden. Die von Neubaugebieten umschlossenen Altstädte werden von dem als Ausgleich notwendigen Grünraum abgeschnitten; sie werden in hygienischer Hinsicht entwertet und sinken zum Slum ab. Wer etwas auf sich hält, zieht in die Stadtrandvilla und beschleunigt damit den Fäulnisprozeß der Stadtkerne, denen buchstäblich die Luft abgeschnitten wird. Die Relation zwischen Stadtgröße, Bebauungsdichte und Freiraum wird den für die Stadterweiterungen zuständigen Behörden erst bewußt, als die von Luft, Licht und Grün ausgesperrte Bevölkerung zu revoltieren beginnt und die gewissenlose Dummheit der »Planung« damit offenbar wird (Bild 1, 2, Seite 22). Wie jede Mangelerscheinung eine Überbewertung des unter normalen Umständen vorhandenen Guten hervorruft, läßt sich das mächtige Anschwellen der Gartenstadtbewegung ableiten aus der Mißachtung der zwischen Bebauung und Grünraum bestehenden Gesetzmäßigkeit. Den in seiner Gesundheit bedrohten Städter zieht es aufs Land, als Ideal schwebt ihm der Ausblick auf eine unbebaute Landschaft vor, wie sie das Kopenhagener Beispiel (Bild 87) bietet; eine Wohnlage wie in Blackheath (Bild 88) wird als noch erträglich akzeptiert. Doch einer Millionenstadt-Bevölkerung können diese Vorteile nicht in gleicher Weise geboten werden. Bei dichter Bebauung sind andere Formen der Verknüpfung des Außenraumes mit der Wohnebene erforderlich. Selten ist die Einsicht der Planer in die Nöte der heranwachsenden Jugend so groß wie in jenen schwedischen Siedlungen, wo innerhalb des Wohngebietes ein Stück »Wildnis« Spielmöglichkeiten offenhält, wie sie kein noch so kunstvoll arrangierter Spielplatz zwischen schönen Rasenflächen, deren Betreten verboten ist, zu bieten vermag (Bild 86). Wenn jedoch jede zweite Stockholmer Familie die drei Monate dauernde Schulferienzeit im Sommerhaus oder Sommerboot verbringt, wird natürlich in der Stadt eine größere Verdichtung möglich; die zur Wohnung gehörende Freifläche kann kleiner sein, sie wird durch den regelmäßigen Ortswechsel ersetzt. In den Städten der übrigen europäischen Industrieländer kann mit einer Transponierung des Dranges nach Naturverbundenheit auf die Sommerwohnung nicht in gleichem Maß gerechnet werden; die Aufnahmefähigkeit der sie umgebenden Landschaft für Wochenend- und Sommerhäuser ist ohnehin fast erschöpft.

Balkone und Dachterrassen

Eine Forderung ist Allgemeingut geworden: Jede Wohnung erhält einen Platz im Freien; Terrasse, Loggia oder Balkon ermöglichen den Aufenthalt außerhalb der eingeschlossenen Wohnräume. Oft nur an wenigen Tagen oder Wochen im Jahr

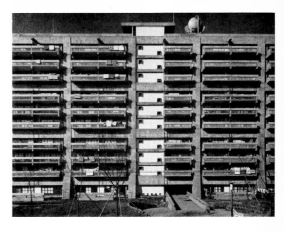

89 Haruni Apartment House, architect Mayekawa
90 Tonelli Apartment House, Mozambique, architect Guedes

89 Haruni-Appartementhaus, Architekt Mayekawa
90 Appartementhaus Tonelli in Mosambik, Architekt Guedes

ditioned by the climate, are mainly designed to provide protection against the sun (Fig. 90). In contrast, Central European housing ideals are reflected in the example of the balconies of the pentagon tower blocks in Basle (Fig. 91). Combining openness with seclusion, these balconies form an extension (albeit, during the winter, merely an optical extension) of the living room from which they are separated by a glass curtain. The flower box affords protection against a direct downward view which might cause giddiness, and the 4'9'' width is just enough to provide normal balcony facilities; a distanze of 5'3'' between wall and parapet would be preferable.

Those who used to be able to enjoy, in an old building, the advantages of a roof terrace of 120 sq.ft. or so will wonder why the architects, who are so fond of trying to appear modern, have not long ago included in the catalogue of specifications for a town dwelling the advantages of an outdoor space measuring at least 8''3' × 10' (Fig. 92). The small bird's nest balconies, hardly large enough for a deck-chair, are no substitute for the outdoor living room of the garden terrace, conspicuous by its absence from multi-storey housing. The struggle of men such as Le Corbusier and Adolf Loos for high level gardens (Figs. 93/94), then rejected by the public as whims of an eccentric, must be resumed; the size of our future conurbations leaves no other option. In this respect, developers and architects lag far behind technical development. Where billions can be spent on roads and transport facilities, it should not be unduly difficult to create a minimum of open space in the towns, at least on the roofs. The results of surveys and investigations into urban environments should long ago have found their way into the building bye-laws of all European cities, laying down that no building with three or more storeys should be built without roof gardens. In view of their beneficial effect in neutralising extreme temperatures and humidities, the provision of such roof gardens is no more expensive than the removal of a population, deprived of all vegetation and exposed to a stuffy urban atmosphere, into the more hygienic suburbs where the high costs of development must be borne by the public at large.

On the roofs of Milan, a roof garden landscape is being created by private initiative, backed by strong capital; the example of a roof garden on the office block of a publishing house is here reproduced in detail (p.61). Roof gardens in London, Oldenburg, (Figs. 95/96) and even in Helsinki prove that, nowadays, there are no longer any technical problems in providing a roof garden under Central European climatic conditions. The financial budgets would have to cover the higher costs for the roof garden in just the same way as they were able to cover the costs for refuse shafts, lifts, garages etc. which have likewise not always been provided voluntarily but because of conditions imposed by the authorities. The inertia and incomprehesion of the public can never be overcome before the damage caused by the failure to take timely action has become obvious. When London, for instance, experienced a fatality rate of 4000 people during one week of "smog", the public began to appreciate that the toxic gases which can, without misgivings, be released into the atmosphere from *one* fireplace are no longer harmless but deadly if hundreds of thousands of fireplaces are concentrated in the same area.

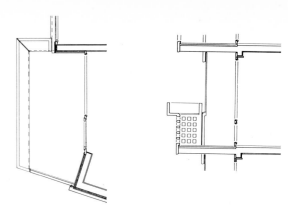

91   Balcony of a tower block of flats, Basle, architect Otto Senn, plan and section, 1 in 100 (cf. page 156)

91   Balkon an einem Turmhaus in Basel, Architekt Otto Senn, Grundriß und Schnitt, 1:100 (siehe Seite 156)

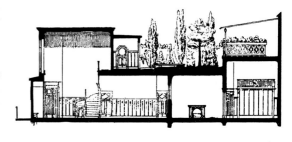

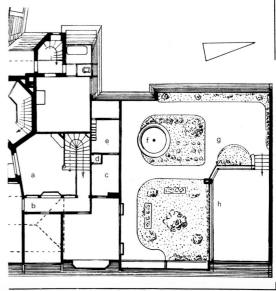

92   Roof garden at Wilmersdorf, Berlin, approx. 1910, architect Alfons Anker, plan and section of the roof storey, situated 65 ft. above street level
a Hall, b Gallery, c Ante-rooms, d Meals hoist, e Bird cage, f Fountain, g Children's playground with sandbox, h Covered terrace

92   Dachgarten in Berlin-Wilmersdorf etwa 1910, Architekt Alfons Anker, Grundriß und Schnitt des 20 m über dem Straßenniveau gelegenen Dachgeschosses
a Diele, b Galerie, c Vorräume, d Speisenaufzug, e Volière mit Winterstall, f Springbrunnen, g Kinderspielplatz mit Sandhaufen, h überdachte Terrasse

voll benutzbar, gibt dieser Platz dem von der Landschaft ausgeschlossenen Städter doch die Freiheit, auch im mehrgeschossigen Haus dem »künstlichen« Klima der Wohnung zu entfliehen, und sei es wie im Winter nur für einen Augenblick. Der praktische Nutzen des Balkons während der günstigen Jahreszeit wird potenziert durch das psychologische Moment, vom natürlichen Rhythmus der Jahreszeiten nicht völlig ausgesperrt zu sein. So ist Mayekawas Haruni-Appartementhaus ein Versuch, die übereinander geschichteten Einfamilienhauszellen, die sich aus klimatischen Gründen an beiden Frontseiten voll öffnen lassen müssen, mit dem Betonformenkanon in Einklang zu bringen (Bild 89). Das Durchlüften der Wohnung wie der Einrichtung und des Hausrats – die vielen auf der Balkonbrüstung ausgebreiteten Bettdecken zeigen es – ist in Japan eine hygienische Notwendigkeit. Die breiten Balkone sind also nicht eine Spielerei des Architekten, sondern eine Funktion des feuchtwarmen Klimas. Die Loggien des afrikanischen Appartementhauses sind, ebenfalls durch das Klima bedingt, in erster Linie Sonnenschutz (Bild 90). Von den Wohnvorstellungen des Mitteleuropäers ist dagegen zum Beispiel der Balkon an den Basler fünfeckigen Turmhäusern bestimmt (Bild 91). Zugleich Offenheit und Intimität bietend erweitert er den Wohnraum, von dem er durch eine Glaswand getrennt ist, auch während der kalten Jahreszeit wenigstens optisch. Die Blumenbank schützt gleichzeitig gegen den schwindelerregenden lotrechten Blick in die Tiefe, die 1,45 m breite Fläche bietet das zu fordernde Minimum an Nutzungsmöglichkeiten; besser wären 1,60 m Abstand zwischen Wand und Brüstung.

Wer in einem Altbau die Vorzüge einer 12 m² großen Dachterrasse genießen konnte, wundert sich, warum die Architekten, die sich gern so modern gebärden, die Vorteile eines wenigstens 2,5 × 3,0 m großen Freiraums nicht längst in den Katalog der Forderungen für eine Stadtwohnung eingereiht haben (Bild 92). Die kaum einen Liegestuhl fassenden Schwalbennester können das im mehrgeschossigen Haus fehlende »Grüne Zimmer«, die Gartenterrasse, nicht ersetzen. Der Kampf eines Le Corbusier und Adolf Loos um »hängende Gärten« (Bild 93, 94) – damals als Spielereien eines Phantasten von der Allgemeinheit abgelehnt – muß wieder aufgenommen werden; die Größe der zukünftigen Stadtgebilde läßt uns keine andere Wahl. Bauherren und Architekten hinken hier weit hinter der technischen Entwicklung her. Wenn Milliarden für den Bau von Straßen und Verkehrsmitteln aufgebracht werden, so müßte es ein leichtes sein, in den Städten zumindest auf den Dächern ein Minimum an grünen Flächen zu schaffen. Untersuchungen und Überlegungen zum Stadtklima sollten längst in allen Bauordnungen europäischer Städte in der Vorschrift ihren Niederschlag gefunden haben, daß kein Gebäude mit drei und mehr Geschossen ohne Anpflanzungen auf Dachgartenflächen gebaut werden darf. In Anbetracht ihrer wohltätigen, Temperatur und Feuchtigkeit ausgleichenden Wirkung ist die Anlage dieser Dachgärten nicht aufwendiger als der Auszug der allen Grüns beraubten und einer stickigen Innenstadtluft ausgesetzten Bevölkerung in die hygienischeren Vorstädte, deren hohe Kosten für Aufschließung und Folgelasten der Gemeinschaft aufgebürdet werden.

Über den Dächern von Mailand ist eine Dachgartenlandschaft aus privater (kapitalkräftiger) Initiative im Entstehen; das Beispiel des über einem Verlagsgebäude angelegten Dachgartens ist hier (S. 61) im Detail wiedergegeben. Dachgärten in London, Oldenburg (Bild 95/96) und selbst in Helsinki beweisen, daß heutzutage die Anlage des Dachgartens im mitteleuropäischen Klimagebiet technisch keine ungelösten Probleme mit sich bringt. In den Finanzierungsplänen können die höheren Kosten für den grünen Dachraum ebenso untergebracht werden, wie das bei den Kosten für Müllschlucker, Aufzüge, Garagen usw. möglich war, die auch nicht immer aus eigener Einsicht, sondern entsprechend den Auflagen der Behörden eingebaut wurden. Aus ihrer Trägheit und Denkfaulheit wird die Allgemeinheit immer erst aufgerüttelt, wenn die durch Versäumnisse hervorgerufenen Schäden offensichtlich werden. Wenn zum Beispiel wie in London viertausend Menschen in einer Woche im Smog sterben, beginnt man einzusehen, daß die giftigen Gase, die aus *einem* Kamin unbedenklich in die Atmosphäre entlassen werden können, bei einer Konzentration von hunderttausend Kaminen auf gleichem Raum eben nicht mehr unbedenklich sondern tödlich sind.

93 Project for an apartment house with two-storey terraces, 1924, architect Le Corbusier
94 Project for a block of flats with terraces, 1924, architect Adolf Loos

93 Appartementhaus-Projekt mit zweigeschossigen Terrassen, 1924, Architekt Le Corbusier
94 Miethaus-Projekt mit Terrassen, 1924, Architekt Adolf Loos

95 Roof terrace on a three-storey block at Oldenburg, 1961, architect Rainer Herrmann
96 Plan of third floor and roof storey, 1 in 500, of the block at Oldenburg

95 Dachterrasse auf einem dreigeschossigen Haus in Oldenburg, 1961, Architekt Rainer Herrmann
96 Grundriß 3. Obergeschoß und Dachgeschoß, 1:500, des Hauses in Oldenburg

97–99 Suspended balconies at the tower blocks of flats at
Vaxjö, Sweden, architect Ralph Erskine (cf. page 18)
100 Plan, elevation and section, 1 in 100
101 Details of the rope suspension of the balconies, 1 in 5

97–99 Vorgehängte Balkone an den Turmhäusern in Vaxjö,
Schweden, Architekt Ralph Erskine (siehe Seite 18)
100 Grundriß, Ansicht und Schnitt, 1:100
101 Detailpunkte der Aufhängung an Stahlseilen, 1:5

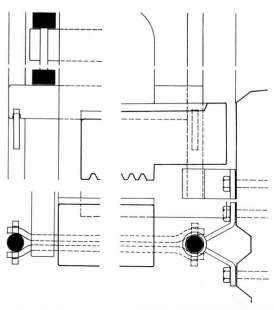

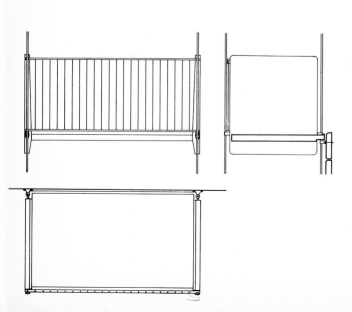

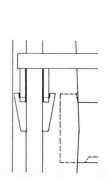

102–104 Roof garden on the building of a publishing house
in Milan, architects L. Figini and J. Pollini
105 Detail section of the roof garden, 1 in 50
a Concrete floor, b Smoothing layer with insulation,
c Two asphalt coatings protected by concrete, d Earth
cover, e Concrete slabs with open joints forming a sub-
floor, f Ceramic bench, g Flower box, h Balustrade,
i Wall behind seat
106 Plan and isometric drawing of the roof garden, 1 in 500
a Study, b Seat with pergola roof, c Fountain

102–104 Dachgarten auf einem Verlagsgebäude in Mailand, Architekten L. Figini und J. Pollini
105 Detailschnitt durch den Dachgarten, 1:50
a Betondecke, b Ausgleichsschicht mit Isolierung,
c zwei Asphaltschichten mit Schutzbeton, d Erdschicht,
e unterlegte Betonplatten mit offenen Fugen, f Keramik-
bank, g Pflanzenschale, h Brüstung, i Sitzplatzwand
106 Grundriß und Isometrie des Dachgartens, 1:500
a Studio, b pergolaüberdachter Sitzplatz, c Springbrunnen

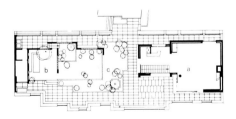

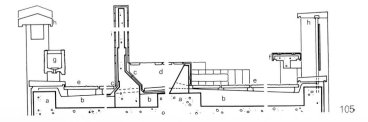

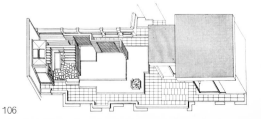

105   106

Artists' Studios

With the provision of roof gardens, it again becomes possible to remember the artists, architects and bon-viveurs who prefer a small studio flat in town to the more hygienic but sterile lodgings in standardised suburbia and who, because of their small number, have been overlooked in normal multi-storey housing. These are members of the public who, because of their somewhat eccentric mode of life, are shunned by landlords and estate agents: "Will he pay his rent punctually? ... and some of them even prefer to work or make merry all night – what will the other tenants say?". These considerations, absurd as they may be, are unfortunately still put forward in earnest.

Details are shown of the studio flat of a Polish professor of architecture in Warsaw which has been created under strict regulations limiting the maximum floor area, and at minimum cost (Figs. 108–114). The space is conceived as a body which contracts and expands and which, through the open space of the roof terraces, is enlivened by the breath of nature. It is no doubt cheaper to build a system of prefabricated, self-contained bunker cells covered by roofing felts arranged in rows; to urban life, however, these are like bread without salt: – insipid, nondescript, and ultimately nauseating.

Atelierwohnungen

Mit dem Ausbau der Dachgärten kann der im normalen Geschoßwohnungsbau vergessenen, weil statistisch unerheblich kleinen Zahl der Künstler, Architekten und Lebenskünstler gedacht werden, die eine kleine Atelierwohnung in der Stadt der hygienischen, aber sterilen Unterbringung im schablonisierten Stadtrandviertel vorziehen; eines Bevölkerungsteils also, um den Vermieter und Vermieterkorporationen wegen seiner unheimlichen, »extravaganten« Lebensweise lieber einen weiten Bogen machen: »Ob er die Miete pünktlich zahlen wird? ... Und dann gibt es darunter solche, die gern nachts arbeiten oder die ganze Nacht feiern – das ist den Mitbewohnern nicht zuzumuten!« Diese Hinweise klingen lächerlich, werden aber leider noch allen Ernstes vorgebracht.

Ausführlich dargestellt ist die Atelierwohnung eines polnischen Architekturprofessors in Warschau, die unter den strengen Einschränkungen der Wohnflächenberechnung und mit geringstmöglichem Aufwand entstanden ist (Bild 108–114). Das Raumvolumen ist als Körper aufgefaßt, der sich verengt und weitet und über die Freiräume der Dachterrassen mit dem Atem der Natur belebt ist. Sicher ist ein System vorgefertigter, abgeschlossener Bunkerzellen, mit Pappdächern reihenweise zugedeckt, billiger; für das Leben der Stadt sind diese wie Brot ohne Salz: fade, nichtssagend und am Ende ekelerregend.

107 Roof terrace with flower window on the Romeo tower block, Stuttgart (cf. pages 162 ff.)

107 Dachterrasse mit Blumenfenster auf dem Hochhaus »Romeo« in Stuttgart (siehe Seite 162 ff.)

108 Sections of a flat with roof terrace in Warsaw

108 Schnitte durch eine Wohnung mit Dachterrasse in Warschau

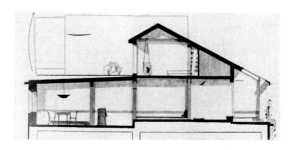

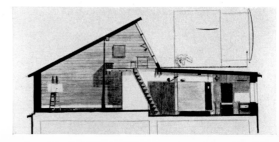

109 Utilisation of the attic of a normal four-storey block, architects Oskar Hansen and Zofia Hansen, plans at main floor and gallery floor levels, 1 in 200
110 Studio at gallery level, seen from the nursery
111 Nursery with balcony
112 Lower studio
113 Stairs leading to the gallery, with the sitting room in the background
114 Gallery, seen from the studio

109 Ausbau des Dachgeschosses eines üblichen viergeschossigen Wohnhauses, Architekten Oskar Hansen und Zofia Hansen, Wohngeschoß- und Galeriegeschoßgrundriß, 1:200
110 Blick vom Kinderzimmer zum Galerie-Atelier
111 Kinderzimmer mit Blick auf den Balkon
112 Unteres Atelier
113 Treppe zur Galerie, Blick in den Wohnraum
114 Die Galerie vom Atelier aus gesehen

110

109
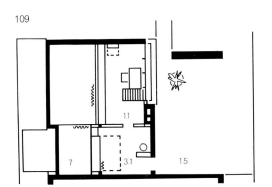
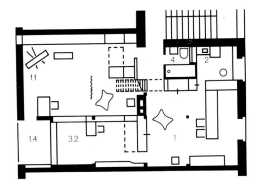

111

112

113

114

"Many of the first employments of these gifts of science have been vulgar, tawdry, stupid or horrible".
H. G. Wells, 1920

"Modern Age was inclined to justify technical measures by their usefulness to the well-being of mankind. This was to conceal the devastations caused by its brutality".
Romano Guardini, 1950

" Well for him who invented nothing,
Well for him who probed nothing,
Well for him who conquered nothing!"
Aimé Césaire, 1939

Town and Residential District

Our present cities are transition products. They were laid out in the era of the pedestrian and horseman – even in the 18th century, a journey from London to Edinburgh still took eight days – and their gradual adaptation to the speeds of locomotion made possible by modern means of transport has proved to be an exceedingly laborious process, restricted by a thousand limitations and prerogatives. Planning for the future is slow in crossing communal and national boundaries. Home and workplace are often separated by the territory of several local authorities.

The boundaries conform to conditions which may still have existed a few decades ago, but not to the general development. For instance, the local problems of the Mannheim conurbation must be decided upon in the capital cities of three German Regions: Mainz, Wiesbaden and Stuttgart. In spite of all the historical, sociological or political differences, however, the problems arising from civilisation are the same in Paris, London, Moscow, Tokyo, in the Dutch and Rhine-Ruhr conurbations and in Chicago: Railways and motor cars have not brought about a decentralisation of residential areas over the whole country – which would have been possible in theory– but have given rise to completely novel types of concentrations which have nothing but the name in common with the cities of the 19th century. In the United States, coherent settlements are being formed which extend across several States, such as the Atlantic Seabord Region covering an area of about 44,000 sq. miles in which the City of Frankfurt-on-Main could be accommodated 58 times. The map of the United States (Fig. 119), on which these Regions are indicated, shows more clearly than any theoretical considerations that these new cities are not radially orientated but ribbon-shaped. Radial road patterns, possibly at one time decreed by an autocratic renaissance princeling, are bound to lead to traffic chaos (Paris!). How difficult it is to free oneself from outdated ideas is demonstrated by Le Corbusier's plan of an "Ideal City", dating back to 1922: Modern buildings are pressed into a conventional ornamental pattern, the plan still has all the shortcomings of the concentric arrangement, the Ring Road is replaced by diagonal roads (Fig. 118). Later, Le Corbusier developed the idea of the Linear City, with industrial, residential, traffic and recreational zones strictly separated in keeping with the C.I.A.M. formula which, though seemingly logical enough, tends to over-simplify the activities of a town.

In 1947, after the complete destruction but before the political partition of Berlin, a team of planners began to work out a far-sighted plan for a New Berlin, designed for the demands of the future, based on a modified version of the Linear City idea, and aiming to provide a link between Western and Eastern Europe, free from political fetters (Fig. 116). This structure is surprisingly similar to the conurbations which, in the United States, began to grow spontaneously ten years later. A wide-mesh network of high-speed roads provides connections in all directions. In ring road systems, the main objectives are by-passed. Whilst the capacity of the Outer Ring is generally not utilised to the full, the traffic chaos in the central area is not relieved. In a well-nigh magical manner, ring roads lead to a concentration of all activities in the town centre and retard the spread in the natural direction of expansion.

Every single dwelling is affected by the efficiency, or lack of efficiency, of the organism of the city as a whole. The best layout plan, the most perfect detail, the most

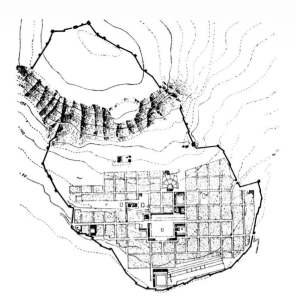

115 Greek "Polis"; a city for pedestrians (Priene). The rigidity of the rectangular road pattern is mitigated by many irregularities, especially near the centre ("Agora")

115 Die griechische Polis; eine Fußgängerstadt (Priene). Rechtwinkliges Rastersystem der Straßen, das durch Abweichungen vom Schema an vielen Punkten, vor allem im Bereich des Ortsmittelpunktes, der Agora, seine Starrheit verliert

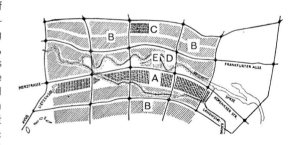

116 Plan for the reconstruction of Berlin, prepared in 1946 by the planning team of the City (at that time still under unified four-sector administration) consisting of Messrs. Ebert, Friedrich, Herzenstein, Lingner, Scharoun, Seitz, Selmanagic, Weinberger. The urban railway system is supplemented by a high-capacity motorway network with a mesh which is, in terms of time, roughly equivalent to that of the old pedestrian road network
A Commercial and industrial areas, B Residential areas,
C Old industrial district, D City administration,
E Museum precinct, open spaces along the watercourses
(River Spree, Landwehr Canal)

116 Plan aus dem Jahre 1946 für den Wiederaufbau Berlins. Berliner Planungskollektiv (der noch einheitlich verwalteten Vier-Sektoren-Stadt): Ebert, Friedrich, Herzenstein, Lingner, Scharoun, Seitz, Selmanagic, Weinberger. Als Ergänzung zur Schnell- und Untergrundbahn ein leistungsfähiges Verteilernetz für den Kraftwagenverkehr, dessen Abstände dem zeitlichen Rhythmus des alten Fußgängernetzes etwa gleichzusetzen sind
A Arbeitsgebiete, B Wohnzonen, C bestehendes altes Industriegebiet, D Stadtverwaltung, E Museumsstadt, Grünräume entlang der Gewässer (Spree, Landwehrkanal)

Die Anwendung dessen, was uns die Wissenschaft geschenkt hat, ist bisher oft gemein, dumm, oberflächlich oder schrecklich gewesen.   H. G. Wells, 1920

Die Neuzeit liebte es, die Maßnahmen der Technik mit ihrem Nutzen für die Wohlfahrt der Menschen zu begründen. Damit deckte sie die Verwüstungen zu, welche ihre Skrupellosigkeit anrichtete.   Romano Guardini, 1950

Wohl dem, der nichts erfunden
Wohl dem, der nichts erforscht
Wohl dem, der nichts bezwungen hat!
         Aimé Césaire, 1939

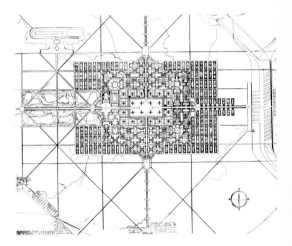

117/118 Le Corbusier's ''Ideal City'' of 1922, and perspective view along the central avenue

117/118 Le Corbusiers Plan für eine Großstadt, 1922, und Perspektive der Straße in der Hauptachse

Stadt und Wohnquartier

Die Städte unserer Tage sind Übergangsprodukte. Angelegt nach dem Lebens- und Verhaltensschema der Fußgänger- und Reiterepoche – zur Reise von London nach Edinburg benötigte man noch im 18. Jahrhundert acht Tage – erweist sich die schrittweise Anpassung an die heute mögliche Schnelligkeit des Ortswechsels mit vielerlei Verkehrsmitteln als zu schwerfällig und von tausend Grenzen und Rechten eingeengt. Planungen für die Zukunft greifen nur zögernd über kommunale und Ländergrenzen hinaus. Zwischen Arbeitsplatz und Wohnsitz liegen oft mehrere Gemeinden. Die Grenzziehungen entsprechen dem Stand, wie er vor Jahrzehnten vielleicht noch vorhanden war, aber nicht der allgemeinen Entwicklung. So muß über »kommunale« Probleme der Agglomeration um Mannheim in den Hauptstädten dreier deutscher Bundesländer, in Mainz, Wiesbaden und Stuttgart, entschieden werden. Gleiche Errungenschaften der Zivilisation laden trotz aller geschichtlichen, gesellschaftlichen oder politischen Unterschiede Paris, London, Moskau, Tokio, der »Randstadt Holland«, der Rhein-Ruhr-Agglomeration oder Chikago die gleichen Sorgen auf: Schienenbahnen und Autos bewirken nicht eine theoretisch mögliche Dezentralisierung der Wohngebiete über das ganze Land, sondern völlig neuartige Konzentrationen, die mit den Städten des 19. Jahrhunderts nur noch den Namen gemein haben. In den USA bilden sich zusammenhängende Siedlungsgebiete, die über mehrere Unionsstaaten hinweggreifen, wie etwa die 113000 km² umfassende »Atlantic Seabord Region«, ein Gebiet, in das die Stadt Frankfurt am Main achtundfünfzigmal hineinpaßt. Eindeutiger als alle Überlegungen beweist die Karte der USA (Bild 119), in der diese Regionen eingezeichnet sind, daß diese neuen »Städte« nicht radial, sondern bandförmig angelegt sind. Radial ins Stadtzentrum geführte Straßen, Ausdruck des Herrschaftswillens eines Renaissancefürsten, müssen zum Verkehrschaos führen (Paris!). Wie schwer es ist, sich von überholten Vorstellungen zu lösen, bezeugt Le Corbusiers Idealstadtplan von 1922: Moderne Gebäude sind in ein traditionelles ornamentales Muster gepreßt; der Plan enthält noch alle Fehler der konzentrischen Ordnung – Diagonalstraßen ersetzen den »Ring« (Bild 118). Später entwickelt »L.C.« die Idee der Bandstadt mit den streng nach C.I.A.M.-Schema getrennten Zonen für Arbeiten, Wohnen, Verkehr und Erholung; eine sehr logisch erscheinende, das Leben in der Stadt jedoch zu stark vereinfachende Formel.

Nach der völligen Zerstörung Berlins geht 1947 ein Planungskollektiv der noch nicht gespaltenen Stadt daran, einen großzügigen, auf die Bedürfnisse der Zukunft zugeschnittenen Vorschlag für ein neues Berlin auszuarbeiten, der eine Modifizierung der Bandstadtidee darstellt und auf eine von politischen Hemmnissen freie Verbindung West- und Osteuropas zielt (Bild 116). Auffallend ist die Verwandtschaft dieses Strukturbildes mit den Städtegebilden, die sich planlos zehn Jahre später in den USA herausbilden. Ein weitmaschiges Straßennetz schafft allseitige Verbindungen. – In den Ringstraßensystemen wird der Zielpunkt umfahren. Während der äußere Ring daher meist nicht ausgelastet ist, wird im Kreiszentrum das Verkehrschaos nicht beseitigt. In fast magischer Weise konzentrieren Ringstraßen das Geschehen auf den Kreismittelpunkt und hemmen die natürlich gegebenen Ausbreitungsrichtungen.

Jedes einzelne Wohnhaus ist vom Funktionieren (oder Versagen) des Gesamtorganismus der Stadt mitbetroffen. So ändert der beste Grundriß, das gelungenste

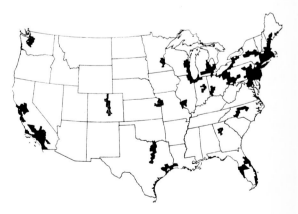

119 High-density areas along main traffic arteries in the United States

119 Verdichtungsräume entlang der Hauptverkehrsadern in den USA

favourable financial arrangement cannot prevent the depreciation of a dwelling, house or property, if the traffic noise robs the occupants of their sleep, if the smoke-laden air prevents them from using their balcony or leaving their windows open, if there are no shopping facilities in the vicinity, or if the site is isolated from the town by poor traffic facilities. The most conspicuous of these factors is generally the transport problem. At a car ownership rate of one car for every three inhabitants, the capacity of the streets is generally exhausted. It is only public transport which can satisfy the passenger mileage requirements of a large city, and especially the underground railways which can use a second level independent of general traffic. This thesis is confirmed by recent American surveys. Stockholm's new suburbs are built along the new underground railways. Most of the other major conurbations in Europe are still lagging behind in this respect.

The motor car itself is an old-fashioned machine by modern scientific standards: a modern vehicle should neither exude concentrated clouds of poisonous fumes nor cause so much noise. Why must the banging of a car door in a residential car park interrupt the sleep of three dozen families? An improvement of these imperfect machines could have far-reaching effects on town planning and housing. In 1947, Hugo Häring proposed the introduction of battery-driven cars in residential areas, of the kind at present used by shoppers in a pedestrian mall at Miami Beach. The noiseless vehicle, free from exhaust gases, could be taken, without misgivings, much closer and with much greater freedom of movement to the residential building themselves than appears to be desirable with the present-day car models. The process would be comparable to the transition from gas to electric lighting. In this way, it would be possible to eliminate a major obstacle to the greater integration of homes and workplaces which are at present far too dogmatically separated from each other.

Mutatis mutandis, the principles laid down in the Athens Charter are still valid to-day; but if they are literally applied, e.g., to the separation of home, workplace and sportsground, they are wrong. A residential district should be able to cater for all jobs other than those constituting a nuisance. Anyone compelled to take a twenty minutes' walk to buy his paper, cigarettes, bread or milk will not regard his dwelling as ideal. If, among the 5000 residents of a housing estate in the outskirts, there is not a single painter or decorator, nor a tailor or cobbler, the value of the town-planning principle of a "pure" residential area must be doubted.

How far the British, with their "New Town" experience, are ahead of the Germans in this respect is proved by the plan for Hook. The planners became convinced that the civic amenities of urban life can only be achieved if the population density is at least 100 persons per acre, and that the residential areas must be closely inter-linked with the 'activity strip' which must not be a stagnant centre but a roadway if this centre is not to remain dead and empty before and after office hours (Fig. 120). The plans for Hook provided for an ultimate population of 100,000 (the LCC report on the extremely detailed surveys into all the different aspects can be regarded as a reference book on town planning). One relationship, however, being undesirable, was not sufficiently taken into account, the dependence on London. That a medium-sized town within the influence zone of a metropolitan city can remain self-contained is a utopian fallacy. In future, a conurbation will be deemed to include the entire area served by local public transport, irrespective of any communal boundaries, and its hinterland will comprise all the land from which a return journey can be made without excessive effort or costs. With a motorway link, this may apply to places as far as 120 miles apart. It is on this background that the sociological classification of the population must be viewed. This classification also has an influence on the percentage distribution of the different types of dwellings required for a healthy structure of individual housing schemes. The age distribution should be similar to that in the conurbation as a whole so that the user of public institutions is evenly balanced (Fig. 127).

Sizes and types of dwellings must be similarly classified if a new district is not to retain the Wild West character of a pioneer settlement for a whole generation.

Any monotony is detrimental to life. If the Hansa District in Berlin had been built by just one of the architects represented in it, it might have become the prototype of a monotonous multi-storey housing scheme. It is from the variety in the buildings

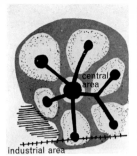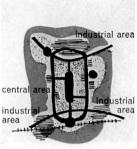

120 The earlier practice of dispersing neighbourhoods as radial satellites around a town centre (left) makes way to the principle of a greater integration of the different zones. (Hook, cf. pages 182 f.)
121 Typical old-type residential area with tenement houses along the streets and in the backyards, Charlottenburg, Berlin
122 Housing scheme with intermittent blocks along the streets and at right angles, Neue Vahr, Bremen, 1957

120 Das satellitenartige Anhängen von Nachbarschaften an ein Kreiszentrum (links) weicht einer stärkeren Ver-flechtung der Bereiche (Hook, siehe Seite 182 f.)
121 Blockrandbebauung mit »Gartenhäusern« in Berlin-Charlottenburg
122 Aufgebrochene Blockrandbebauung und Zeilenbau in Bremen-Neue Vahr, 1957

Detail, die günstigste Finanzierung nichts an der Wertminderung der Wohnung, des Hauses und Grundstückes, wenn der Straßenlärm den Bewohnern die Nachtruhe raubt, die abgasgeschwängerte Luft den Aufenthalt auf dem Balkon oder bei offenem Fenster unmöglich macht, Einkaufsgelegenheiten in der Nachbarschaft fehlen oder die Verkehrsverhältnisse das Haus von der Stadt isolieren. Am augenfälligsten ist allgemein das Verkehrsproblem. Bei einer Dichte von 1:3, einem Auto auf drei Einwohner, ist das Fassungsvermögen der Straßen durchweg erschöpft. Nur öffentliche Verkehrsmittel, vor allem die in einer zweiten, unabhängigen Verkehrsebene geführten Untergrundbahnen, können die in der Großstadt benötigten »Personenkilometer« aufbringen. Neueste amerikanische Untersuchungen bestätigen diese Meinung. Stockholm baut seine Vororte entlang neuer »Tunnelbahn«-Linien; in den meisten Städteagglomerationen Europas sind die Versäumnisse auf diesem Gebiet groß.

Das Automobil selber ist im Vergleich mit dem Fortschritt der Wissenschaften eine altmodische Maschine; ein zeitgemäßes Fahrzeug dürfte weder konzentrierte Giftschwaden ausstoßen noch derartigen Lärm verursachen. Warum muß das Zuschlagen einer Autotür auf einem Parkplatz zwischen Wohnhäusern mindestens drei Dutzend Familien aus dem Schlaf schrecken? Eine Verbesserung dieser unvollkommenen Maschinen kann für den Städte- und Wohnungsbau weitreichende Folgen haben. Hugo Häring schlug 1947 zur Versorgung von Wohngebieten Elektrowagen vor, wie sie jetzt auf einer Fußgänger-Einkaufspromenade in Miami Beach zur Beförderung der Kauflustigen benutzt werden. Der lautlose und abgasfreie Wagen könnte bedenkenlos näher und verzweigter an die Wohnhäuser herangeführt werden, als das bei den gegenwärtigen Automodellen ratsam erscheint. Der Vorgang wäre mit dem Übergang von der Gas- zur elektrischen Beleuchtung zu vergleichen. Ein wesentliches Hindernis für die Verflechtung der allzu schematisch getrennten Wohn- und Arbeitsgebiete könnte auf diese Weise beseitigt werden.

Bei sinngemäßer Anwendung haben die Grundsätze der Charta von Athen heute noch Gültigkeit, bei wörtlicher Übertragung der Trennung von Wohnung, Arbeit und Sportflächen zum Beispiel sind sie falsch. Die Wohnstadt muß alle nicht störenden Berufe integrieren können. Wer zum Zeitungs-, Zigaretten-, Brötchen- oder Milcheinkauf 20 Minuten gehen muß, empfindet sein Wohnen nicht als ideal. Wer in einer Stadtrandsiedlung mit 5000 Einwohnern weder einen Anstreicher und Tapezierer, noch einen Schneider oder Schuhmacher findet, zweifelt am Wert des städtebaulichen Prinzips des »reinen« Wohngebiets.

Wie weit die Engländer mit ihren New-Town-Erfahrungen uns Deutschen voraus sind, beweist die Planung für Hook. Man hat sich davon überzeugt, daß städtisches Leben sich erst bei einer Mindestdichte von 250 Einwohnern pro Hektar entfalten kann und daß die Wohngebiete mit dem Aktivitätsstreifen, der kein in sich ruhendes Zentrum sondern »Straße« sein muß, zu verzahnen sind, wenn diese Mittelzone nicht vor und nach den Bürozeiten tot und leer bleiben soll (Bild 120). Die Planung für Hook sah im Endzustand 100000 Einwohner vor (der Bericht des LCC über die nach allen Seiten hin äußerst sorgfältigen Untersuchungen kann als Städtebaulehrgang gelten). Eine Beziehung war allerdings, weil unerwünscht, nicht genügend berücksichtigt: die Abhängigkeit von London. Autarkie einer Mittelstadt im Ausstrahlungsbereich einer Millionenstadt ist eine Utopie. – In Zukunft wird das mit öffentlichen Nahverkehrsmitteln erschlossene Gebiet – unabhängig von bestehenden Grenzziehungen – zur Innenstadt gezählt werden. Zum »Weichbild« ist dann der Bereich zu rechnen, in dem Hin- und Rückfahrt an einem Tag ohne Anstrengung und übermäßige Kosten möglich sind; das können bei Autobahnverbindung 200 km entfernte Orte sein. Die soziologische Gliederung der Bewohner muß unter diesen Voraussetzungen gesehen werden. Sie beeinflußt zugleich im Einzelfall die für einen »gesunden« Aufbau einer Wohnsiedlung notwendige Streuung der Wohnungstypen. Im Altersaufbau ist eine ähnliche Verteilung wie im Gesamtstadtraum vorzusehen, damit die öffentlichen Einrichtungen nicht einseitig überlastet werden (Bild 127).

Wohnungsgrößen und -formen müssen in ähnlicher Weise gestaffelt sein, wenn ein neues Siedlungsgebiet nicht für eine Generation den Wildwest-Charakter einer Pioniersiedlung behalten soll.

Jede Monotonie ist lebensfeindlich. Das Berliner Hansaviertel wäre, hätte es einer der dort vertretenen Architekten allein gebaut, das Muster eines langweiligen Hoch-

123 A view of the Neue Vahr housing scheme, Bremen. The court-yards contain playgrounds of exemplary design for children of all ages
124 Hasenbergl housing scheme, Munich, 1962
125 Ruhr Expressway, Essen, 1961

123 Ausschnitt aus der Neuen Vahr in Bremen. In den Höfen vorbildlich geplante Spielplatzfolgen für Kinder aller Altersstufen
124 München Hasenbergl 1962
125 Ruhrschnellweg in Essen 1961

and from the contrast in the attitudes expressed by them that the district now derives its attraction in spite of serious town planning mistakes.

Even in deciding on the types of dwellings, it is possible to avoid the monotony of a block occupied by families of well-nigh equal size belonging to the same professional and income groups, a monotony which comes easily to standardisation-prone planners, and which the developers regard as economic. The depreciation of such buildings and housing estates will only become apparent when the housing market has come closer to saturation.

Dwelling units which are mass-produced like Chinese coolie jackets all look the same! If the clothing industry were to follow the example of the building industry and concentrate on the exclusive production of standardised Chinese coolie jackets, we would have to wear them just as we now have to put up with the mass-produced types of dwellings. In other words, the marketability of a commodity that is in short supply is no proof of its quality.

Slum Clearance

Perhaps the worst manifestation of such monotony is the method of slum clearance practised in American cities (Figs. 128, 130, 131). The principle of re-housing by income groups is reminiscent of the spontaneous class segregation in the Kaiser's Berlin and creates, in spite of hygienic improvements, an atmosphere of discrimination which poisons the thoughts of the population until they revolt. The buildings erected on the completely cleared sites are more akin to prisons than to homes and recall the attempts of those militarists who want to "improve" civilians by subjecting them to barrack drill.

Slum formation is promoted by small landlords who permit overcrowding and charge exorbitant rents so that, on the advent of slum clearance, they are entitled to high compensation. In 1960, Dr. Brecht warned against the adoption of similar methods in dealing with the slum clearance work due to begin in Germany within the next few years. Isolated slum clearance schemes without proper integration with urban renewal and town planning are doomed to failure. Equally imprudent is the demolition of entire districts which, given sufficient aid, might regenerate themselves spontaneously.

England offers better conditions for urban renewal. While Scotland – in traditional, partly sectarian adherence to French practice – has inherited the sins of continental cities, with entire districts of four- or five-storey tenement houses in Glasgow and Edinburgh much akin to similar districts in Paris or Berlin, English slums look different and are of different origin. For a long time, the land has remained in the possession of the landed gentry and is generally leased for 99 years. It is in the Germanic tradition that the value of the ground and the value of the house are different things. When the leasehold has expired, all the buildings erected on the site accrued to the landlord without compensation. Slum clearance was therefore possible, at intervals of 99 years, without high compensation payments. The snag lies in the fact that, at least during the second half of the leasehold period, the houses are no longer properly maintained; they decay, and as housing schemes are normally developed in major coherent areas, the entire district degenerates into a slum. Small houses used to be the rule; as in the Netherlands and North Germany, they often took the form of terrace houses so that the population density remained low. As a result of extreme ground speculation and of an embargo on basements (so that they should not be used as dwellings), the narrow courtyards behind the houses were not used for gardens but for a motley collection of sheds and mews. In many places, the residential districts with their narrow streets adjoin each other without being relieved by open spaces or public squares. British postwar legislation therefore aimed at unclogging the blighted districts by favouring multi-storey housing and by converting the surplus areas into public open spaces. It was for the rehousing of the overspill population from such districts that the "New Towns" were developed. In recent times, however, because of high death duties, the ground is often acquired by property companies and speculators.

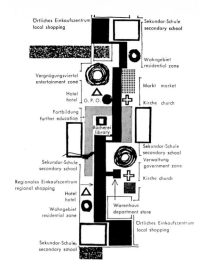

126 Housing should not be completely segregated from all services and other activities. The block diagram shows part of the central area of the Hook project (cf. Fig. 120)

126 Wohnen darf nicht völlig von allen Diensten und anderen Tätigkeiten getrennt werden: Das Schema zeigt einen Ausschnitt des Mittelstreifens im Hook-Projekt (siehe Bild 120)

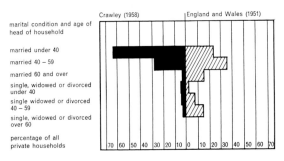

127 Comparison of households in Crawley New Town with those in urban areas of similar size in England and Wales. The unbalanced age structure at Crawley impedes, in many respects, the proper working of the town

127 Vergleich der Haushalte in der neuen Stadt Crawley mit denen anderer Städte in England und Wales. Von oben nach unten: Personenstand und Alter des Haushaltsvorstandes: verheiratet, unter 40 – zwischen 40 und 59 – über 60, alleinstehend, verwitwet oder geschieden, unter 40 – zwischen 40 und 59 – über 60, Prozent aller Privathaushalte. Der unausgeglichene Altersaufbau in Crawley behindert in vielerlei Weise das Funktionieren der Stadt

128 Rehabilitation scheme in Chicago; Housing for medium income groups
129 Slum area in the United States: Blighted, but closely integrated with nature
130 Redeveloped area in Chicago

128 Sanierung in Chikago: Unterkünfte für die mittleren Einkommensklassen
129 Sanierungsreifes Gebiet in den USA: Verkommen, aber naturverbunden
130 »Saniertes« Wohngebiet in Chikago

hausviertels; aus der Mannigfaltigkeit der Bauten und aus der Gegensätzlichkeit der Auffassungen bezieht es heute trotz schwerer städtebaulicher Fehler seinen Reiz.

Schon bei der Festlegung der Wohnungstypen kann die Monotonie des nur von etwa gleich großen Familien aus gleichen Berufsschichten mit fast gleichem Einkommen bewohnten Hauses vermieden werden, die den typisierungsfreudigen Planern so leicht von der Hand geht und mit der die Bauherren Kosten zu sparen glauben. Die Wertminderung derartiger Bauten und Siedlungen wird erst bei einem ausgeglichenen Wohnungsmarkt in Erscheinung treten.

Wohnungen werden produziert wie chinesische Wattejacken, alle sehen gleich aus. Würde die Bekleidungsindustrie ebenso wie die Wohnungsbauindustrie verfahren und einheitlich zur Produktion chinesischer Wattejacken übergehen, wir müßten sie ebenso tragen wie heutzutage das Wohnungsangebot an den Mann gebracht wird. Oder: daß eine Mangelware verkauft wird, ist noch kein Beweis für ihre Qualität.

Sanierung

Was in den amerikanischen Städten bei der Sanierung der Slumviertel geschieht, ist schlimmster Ausdruck dieses Verfahrens (Bild 128, 130, 131). Die nach Einkommensklassen gestufte »Unterbringung« ähnelt dem aus Standesdünkel im wilhelminischen Berlin erwachsenen Sortierungsverfahren und schafft trotz »hygienischer Zustände« Diskriminierungen, die das Denken der Bewohner bis zum Aufruhr vergiften. Auf glattrasiertem Boden entstehen eher zuchthaus- als wohnhausartige Bauformen, die Erinnerungen an die Versuche jener Militaristen wachrufen, die durch abschleifenden Drill aus Zivilisten »bessere Menschen« machen wollten.

Gerissene Unternehmer beschleunigen den Prozeß der Slumbildung durch Überbelegung und halsabschneiderische Mieten, die ihnen bei der Sanierung dann hohe Abfindungssummen einbringen. 1960 warnte Dr. Brecht vor ähnlichen Verfahrensweisen bei den in den nächsten Jahren in Deutschland beginnenden Sanierungen. Ohne Einbindung in einen Plan zur städtischen und städtebaulichen Neuordnung sind »Objektsanierungen« Fehlinvestitionen. Ebenso unklug dürfte das Abreißen ganzer Quartiere sein, die sich bei geeigneter Unterstützung von selber regenerieren.

Großbritannien bietet für die Sanierung der Städte günstige Voraussetzungen. Während Schottland in traditioneller, zum Teil konfessionell bedingter Anlehnung an Frankreich die Sünden kontinentaler Großstädte übernommen hat – vier- und fünfgeschossige Wohnviertel mit Randbebauung in Glasgow und Edinburg gleichen ähnlichen Quartieren in Paris oder Berlin –, haben englische Slums ein anderes Gesicht und sind aus anderen Gründen entstanden. Der Boden war lange Zeit im Besitz der alten Adelsschicht geblieben und wurde, meist auf 99 Jahre, in Erbpacht vergeben. Bodenwert und Wert des Hauses bilden nach germanischer Tradition keine Einheit. Nach Ablauf der Pachtzeit fielen durchweg alle auf dem Grundstück stehenden Bauwerke entschädigungslos dem Besitzer anheim. Alle 99 Jahre war eine Sanierung ohne hohe Entschädigungskosten möglich. Der Pferdefuß lag darin, daß zumindest in der zweiten Hälfte der Pachtzeit die Häuser nicht mehr instandgehalten wurden, verkamen und, da normalerweise große zusammenhängende Flächen gleichzeitig von Unternehmern bebaut wurden, die ganze Gegend zum Slum absank. Einfamilienhäuser waren die Regel, wie in Holland und Niederdeutschland oft als Reihenhäuser angelegt, so daß die Bevölkerungsdichte begrenzt blieb. Bei der spekulativ bis zum äußersten getriebenen Ausnutzung der Baugelände und dem Verbot, Keller zu bauen (damit dort niemand wohnen konnte), entstanden in den engen Höfen hinter den Häusern keine Gärten, sondern ein Sammelsurium von Ställen und Verschlägen. Vielfach reihten sich die Wohngebiete mit engen Straßen ohne Einschaltung von Grünzonen oder -plätzen aneinander. Die Nachkriegsgesetzgebung in England zielte daher auf eine Auflockerung der Sanierungsgebiete durch mehrgeschossige Bauweisen und durch die Umwandlung der frei werdenden Flächen in Grünanlagen. Für die überzählige Bevölkerung der Sanierungsgebiete wurden die Neustädte, die New Towns, angelegt.

Der Boden geht infolge sehr hoher Erbschaftssteuern in der letzten Zeit allerdings vielfach in den Besitz von Grundstücksgesellschaften – und Spekulanten – über.

Prospects
In view of the distressingly inadequate planning efforts of many European cities and the effects of land speculation, Dr. Brecht's warnings appear to be amply justified. On the Continent of Europe, town planning is still too much regarded as a static phenomenon. The time factors and therefore the continual regeneration of the structural shape of a city are ignored in favour of a vision which, in the ultimate stage, does not admit any corrections or modifications. The variability of shape, so well understood by the Fine Arts, will undoubtedly also exert its influence on building activities. More than before, the supremacy of the living over the petrified (borne out, inter alia, by the status of the motorist) will be reflected in the design of the dwelling. The way to a continual process of urban renewal will be cleared. That, in this process, the aberrations of commercial exploitation will give rise to many ugly features is just as inevitable as the so-called Modern Architecture which happened to accompany the great evolution of building in our time. The little poem by Aimé Césaire of Martinique (page 64) shows how little European mentality alone is able to provide a basis for town planning in African or, for that matter, Asiatic countries. More important than stone monuments is a healthy life which, according to Paul Valéry, must be regarded as the narrow and difficult path of mankind, threatened just as much by Chaos as by Orderliness.

131 In America, lack of proper maintenance, segregation of population classes and overcrowding cause originally satisfactory and uncongested residential areas to decay into slums

131 Fehlende Bauunterhaltung, Entmischung der Bevölkerungskategorien und Überbelegung verwandeln in den USA gute, ursprünglich nicht zu dicht besiedelte Wohngebiete in Slums

Ausblick

Die erschreckend unvollständigen Planungen europäischer Städte und die Auswirkungen der Bodenspekulation lassen die oben zitierten Warnungen Dr. Brechts nur allzu berechtigt erscheinen. Städtebau wird auf dem Kontinent noch viel zu statisch gesehen. Der Zeitfaktor und damit die fortlaufende Regeneration der baulichen Gestalt einer Stadt werden vernachlässigt zugunsten einer Formvorstellung, die als Endziel keine Korrekturen oder Veränderungen mehr zuläßt. Die von den bildenden Künsten begriffene Veränderlichkeit der Form wird unzweifelhaft auch das Bauen erfassen. Das Primat des Lebendigen vor dem Versteinerten (von dem unter anderem das Prestige des Autofahrers zeugt) wird mehr als bisher die Hausformen prägen; der Weg zu einer andauernden Erneuerung der Stadt wird frei. Daß dabei die Fehlleistungen kommerzieller Ausnutzung manche Häßlichkeit darbieten werden, ist ebenso unvermeidlich wie die sogenannte »moderne Architektur«, die den Weg des Neuen Bauens begleitet hat. Das Gedicht von Aimé Césaire, Martinique (Seite 65), deutet an, wie wenig europäische Denkkategorien allein geeignet sind, Grundlage für den Städtebau in afrikanischen oder auch asiatischen Ländern zu sein. Wichtiger als Denkmäler ist ein gesundes Leben, das nach Paul Valéry anzusehen ist als »der schmale, heikle Pfad des Menschlichen, der doppelt bedroht ist, vom Chaos und von der Ordnung«.

132 ''New Look'', after rehabilitation, of an area like that shown in Fig. 131: clean, hygienic flats for low-income families in Chicago. This approach to housing problems is similar to that which resulted in the Berlin backyards of the 19th century (Page 22). If the Berlin backyards ignored the hygienic requirements, the modern development, shown here, ignores sociological facts. The mentality behind both examples provides dynamite for the revolt of the underprivileged

132 Nach der Sanierung sieht ein Gebiet wie in Bild 131 dann so aus: Saubere, hygienische Wohnungen für weniger bemittelte Bürger in Chikago. Ein Ergebnis, das die gleiche Einstellung zu den Wohnproblemen dokumentiert wie die Berliner Hinterhöfe des 19. Jahrhunderts (Seite 22); wurden damals die hygienischen Forderungen mißachtet, so sind es hier und heute die soziologischen Erkenntnisse. Diese Einstellung erzeugt hier wie dort den Zündstoff für das Revoltieren der Diskriminierten

Examples

Scandinavian Housing

The following 47 examples are divided into seven groups. The first of them is almost exclusively concerned with Scandinavian housing. The only exception is the Horner Geest housing estate in Hamburg where the blocks are assembled in accordance with the Danish Larsen & Nielsen system.

The Scandinavians, well-known as sober calculators, are not prepared to subordinate housing construction to any ideology. The examples in this group may therefore already demonstrate the variety in design possible for buildings serving the same purpose. The two-storey house (Eskemosegaard or, on stanchions, Lauttasaari) is not necessarily confined to a single-family dwelling; a four-storey three-unit type of building (Tapiola) may be so well designed that none of the flats is at a disadvantage.

All the buildings in this group conform to a rectangular plan – a statement no more indicative of quality than, for instance, a mention of the material, such as bricks, concrete or prefabricated concrete slabs. It so happens that the most modern examples (for buildings erected of prefabricated wall and floor units) have the poorest plans although, for serial production, only the best should be good enough. It would seem that here, as in many similar cases, all the mental energy was consumed by the efforts to solve the technical problems.

With such "economic" mentality, essential features such as the planning of layouts and urban environments are bound to suffer.

The street block with buildings lining the roads, previously on a pedestrian scale and now on a motorised scale, is still merrily holding sway in Sweden. Here, again, it is found that, no matter how many individual improvements may have been introduced, a new spiritual overall concept as a basis for a new approach to building construction has not yet been found.

Beispiele

Skandinavische Wohnformen

Die 47 Beispiele sind in sieben Gruppen gegliedert, deren erste fast ausschließlich skandinavische Häuser umfaßt. Einzige Abweichung sind die nach dem System Larsen & Nielsen in Hamburg montierten Häuser, also auch dänische Produkte.

Die Skandinavier, bekannt als nüchterne Rechner, sind nicht gewillt, den Wohnungsbau einer Ideologie unterzuordnen. Es läßt sich daher an den Beispielen dieser Gruppe bereits ablesen, wie verschiedenerlei Gestalt die dem gleichen Zweck dienenden Häuser haben können. Das zweigeschossige Wohnhaus (Eskemosegaard; auf Stützen: Lauttasaari) muß durchaus nicht immer ein Einfamilienhaus sein; ein viergeschossiger Dreispännertyp (Tapiola) kann so gut überlegt sein, daß keine Wohnung benachteiligt wird.

Die Häuser dieser Gruppe sind alle im rechtwinkligen Grundrißschema angelegt, was ebensowenig ein Werturteil bedeutet wie die Materialangaben »Ziegel«, »Beton« oder »vorgefertigte Betonplatten«. Zufällig haben hier die »modernsten« Beispiele (aus vorgefertigten Wand- und Deckenelementen) die schlechteren Grundrisse, obwohl für die Serienproduktion nur die besten Erzeugnisse gut genug sein dürften. Offenbar haben wie in vielen ähnlichen Fällen die Bemühungen um die technischen Probleme alle Kraft aufgezehrt. Das Wesentliche, die Arbeit an Grundriß und Stadtplan, kommt bei diesem sogenannten ökonomischen Denken dann zu kurz.

Die Blockbebauung – früher im Fußgängerblock, heute im Autofahrerblock – feiert in Schweden fröhliche Urständ. Auch dort zeigt sich: So groß die Zahl der Neuerungen auf Einzelgebieten auch ist, ein neues geistiges Gesamtkonzept als Grundlage für ein Neues Bauen wurde noch nicht gefunden.

Eskemosegaard near Copenhagen, 1960 · Housing estate, based on a competition project of 1952
Architects: Henning Jensen and Torben Valeur

A brick building with tiled roof is readily dismissed as old fashioned. In this case, the architects – having shown elsewhere that they are just as ready to work with concrete components – have proved that a building erected by conventional means can also be modern. Apart from a longitudinal pipe duct, the flats have no basements. The zone around the stairs is skilfully utilised for ancillary rooms, which has also enabled the architects to avoid the three-flats-per-landing arrangement so difficult to design without doing violence to the plan. In the entrance hall, all the gas and water installations, placed above the plaster, are concealed behind a cupboard yet are readily accessible for repairs. In view of this ingenious idea, one is prepared to excuse the symmetric arrangement of the kitchens. Sitting room and dining kitchen are separated by a glass partition which can be completely opened. The bedrooms of the inside flats can be kept very small (approx. 10 × 11 ft.) because of the built-in cupboard room. In the roof-storey flats, the dormitory area is divided into several smaller bedrooms, though some of them are only accessible from the kitchen.

Eskemosegaard bei Kopenhagen, 1960 · Siedlung nach einem Wettbewerbsentwurf, 1952
Architekten: Henning Jensen und Torben Valeur

Ein Backsteinbau mit Ziegeldach wird leicht als etwas sehr Altmodisches abgetan. Hier beweisen die Architekten, die andernorts ebenso gern mit Betonteilen arbeiten, wie zeitgemäß ein handwerklich hergestellter Bau sein kann. Die Häuser sind – bis auf einen Rohrkanal in Längsrichtung – nicht unterkellert. Der Treppenhausbereich ist geschickt für die Nebenräume genutzt; man hat so gleichzeitig die oft nur gewaltsam gewonnene Dreispänneranordnung vermieden. Im Hauseingangsflur verbirgt sich die gesamte, auf Putz verlegte Gas- und Wasserinstallation hinter einem Wandschrank und ist bei Reparaturen jederzeit zugänglich. Angesichts dieses Einfalls verzeiht man die spiegelbildliche Anordnung der Küchen. Wohnraum und Eßküche sind durch eine Glaswand getrennt, die auch ganz geöffnet werden kann. Bei den innenliegenden Wohnungen erlaubt die eingebaute Kleiderkammer, die Schlafräume sehr klein zu halten (3,00 × 3,40 m). In den Giebelwohnungen ist der Schlafbereich in mehrere Kammern aufgeteilt, die allerdings zum Teil nur von der Küche aus zugänglich sind.

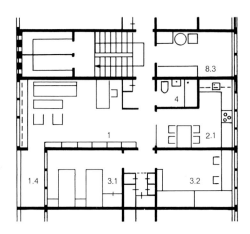

1 Plan, 1 in 200 (section A in Fig. 3). The plan is based on a square module, inserted between the bearing crosswalls of 60 cm (approx. 2 ft.) side length, corresponding to the aggregate thickness of the two outer walls. End walls and balustrades are double walls with an air gap filled by 2″ thick insulating mats

1 Grundriß, 1:200 (Bild 3, Ausschnitt A). Dem Grundriß liegt ein zwischen die tragenden Querwände eingespannter Raster zugrunde, Seitenlänge der Quadrate 60 cm = 2 Außenwanddicken. Giebelwände und Brüstungen sind zweischalig gemauert mit einer 5 cm dicken Isoliermatte im Luftzwischenraum

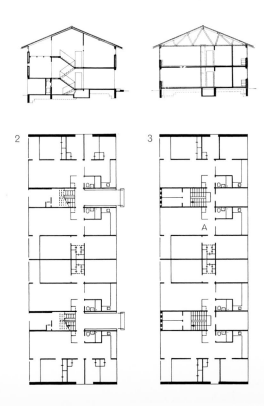

Key to plans see page 213
Legende zu den Grundrissen siehe Seite 213

2 Ground floor plan and section of stair well, 1 in 500. The garden exit, leading to the wind-protected playground for toddlers, is flanked by a pram port and dustbins
3 Plan of upper floor and cross-section of the block, 1 in 500. The nailed beams of the roof structure rest on steel girders which are wrapped in rockwool and enclosed in wooden shutters

2 Erdgeschoßgrundriß und Schnitt durch das Treppenhaus, 1:500. Am Gartenausgang zum windgeschützten Kleinkinderspielplatz ist ein Platz für Kinderwagen und Müllbox
3 Obergeschoßgrundriß und Schnitt durch die Wohnung, 1:500. Die Nagelbinder des Dachstuhls ruhen auf Stahlträgern, die mit Steinwolle und einer Holzschalung umhüllt sind

4 View from north-west on the oldest part of the estate
5 Site plan of the western part of the estate, 1 in 10000.
A Shopping parade, B Service station, C Kindergarten,
D Old houses
6 The entrance zone shows the harmony of the materials

4 Blick von Nordwesten auf den ersten Bauabschnitt der Siedlung
5 Lageplan des westlichen Teils der Siedlung, 1:10000.
A Ladengruppe, B Service-Station, C Kindergarten,
D alte Bebauung
6 Die Eingangspartie zeigt den Zusammenklang der Materialien

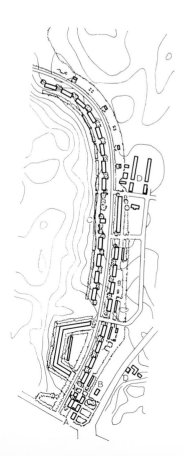

7 The open view over the green valley, designated as a permanent open space, can only be enjoyed from the west-side flats. Due to the large window and the glass partition on the kitchen side in the rear of the observer, the sitting rooms do not appear to be unduly narrow though they are no more than 12 ft. wide

8 Detail of window, 1 in 10. Some of the windows cannot be opened; these can be cleaned from inside by a wiper in the shape of an angle iron measuring approx. $3/4'' \times 1^1/_4'' \times 1/_8''$. Window, concrete lintel and concrete plinth as well as the wooden cladding of the cross-wall ends and roof beams are placed about 1" behind the brick front

9 Brick, timber, glass. A narrow concrete ribbon projecting from the structural floor downwards has an inside insulation of insulating boards

7 Nur die westliche Reihe der Häuser hat diesen freien Blick auf das Wiesental, das nicht zugebaut wird. Durch das große Fenster und die Glaswand zur Eßküche im Rükken des Betrachters wirken die nur 3,60 m breiten Wohnräume nicht eng

8 Fensterdetail, 1:10. Zum Teil sind die Fenster fest verglast und haben innen einen Reinigungsflügel aus einem Stahlwinkel 20 × 30 × 4 mm. Fenster, Betonsturz und -sockel sowie die Holzverkleidung der Querwandenden und Dachträger liegen in einer Ebene 3 cm hinter der Backsteinfassade

9 Ziegel, Holz, Glas. Ein schmaler, aus der Decke nach unten verkröpfter Betonstreifen ist innen durch Dämmplatten isoliert

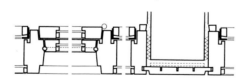 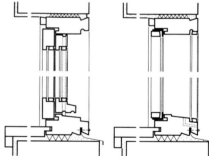

Copenhagen, 1960/61 · Bellmansgade housing estate
Architect: City Architect, Copenhagen

One five-storey block and two eight-storey blocks, erected with prefabricated Larsen & Nielsen units, together contain 243 flats. In the two-storey annex linking the blocks is a kindergarten; in the ground floor of the five-storey block are shops. Although 20 flats are reserved for physically handicapped people and old-age pensioners, the lack of differentiation in the size of the flats is a shortcoming which has unfortunately become general throughout Europe.

Kopenhagen, 1960/61 · Siedlung Bellmansgade
Architekt: Stadtbauamt Kopenhagen

Ein fünfgeschossiger und zwei achtgeschossige Baublöcke aus vorgefertigten Elementen nach dem System »Larsen & Nielsen« enthalten 243 Wohnungen. In dem zweigeschossigen Verbindungsglied ist ein Kindergarten und im Erdgeschoß des fünfgeschossigen Teiles sind Läden eingerichtet. Es sind zwar 20 Wohnungen für Invaliden und Pensionäre vorgesehen, insgesamt ist die zu geringe Differenzierung in den Wohnungsgrößen aber ein Fehler, der leider in Europa üblich geworden ist.

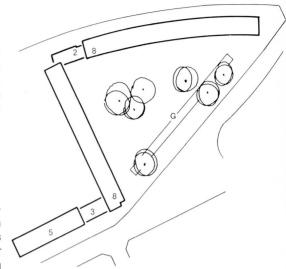

1 Site plan, 1 in 2000. The figures indicate the number of storeys. The 27 garages, marked G, are placed at a lower level
2 View from south-west
3 Interior of a sitting room
4 Plan, 1 in 200. A prominent feature is the small washing room. The space is, however, adequate for the later installation of a shower bath

1 Lageplan, 1:2000. Die Ziffern bezeichnen die Stockwerksanzahl. Die 27 Garagen (G) sind tiefer gelegt
2 Ansicht von Südwesten
3 Blick in ein Wohnzimmer
4 Grundriß, 1:200. Auffallend ist der kleine Waschraum. Der Platz reicht aus, um nachträglich eine Dusche einzubauen

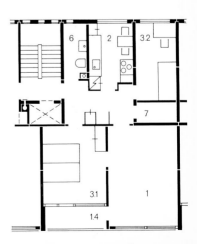

Hamburg, 1961 · "Horner Geest" housing estate, developed by Freie Stadt Ltd.
Architects: Gerd Pempelfort, K. Gerhard Wilhelmi

In this case, the Danish type plans of the Larsen & Nielsen system have been adapted to German conditions and bye-laws.
The "laboratory type" kitchens are very small; their floor area of 45 or 50 sq. ft. is barely sufficient to permit the installations of the domestic appliances needed to ease the housewife's burden. Symmetric arrangement of the kitchens has been avoided; in every third flat, however, the walk from the kitchen to the dining area in the sitting room is across the whole flat.
The details reveal the weaknesses of the prefabrication system: at many points, it is still necessary to resort to manual work for the installation of the insulation strips and for the filling of the joints. There are thus still many potential trouble spots.

Hamburg, 1961 · Siedlung »Horner Geest« der »Freien Stadt GmbH«
Architekten: Gerd Pempelfort, K. Gerhard Wilhelmi

Die dänischen Grundrisse des Bausystems »Larsen & Nielsen« werden hier deutschen Verhältnissen und Vorschriften angepaßt.
Die »Laborküchen« sind sehr klein; bei 4,12 oder 4,73 m² Grundfläche können die zur Erleichterung der Hausfrauenarbeit notwendigen Apparaturen kaum montiert werden. Eine spiegelbildliche Anordnung der Küchen ist zwar vermieden, aber in jeder dritten Wohnung muß dafür von der Küche zum Eßplatz im Wohnraum ein Weg quer durch die ganze Wohnung zurückgelegt werden.
Die Details lassen die schwachen Stellen im Vorfertigungssystem erkennen: An zahlreichen Stellen ist noch Handarbeit beim Anbringen der Isolierstreifen und Fugenfüllungen erforderlich. Die Zahl möglicher Fehlerquellen ist damit noch relativ hoch.

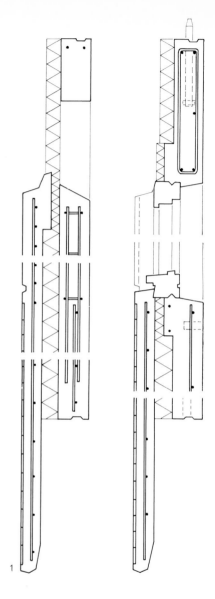

1

2

3

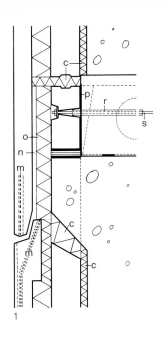

1

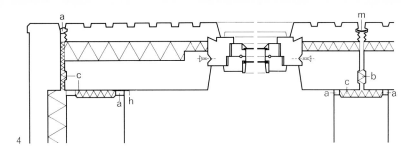

4

1 Sections of a solid panel at the suspension point, of a window panel, and of panel suspension at the cross-wall, 1 in 10
2 The blocks seen from the staircase side
3 Plan, 1 in 200
4 Horizontal section of wall and window
5 Longitudinal section and cross section of the eaves, 1 in 10
6 The blocks seen from the balcony side

Key to detail plans:
a "Secomastic" lining, b Glass wool cord, c Glass wool packing, d "Styropor", e Neoprene, f Galvanised steel plate, g Plastic foil, h Coat of paint, i M 20 bolt, k Pipe with weld-assembled sleeve, l Concrete filling, m Vertical joint at stanchions with neoprene sealing; the grooves in the concrete are inclined, n Expansion joint (air circulation), o Glass wool, applied after the assembly of the lower panel, p Cardboard strip, r Plastic tube, s Anchor bolt, t Tiles or mosaic, u Plastic material inserted from above

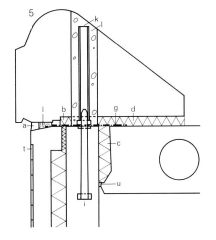

5

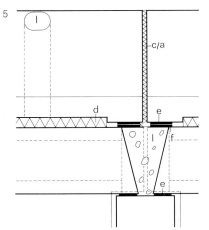

5

6

1 Schnitte durch eine Vollwandplatte am Aufhängepunkt, durch eine Fensterplatte und durch die Aufhängung der Platte in der Querwandebene, 1:10
2 Die Treppenhausseite der Baublöcke
3 Grundriß, 1:200
4 Horizontalschnitt durch Wand und Fenster
5 Schnitt durch das Dachgesims, längs und quer, 1:10
6 Die Loggienseite

Legende zu den Detailplänen:
a Secomastic-Verstrich, b Glaswolleschnur, c Glaswolle gestopft, d Styropor, e Neoprene, f Stahlblech verzinkt, g Plastikfolie, h Anstrich, i Schraube M20, k Rohr mit aufgeschweißter Mutter, l Betonfüllung, m senkrechte Fuge an Stützen mit Neoprene-Dichtung; im Beton Rillung schräg nach unten, n Bewegungsfuge (Luftzirkulation), o nach Montage der unteren Platte angeklebte Glaswolle, p Pappstreifen, r Plastikrohr, s Ankereisen, t Kacheln oder Mosaik, u Plastikmaterial von oben eingelegt

1 A photograph which might well have been taken from a Ministry of Health leaflet. Unfortunately, the need for playgrounds where children can play freely and to their hearts' delight is still ignored in all but a few central and western European housing schemes. Soil, once cultivated, requires ten years or more to become "natural" again
2 View from one of the flats towards south, overlooking the kindergarten, the footpath to the shopping centre, and the small, about 15 ft. high wooded hillock which is also shown on page 56

1 Ein Bild wie aus dem Prospekt eines Familienministeriums. Leider ist in den wenigsten mittel- und westeuropäischen Siedlungen an die Notwendigkeit eines freien, ungezwungenen Spiels der Kinder gedacht. Ein planierter Boden braucht über ein Jahrzehnt, um wieder »natürlich« zu werden
2 Blick aus einer Wohnung nach Süden auf den Kindergarten, den Weg zum Ladenzentrum und den 5 m hohen, bewaldeten Hügel, der auch auf Seite 56 gezeigt ist

Baronbackarna, Örebro (Sweden), 1955 · Meander type housing estate
Architects: Per Axel Ekholm and Sidney White, Bruno Alm, Rune Falk

The far-reaching rationalisation of Swedish housing construction leaves little freedom to the architect's imagination. To prevent stagnation, some 10 per cent. of all State-aided dwellings are designated as experimental. One such experiment, which has yielded excellent results, is Baronbackarna. The housing estate is situated about 1½ miles from the town centre on a site of about 67 acres, accessible from the surrounding roads. The blocks are arranged in meandering rows around a central open space which contains two kindergartens and a school. The central heating plant in the north-east, the four garages accommodating 137 cars, and the car parks with space for 710 cars are outside the pedestrian zone. A shopping centre at the southern edge of the estate (distinguished, in the aerial photograph, Fig. 6, by the bright roofs) is supplemented by shops at two sub-centres.
All the blocks have three storeys (the Swedish bye-laws require lifts for four storeys or more). The problem of interlacing the vehicular and pedestrian zones has been solved very successfully, albeit at the price of having to place many of the bedrooms on the north side. It was not yet possible to arrange for a staggering in height.

Örebro-Baronbackarna (Schweden), 1955 · Mäander-Siedlung
Architekten: Per Axel Ekholm, Sidney White, Bruno Alm und Rune Falk

Der weitgehend durchrationalisierte schwedische Wohnungsbau setzt dem Spielraum der Architektenphantasie enge Grenzen. Um ein Stagnieren der Entwicklung
zu verhindern, werden etwa 10% der staatlich geförderten Wohnungen als Experimentierwohnungen gebaut. Baronbackarna ist ein solches »Experiment« mit vor-
züglichen Ergebnissen. Die Siedlung liegt 2 km vom Stadtzentrum entfernt auf
einem etwa 27 Hektar großen Gelände, das von außen her erschlossen ist. Die
Wohnblöcke umschließen mäanderförmig den inneren Grünbereich, in dem zwei
Kindergärten und eine Schule liegen. Die Heizzentrale am Nordostrand, 4 Garagen
mit 137 Plätzen und 710 Wagenabstellplätze liegen außerhalb der Fußgängerzone.
Ein Ladenzentrum am Südrand der Anlage (im Luftbild 6 mit hellen Dächern) wird
durch Läden an zwei weiteren Punkten ergänzt.
Alle Wohnhäuser sind dreigeschossig (vom vierten Wohngeschoß ab sind in
Schweden Aufzüge erforderlich). Die Verzahnung der Bereiche für Fahrverkehr und
Fußgänger ist sehr gut gelungen, wenn auch mit der Nordlage eines großen Teiles
der Schlafräume erkauft. Eine Höhenstaffelung konnte noch nicht gleichzeitig ge-
plant und durchgearbeitet werden.

3   Part of site plan, 1 in 1000 (showing the second courtyard
from the bottom on the right-hand side of the aerial photograph, Fig. 6). The narrowness of the courtyard is compensated by the adjacent open space
4/5   Flat entrances, kitchens, sitting rooms and balconies
face the central area which offers many playing facilities
for children

3   Lageplanausschnitt, 1:1000 (auf dem Luftbild S. 82 der
zweite Innenhof von rechts unten). Die Enge des Hofes wird
ausgeglichen durch den anschließenden Grünbereich
4/5   Hauseingänge, Küchen, Wohnräume und Balkone liegen am Innenhof, der den Kindern vielfältige Spielmöglichkeiten bietet

6 Aerial photograph, seen from the east (north being on the right), reproduced on a scale of approx. 1 in 2500. Inside the area are playgrounds, kindergartens and the elementary school (just above the centre of the picture)
7 Swedish kitchens are always carefully planned. In this experimental dwelling, the washroom (with bath-tub) is separated from the kitchen by a glass partition. The kitchen can also be reached through the sitting room
8/9 Plans of standard type upper floors, 1 in 200. The plans, though composed of similar units, are amazingly flexible. The sanitary installations are very successfully combined with the kitchen (although the arrangement is, unfortunately, symmetric). The bedrooms can be partitioned at will by means of cupboard walls. The flat entrance doors are double doors with sills. There is, in Sweden, no objection to a direct access to the bedrooms from the sitting room. The flats have a floor area of 620 sq. ft. and 940 sq. ft.

6 Luftbild von Osten gesehen (Norden ist rechts), etwa 1:2500 wiedergegeben. Im Innenbereich liegen Spielplätze, Kindergärten und die Volksschule (oberhalb der Bildmitte)
7 Die Küche ist in schwedischen Wohnungen stets sorgfältig geplant. In diesen Experimentierwohnungen verbindet eine Glaswand den Waschraum (mit Badewanne) mit der Küche. Die Küche ist außerdem über den Wohnraum zu erreichen
8/9 Grundrisse normaler Obergeschosse, 1:200. Die aus gleichartigen Elementen aufgebauten Grundrisse sind erstaunlich variabel. Sehr günstig ist die sanitäre Gruppe mit der Küche kombiniert (leider spiegelbildlich). Die Schlafzimmer können durch die Schrankwände nach Bedarf unterteilt werden. Die Wohnungstüren sind Doppeltüren mit Schwelle. Der Zugang zu den Schlafräumen aus dem Wohnraum heraus wird in Schweden nicht bemängelt. Die Wohnungen haben 58 m² und 88 m² Wohnfläche

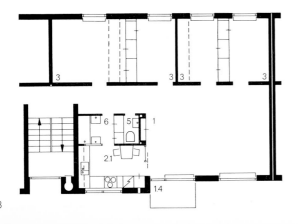

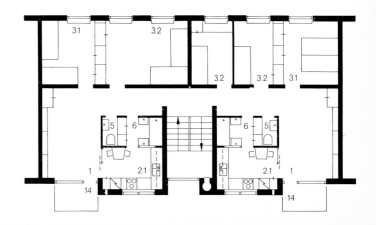

Markbacken, Örebro (Sweden), 1959–62 · Housing estate built by A. B. Marks Hyresbostäder
Architects: White and Associates (Sidney White, Bruno Alm, Rune Falk)

The experience gained by the architects at Baronbackarna has been utilised in this scheme. Facing the noisy car parks are the stairwells, bathrooms and television lounges where the traffic noise is less troublesome than in the bedrooms. Also on the noisy side are, at ground floor level, the "Moped" sheds. Facing the courtyard are the kitchen with dining and working area, balcony, and bedrooms of each flat. The nursery is thus in direct contact with the housewife's working zone whilst the sitting room, mainly used during leisurely evenings, is more isolated. The whole layout is more concentrated and rather more rigid in form, the open space more secluded and, unfortunately, not as variegated as at Baronbackarne.
Of the 1285 flats, 11 per cent. have one room (not counting the kitchen), 37 per cent. two rooms, 42 per cent. three rooms, 4 per cent. four rooms and 6 per cent. five rooms. In addition, terrace houses for large families are built on the north side of the main road.

Örebro-Markbacken (Schweden), 1959–1962 · Siedlung der AB Marks Hyresbostäder
Architekten: Architekturbüro White (Sidney White, Bruno Alm und Rune Falk)

Die Erfahrungen, die der Architekt in Baronbackarna sammelte, wurden in dieser Siedlung ausgewertet. Zu den geräuschvollen Parkplatzhöfen hin liegen Treppenhäuser, Bäder und Fernseh-(Wohn-)Räume, in denen der Außenlärm weniger stört als in den Schlafräumen. An der lauten Seite sind im Erdgeschoß auch die Moped-Abstellräume. Zum Innenhof hin sind jeweils die Küche mit dem Eß- und Arbeitsplatz, der Balkon und die Schlafräume orientiert. Das Kinderzimmer steht so in direktem Kontakt zum Hausfrauen-Arbeitsbereich, das Wohnzimmer ist als »Feierabendraum« etwas mehr ausgesondert. Die ganze Anlage ist konzentrierter und in der Form starrer, der Grünbereich abgeschlossener und nicht mehr so vielfältig gegliedert wie in Baronbackarna.
Die Größen der 1285 Wohnungen, jeweils mit Küche, sind nach folgendem Schlüssel ausgewählt: 1 Zimmer 11%, 2 Zimmer 37%, 3 Zimmer 42%, 4 Zimmer 4%, 5 Zimmer 6%. Für große Familien werden außerdem nördlich der Hauptstraße Reihenhäuser gebaut.

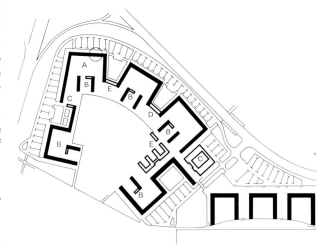

1 Site plan, 1 in 10000.
A See plan, B Laundry, C Shops, D Kindergarten, E Elementary school. The only vehicles permitted to use the inner courtyard are bicycles
2 Children can play in the pedestrian zone, free from danger
3 Ground floor plan, upper floor plan and section, 1 in 500

1 Lageplan, 1:10000.
A siehe Grundriß, B Waschküche, C Läden, D Kinderschule, E Volksschule. Nur Fahrräder dürfen in den Innenhofbereich
2 Ungefährdetes Spielen im Fußgängerbereich
3 Grundrisse Erd- und Obergeschoß und Schnitt, 1:500

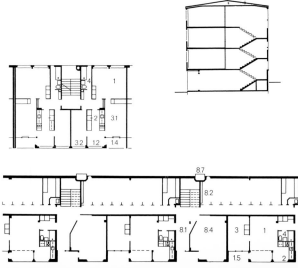

1 View from north-west on entrance side. On closer approach, the horizontal lines (cf. Fig. 3) reveal a well balanced profile treatment
2 Site plan, 1 in 1000

1 Blick von Nordwesten auf die Zugangsseite. Bei näherem Herantreten lösen sich die Horizontalen (siehe Bild 3) in eine wohlabgewogene Profilierung auf
2 Lageplan, 1:1000

Tapiola, Helsinki, 1961 · Riistapolku blocks of flats
Architect: Aulis Blomstedt

Low-rent housing need not be monotonous, depressing or nondescript. In Finland, too, there are restrictive regulations and some less successful housing schemes. But Finnish architects have been able to free themselves from the tasks of building site supervision, property deals and financing and can therefore devote all their efforts to their tasks as planners and architects right down to the finest details. One housing scheme is typical for many.
The ground floor is clearly recessed. The ancillary rooms can be recognized from the glass brick window ribbons. The appearance of heaviness is reduced. The west elevation is featured – without giving the impression of being overloaded – by the loggia recesses, the projecting balcony balustrades, the uniform flower boxes, the balcony side screens, and the widely overhanging roof. The sure touch in choosing the right proportions is also apparent in the plan. The insertion of the third flat, resulting in a three-unit system, does not harm the two larger flats – a rare case!

Helsinki-Tapiola, 1961 · Wohnhausgruppe Riistapolku
Architekt: Aulis Blomstedt

Sozialer Wohnungsbau muß nicht eintönig, trost- und formlos sein. Auch in Finnland gibt es einschränkende Bestimmungen und auch weniger geglückte Wohnungsbauten. Die finnischen Architekten haben sich jedoch von der Bauleitung, dem Grundstückshandel und den Finanzierungsgeschäften freizumachen verstanden, können sich folglich bis ins letzte Detail hinein ihrer Aufgabe als Planer und Architekten widmen. Ein Haus-Beispiel steht hier für viele.
Das Erdgeschoß ist deutlich zurückgesetzt. Die Nebenräume sind an den Fensterbändern aus Glasbausteinen zu erkennen. Der ganze Bau scheint weniger auf dem Boden zu lasten. Die westliche Fassade ist durch die Rücksprünge der Loggien, die herausgeschobenen Balkonbrüstungen, die einheitlichen Blumenkastengitter, die seitlichen Blenden an den Balkonen und das weit vorspringende Dach gegliedert, ohne überladen zu wirken. Die Sicherheit in der Wahl der Proportionen fällt auch im Grundriß auf. Das Einfügen der dritten Wohnung in den Dreispännertyp bringt für die beiden größeren Wohnungen keine Nachteile mit sich (ein seltener Fall!).

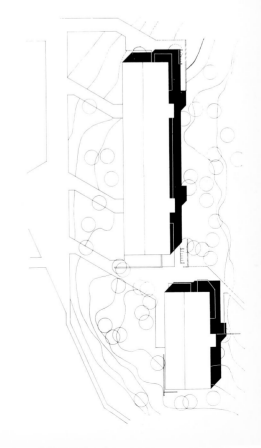

3

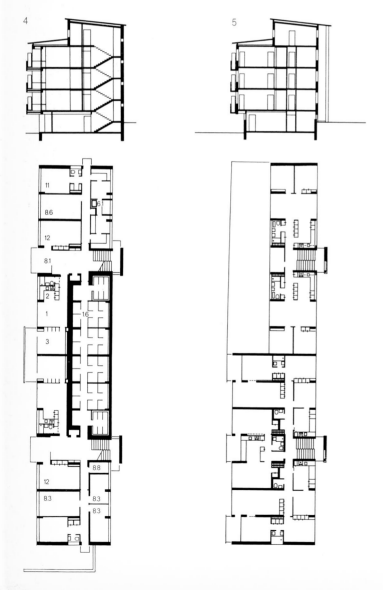

4

5

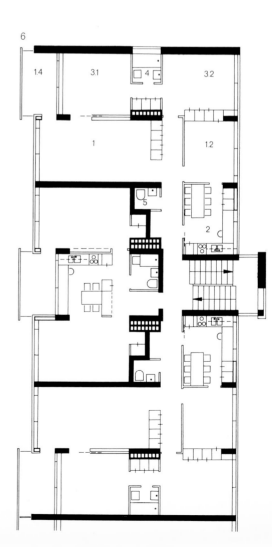

6

3 West elevation. The dominating feature is the landscape which, at Tapiola, it has been possible to preserve as the population density is no greater than about 65 persons per acre. The quiet horizontal layers of the block form an attractive contrast to the scattered pine trees

4 Ground floor plan and section, 1 in 500. The ground floor contains, inter alia, a hobby room, premises for sports implements, a laundry with drying and wringing facilities as well as a Sauna with its ancillary rooms

5 Plan of standard floor (bottom half of plan) and roof storey (top half), with section, 1 in 500

6 Plan of upper floor with three-flat unit, 1 in 200. The light, non-bearing partitions are merely shown in outline. Main entrance and balcony doors are double doors with thresholds. The kitchen includes a breakfast recess; next to it, in the larger flats, is a dining room, also used for housework

7 The profile of the house

8 East side with the projecting stairwell

3 Die Westseite der Baugruppe. Bestimmend ist die Landschaft, die in Tapiola bei einer Dichte von etwa 65 Einwohnern je Hektar gut erhalten werden kann. Die ruhigen horizontalen Schichtungen des Hauses stehen in reizvollem Kontrast zu dem dünnen Kiefernbestand

4 Grundriß des Erdgeschosses und Schnitt, 1:500. Im Erdgeschoß liegen unter anderem ein Hobbyraum, Sportgeräteräume, die Waschküche mit Trocken- und Mangelräumen sowie eine Sauna mit den dazugehörigen Nebenräumen

5 Grundriß (je zur Hälfte) Normalgeschoß und Dachgeschoß, und Schnitt, 1:500

6 Der Dreispännertyp, Obergeschoßgrundriß, 1:200. Die leichten, nichttragenden Wandteile sind nur umrandet gezeichnet. Wohnungs- und Balkontüren sind Doppeltüren mit Schwelle. In der Küche ist ein Frühstücksplatz; daran schließt sich in den größeren Wohnungen ein Eß- und Hausarbeitsraum an

7 Das »Profil« des Hauses

8 Die Ostseite mit dem vorgezogenen Treppenhaus

7

8

1 North side of the blocks. From the nurseries and bedrooms, there is a wide view over the landscape
2 South side. The hard edges of the three coherent blocks are in contrast to the undulating woodland
3–5 Ground floor and upper floor plans and section, 1 in 200. The light insulating partitions are merely shown in outline. In the nurseries, the north position is compensated by the view on the sunlit landscape
6 Site plan, 1 in 2000. The coastline is indicated in the north.

1 Die Nordseite der Häuser. Aus den Kinder- und Schlafzimmern hat man einen weiten Ausblick auf die Landschaft
2 Südfassade. Hart und kantig im Detail stehen die drei aneinandergebauten Häuser im Gegensatz zu der bewegten Waldlandschaft
3–5 Grundrisse des Erd- und Obergeschosses sowie Schnitt, 1:200. Die leichten, isolierenden Wandteile sind nur umrandet. Der Blick auf die sonnenbeschienene Landschaft muß in den Kinderzimmern für die Nordlage entschädigen
6 Lageplan, 1:2000. Im Norden ist die Küste des Meeresarmes angedeutet.

Lauttasaari, Helsinki, 1961 · Sea-side blocks of flats
Architect: Toivo Korhonen

The blocks are erected in a park-like landscape on a peninsula offering a wide view towards north. As there are plans for constructing a bridge in the vicinity of the site, the floors are placed so high as to retain the fine view over the bay, preserve favourable sunlight conditions, and permit footpaths at ground floor level through the building.
The end walls are plastered; the main elevations have a cladding of asbestos cement slabs. But the sharp-edged cubic form has not been adhered to quite consistently. The section shows how the end walls have been raised above the inclined roof for merely aesthetic reasons. Because of the detachment from the ground and the small number of storeys, the quiet impression of a horizontal orientation has also been achieved in this case.

Helsinki-Lauttasaari, 1961 · Hausgruppe am See
Architekt: Toivo Korhonen

Das Grundstück liegt in einer parkähnlichen Landschaft auf einer Halbinsel mit weiter Aussicht nach Norden. Da geplant ist, in der Nähe des Grundstücks eine Brücke zu bauen, sind die Wohngeschosse so hoch gelegt, daß eine gute Aussicht zum Meer, eine günstige Besonnung und unter dem Gebäude hindurch Fußwege erhalten bleiben.
Die Fassaden sind an den Giebelseiten verputzt und an den Stirnseiten mit Asbestzementplatten verkleidet. Die scharfkantig kubische Form ist allerdings nicht ganz durchgestanden. Der Schnitt zeigt, wie die Giebelwandscheiben nur zur Verzierung über die Dachschräge hochgezogen wurden. Durch das Abheben vom Boden und die geringe Stockwerkszahl wird der ruhige Eindruck einer horizontalen Schichtung auch hier erreicht.

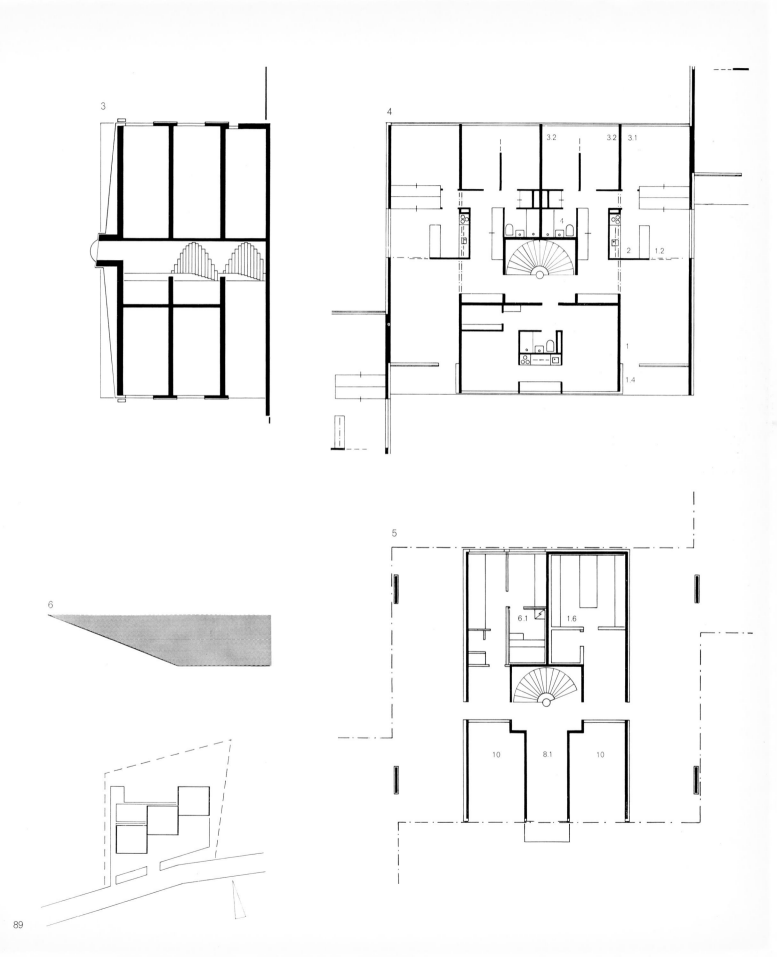

3

4

3.2   3.2   3.1

4

2   1.2

1

1.4

6

5

6.1   1.6

10   8.1   10

Under the Sway of the Rectangular Ground Plan

The examples in this second category still conform to the rectangular plan. With them, the special circumstances affecting the plan are even more obvious than in the variegated picture of the first category.

In England, the regeneration of a residential area governed by the leasehold rhythm is a traditional practice, in contrast to Germany where, e.g. Bernouilli's proposals have often been misinterpreted as "bolshevisation of the most sacred assets of the nation". Germany's town planners would no doubt be very glad if the leasehold system would still be practised in their cities. For example, the tenement houses erected in the Wedding district of Berlin in 1870/80 could then be replaced, without enormous compensation payments, during the years 1969/79.

Among the special cases are new buildings in a former convent garden (Blackheath), in a castle park (Meudon) or on University ground (Yale University), or blocks designed to fill the gaps in building lines (Cologne, London), or a competition proiect for a building that can be erected in any open space.

Im rechtwinkligen Grundrißschema

Die Beispiele der zweiten Gruppe sind ebenfalls dem rechtwinkligen Grundrißschema zuzuordnen. Bei ihnen treten die besonderen Umstände, die auf die Planung einwirken, noch mehr in den Vordergrund als bei dem vielfältigen Bild der ersten Gruppe.

Die Regenerierung eines Wohngebiets im Erbpacht-Rhythmus ist in England Tradition, während zum Beispiel Bernoullis Vorschläge in Deutschland häufig als »Bolschewisierung der heiligsten Güter der Nation« mißdeutet wurden. Wie froh wären doch Deutschlands Stadtväter, wäre das Erbpachtrecht auch in ihren Städten noch üblich: 1870–1880 zum Beispiel im Berliner Wedding Gebautes könnte ohne Milliardenentschädigungen 1969–1979 saniert werden.

Sonderfälle sind weiterhin sowohl Neubauten im Klostergarten (Blackheath), im Schloßpark (Meudon) oder im Universitätsgelände (Yale-Universität), als auch das Ausfüllen von Baulücken (Köln, London) oder ein Wettbewerbsprojekt für eine beliebige grüne Wiese.

Not from Scandinavia, but from South America comes the example of brick architecture (housing scheme at Bogotá, designed by Rogelio Salmona, see page 150).
Car ports at ground floor level, a round tower containing the spiral stairs leading to the access galleries, and plans no less modern than those to be found anywhere in Europe. One more proof that new designs are not necessarily dependent on the use of new building materials.

Nicht aus Skandinavien, sondern aus Südamerika stammt diese Ziegelarchitektur (Wohnbauten in Bogotá von Rogelio Salmona, siehe Seite 150ff.).
Wageneinstellplätze im Erdgeschoß, im runden Turm die Treppe zu den Laubengängen, dazu Grundrisse, wie sie zeitgemäßer in Europa nicht entworfen werden. Ein Beweis mehr, daß neue Bauformen nicht unbedingt an die Verwendung neuartiger Baustoffe gebunden sind

Preston, Lancashire (Britain), 1961 · Slum clearance and redevelopment scheme
Architects: James Stirling and James Gowan

This scheme at Preston, Lancs., has been selected as a typical English example of a rehousing scheme. The often used term slum clearance is in fact a misnomer as we are dealing with new buildings which usually represent a natural or organic renewal after the expiry of the leasehold agreements and the return of the properties to the landlords without compensation. The slum character of such areas is due to the fact that, during the last years of the leasehold period, the lease holders no longer bother to carry out repairs. Even so, the population has formed an attachement to the district and cultivated a community spirit which is absent from the suburban dilution of the garden cities. According to British sociologists and architects, the latter are not suitable as a generally acceptable form of housing in an industrial mass community (T. Harrison, "Britain Revisited. – Mass Observation").
Despite the improvements in the living standard of British workers, there has been little change in their habits or character. It was therefore necessary to trace this character, which is definitely regarded as a positive feature, and to take it into account with new construction. The access gallery, for example, is reminiscent of traditional English alley-yards and street terraces, which made for neighbourliness and communal spirit. Details have been taken over from the industrial world – especially the cotton mills: the brittle surface quality of the brickwork and the bull-nosed sills are reminiscent of industrial buildings.
The local authorities prepare the overall plan for the site and specify the type of dwellings, and then invite tenders from contractors. In general, it is only the big companies who are able to undertake such work on a package deal basis, including the detailed planning of construction work. The architects are merely employees of the contractors, a state of affairs which the younger architects view with alarm. As far as the authorities are concerned, the method is simple; but the quality of the buildings is considerably lowered. Also, there is often little contact between client and architect. In the case of the Preston housing scheme, however, the contractors were supported by a team of highly qualified experts and were therefore able to achieve a result above the average.

1 The new buildings are adapted to the character of the old ones without repeating their disadvantages
2 Site plan, 1 in 2000.
A Three-storey terraces, B Fourstorey blocks,
C Two-storey houses for old people (too isolated, in the architects' opinion), D Play area, E Garages

1 Die neuen Bauten sind dem Charakter der alten Bebauung angepaßt, ohne deren Nachteile zu wiederholen
2 Lageplan, 1:2000.
A dreigeschossige Häuser, B viergeschossige Häuser,
C Altenwohnungen, zweigeschossig (zu sehr ausgesondert nach Meinung der Architekten), D Spielhof, E Garagen

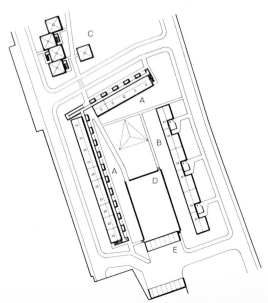

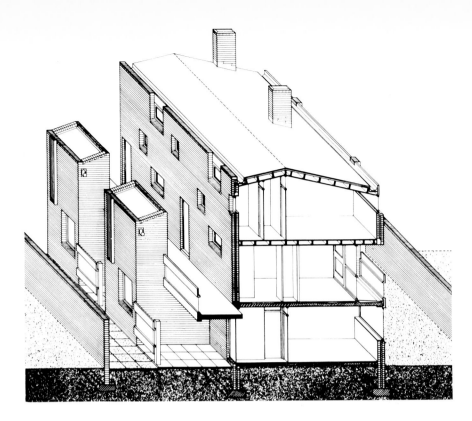

Preston, Lancashire (Großbritannien), 1961 · Abriß und Neubau einer Hausgruppe
Architekten: James Stirling und James Gowan

Die Siedlung in Preston wurde als ein typisches englisches »Rehousing«-Projekt hier ausgewählt. Die häufig gebrauchte Bezeichnung »Sanierung« ist eigentlich fehl am Platz, da es sich um Neubauten handelt, die meist nach Ablauf der Erbpachtverträge und dem entschädigungslosen Anheimfallen der auf den Grundstücken stehenden Häuser als natürliche oder organische Erneuerung notwendig sind. Der Slumcharakter derartiger Gebiete entsteht, weil in den letzten Jahren der Laufzeit des Erbpachtvertrages der Hausbesitzer keinerlei Reparatur mehr ausführen läßt. Die Bevölkerung ist dennoch mit ihrem Wohnbereich verwachsen und pflegt einen Gemeinschaftsgeist, der in der Vorstadtverdünnung der Gartenstädte vermißt wird. Nach Ansicht englischer Soziologen und Architekten eignen sich die stark aufgelockerten Gartenstädte nicht als allgemein gültige Wohnform für die industrielle Massengesellschaft (T. Harrison, Britain Revisited.-Mass-Observation). Trotz der Verbesserungen des Lebensstandards der englischen Arbeiter haben sich die Gewohnheiten und Eigenarten der Bevölkerung nur geringfügig gewandelt. Es galt daher, diesen durchaus positiv empfundenen Eigenheiten nachzuspüren und sie beim Neubau zu berücksichtigen. So ist der Laubengang eine Erinnerung an die engen alten Straßenräume, die einen gewissen Kontakt mit der Nachbarschaft ermöglichten. Details aus der Arbeitswelt – hauptsächlich der Spinnereien – wurden übernommen: Die spröde, herbe Oberfläche der Ziegelbauten und die »stiernasigen« Mauerkappen erinnern an Industriebauten.

Die Grafschaft bereitet die Planung vor und legt die Wohnungstypen fest; dann wird ein Wettbewerb unter den Unternehmern ausgeschrieben. Gemeinhin ist es nur großen Firmen möglich, sich an dieser Ausschreibung der Gesamtarbeiten, einschließlich der Bauplanung, zu beteiligen. Die Architekten treten nur noch als Angestellte des Unternehmers in Erscheinung, ein Zustand, der von der jüngeren Generation als alarmierend empfunden wird. Für die Behörde ist das Verfahren einfach, aber die Qualität der Bauten wird auf diese Weise erheblich herabgemindert. (Die Bauausführung ist in England normalerweise erheblich schlechter als in europäischen Ländern.) Der Kontakt zwischen Bauherrn und Architekt ist ebenfalls erheblich gestört, da der Architekt die Entwurfsrichtlinien oft nur aus dritter Hand erhält. Für die Bauten in Preston hatte der Unternehmer mit einem Team sehr guter Fachkräfte eine überdurchschnittliche Lösung erarbeiten können.

3 Section, 1 in 100, with isometric drawing
4 Footbridge for the access gallery at the ramped entrance

3 Schnitt, 1:100 und Isometrie
4 Die Laubengangbrücke am Rampenaufgang

6

5 East side of the four-storey blocks. Open staircases with drying balconies. By letting the block step with the slope of the site, by placing the bathroom windows at a higher level, and by arranging the front doors on each quarter landing of the staircase, a rhythmic window pattern has been obtained. The brick detailing is reminiscent of nineteenth century industrial buildings
6 Plan of flats in the four-storey block (B), 1 in 500
7 Sitting room side of the three-storey terraces (A)
8–10 Type A plans, 1 in 200. Ground floor flat (Fig. 10) and access gallery type maisonette with bedroom storey (Figs. 8, 9)

5 Die Ostseite des viergeschossigen Baublocks. Offenes Treppenhaus mit Wäschetrockenplatz (zurückliegende Brüstung). Durch die Staffelung der Häuser am Hang, das Höherlegen der Badfenster und das Versetzen der Wohnungseingänge um jeweils drei Stufen in jedem Treppenhaus ergibt sich das rhythmische Spiel der Fensteranordnung. Die Ziegeldetails sind bei den Fabrikbauten des 19. Jahrhunderts entlehnt
6 Grundriß der Wohnungen im viergeschossigen Haus B, 1:500
7 Die Wohnseite der dreigeschossigen Häuser (A)
8–10 Grundrisse Typ A, 1:200. Erdgeschoßwohnung (Bild 10) und Laubengangwohnung mit Schlafgeschoß (Bild 8, 9)

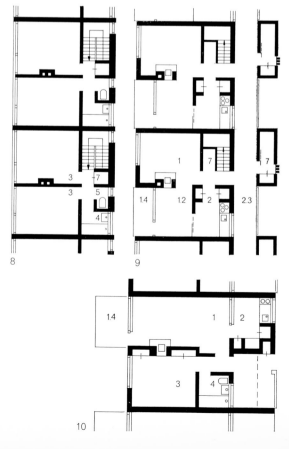

8

9

10

London, 1961 · No. 9/11, St. Petersburgh Place
Architects: Andrews Emmerson and Thomas Harley Sherlock
Civil engineer: James Atherton

A modern luxury flat is distinguished from a normal low-rent flat in about the same way as the technical features of a racing car differ from those of a production line model. The luxury features, which subsequently tend to become standard features, are no longer reflected in large suites of rooms calling for numerous domestic servants, but in the first-class technical equipment of a flat of otherwise normal layout, though perhaps with rather more spacious main rooms. In a few years, this tendency will also be followed in low-rent housing. The block consists of eight storeys with two flats on each floor, served by staircase and lift. The emergency stairs with open landings are placed on the garden side and connected with the main bedrooms. The noisy waterpipes are grouped together around the lift well so that the bathrooms and lavatory insulate the lift noise from the rest of the flat. Kitchen and living room are connected by a "through-unit"; there is no separate dining room or dining area. The balcony, measuring 6' × 13', is spacious enough to accommodate a table and three or four chairs. (Vertical-lift doors have, strangely enough, not yet become popular in Britain.) A quiet position for the bedrooms on the garden side is ensured. Elevations and details are simple, sometimes rather robust and by no means as refined as might be expected with a flat costing £ 9750 plus £ 50 annual ground rent.

London, 1961 · Haus Nr. 9/11 St. Petersburgh Place
Architekten: Andrews Emmerson und Thomas Harley Sherlock
Ingenieur: James Atherton

Eine »Luxuswohnung« (luxury flat) zeichnet sich heute durch Vorzüge aus, die zu denen einer normalen Sozialwohnung etwa im gleichen Verhältnis stehen wie die technischen Neuheiten eines Rennwagens zum Serienmodell. Der Luxus, der in der Folgezeit langsam zum Standard wird, äußert sich nicht mehr in Zimmerfluchten mit Scharen von Bediensteten, sondern in der erstklassigen technischen Ausrüstung einer normal zugeschnittenen Wohnung. Normal bedeutet: weniger beengt in den Haupträumen. Auch Sozialwohnungen werden in einigen Jahren dieser Tendenz folgen. – Treppenhaus und Aufzug erschließen das achtgeschossige Haus wie bei einem Zweispännertyp. Die zweite Feuertreppe mit offenen Podesten ist einfach an die Gartenfront gelegt und jeweils mit dem Elternschlafraum verbunden. Die lärmerzeugenden Wasserleitungen sind zusammengefaßt und bilden mit den sanitären Räumen ein Geräuschpolster gegenüber Aufzug und Treppenhaus. Die Kochküche hat eine Durchreiche zum Wohnraum; ein Eßzimmer oder ein besonderer Eßplatz fehlen. Der Balkon ist mit 1,82 × 3,96 m geräumig genug, um einen Tisch mit 3–4 Stühlen aufzunehmen. Hebetüren haben sich eigenartigerweise in Großbritannien noch nicht eingeführt. Für eine ruhige Lage der Schlafräume an der Gartenseite ist gesorgt. Fassaden und Details sind einfach, teilweise hart, keinesfalls von extremer Raffinesse, die man bei einem Wohnungspreis von £ 9750 zuzüglich £ 50 jährlichem Erbpachtanteil vermuten könnte.

1   Street frontage of the block which, on the right, adjoins a wall of equal height. The basement car park is approached by ramps on each side

1   Die Straßenseite des Hauses, das sich rechts an einen gleichhohen Giebel anlehnt. Die Garagen im Untergeschoß sind über zwei Rampen zu erreichen

2   Typical plan of one of the two flats on each floor, 1 in 200. The load-bearing concrete walls are marked by heavy black lines; those on the outside and at the bedrooms have an inside insulation of rockwool

2   Grundriß einer Zweispännerwohnung, 1 : 200. Die tragenden Betonwände (schwarz angelegt) sind an den Außenwänden und in den Schlafräumen mit Steinwolle von innen isoliert

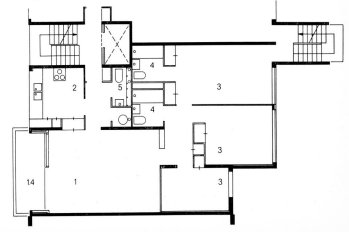

Riehl, Cologne, 1957 · Garthestrasse 18
Architect: Oswald Mathias Ungers

As in the previous example, the design of this building has been governed by the need to fill a gap in the building line; in this case, however, the street is on the south-western side. As a lift serving no more than two flats on each of five storeys would have been rather uneconomic, a third flat has been connected to it by an access gallery. Two of the three bedrooms of each flat face the quiet garden side. The balcony, which has an adequate depth of just over 5 ft. is surrounded by nursery, sitting room and dining area, with the kitchen in the background. A very welcome feature, especially in the event of illness, is the possibility of reaching the bedrooms, bath room and lavatory through intermediate doors directly from the corridor.

Köln-Riehl, 1957 · Haus Garthestraße 18
Architekt: Oswald Mathias Ungers

Eine ähnliche Baulücken-Situation wie im vorhergehenden Beispiel war der Ausgangspunkt für die Planung, jedoch liegt die Südwestfront hier an der Straßenseite. Um den bei fünf Geschossen für einen Zweispännertyp zu aufwendigen Aufzug besser auszunutzen, ist die dritte Wohnung mit einem Laubengang angeschlossen. Zwei der drei Schlafräume einer Wohnung sind zur ruhigen Gartenseite hin orientiert. Um den Balkon herum, der mit 1,55 m ausreichend tief ist, gruppieren sich Kinderzimmer, Wohnraum und der Eßplatz mit dahinterliegender Küche. Sehr günstig, zum Beispiel in Krankheitsfällen, ist die Möglichkeit, direkt vom Flur aus über Zwischentüren die Schlafräume und die Bad-WC-Gruppe zu erreichen.

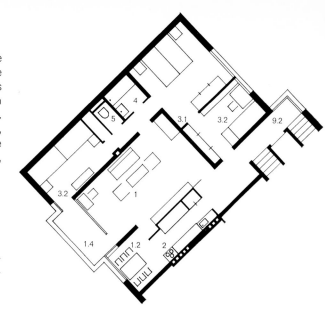

1 Upper-floor plan of the flat adjoining the lift landing, 1 in 200. With some of the flats, a further door leads from the dining area to the balcony
2 South-east side of the block
3 Upper-floor and roof-storey plans (with roof terrace shared by two flats), 1 in 500

1 Obergeschoßgrundriß der Wohnung am Aufzugpodest, 1:200. Bei einem Teil der Wohnungen führt eine weitere Tür vom Eßplatz auf den Balkon
2 Südostseite des Hauses
3 Grundrisse eines Obergeschosses und des Dachgeschosses (mit durchgehender Dachterrasse an 2 Wohnungen), 1:500

Newhaven, Connecticut (USA), 1960 · Flats for married students
of Yale University
Architect: Paul Rudolph

Rudolph's original plans for this westward slope, studded with magnificent trees,
envisaged a kind of Italian terrace city; for economic reasons, however, these had
to be abandoned in favour of a more compact design. Even so, the group of buildings, forming cubes placed on different levels up the slope, still offers many interesting features. The four flats in each block are accessible from a narrow and
rather ugly inside passage which connects the two staircases.

New Haven, Connecticut (USA), 1960 · Wohnungen für verheiratete Studenten
der Yale Universität
Architekt: Paul Rudolph

Auf einem von herrlichen Bäumen bewachsenen, nach Westen abfallenden Hang
plante Rudolph zunächst eine Art italienischer Terrassenstadt, mußte aus Kosten-
gründen dann jedoch für den Bauentwurf eine kompaktere Form wählen. Auch
jetzt ist noch eine sehr abwechslungsreiche Hausgruppe entstanden, deren Kuben
sich den Hang hinauf staffeln. Die vier Wohnungen eines Hauses werden von
einem schmalen, häßlichen Innengang aus erschlossen, der die Verbindung zwischen den beiden Treppenhäusern herstellt.

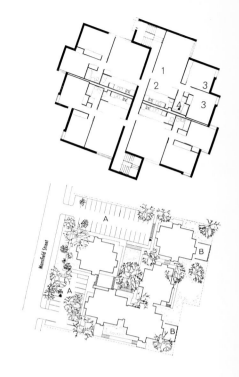

1 Typical floor plan, 1 in 200
2 Site plan, 1 in 2000. A Car park, B Drying space
3 A student's child going for a walk under the old oak
trees

1 Grundriß eines typischen Geschosses, 1:200
2 Lageplan, 1:2000. A Parkplatz, B Trockenplatz
3 Studentensohn spaziert unter alten Eichen

Meudon, Paris, 1957–1959 · Blocks of flats in a park setting
Architects: Henry Pottier and Jean Tessier

Below the large terrace of Meudon, crowned by the Observatory, two blocks of flats have been erected in a 5-acre park together with three detached houses for the previous owners of the ground. The buildings have been so designed and adapted to the park that the ground features have been largely preserved. What was said about the luxury flats filling the gap in the London building line (page 95) also applies to these flats. To the good technical equipment must here be added the park setting. Especially in the staggered blocks, the flats offer many advantages of a detached house. The garages are placed outside the residential zone proper. The entrance side of the three-storey blocks attractively reveals one aspect of French mentality which, in the grands ensembles of the large new residential areas around Paris, has often been exaggerated, viz. the pleasure at playing with structural design. It is not for nothing that the French prefer to talk of "construire" – constructing – rather than "bâtir" – building.

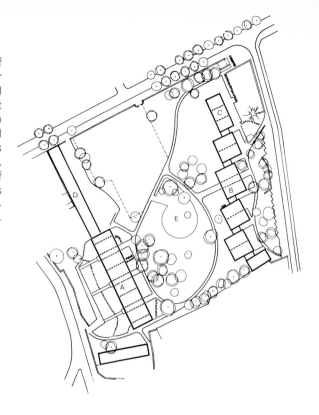

1 Site plan, 1 in 2000.
A Three-storey block, B Four-storey block, C Terrace houses, D Garages, E Playground
2 Entrance side of four-storey block (B). The end walls and the heads of the bearing walls are of brick which are, on the sitting room side, insulated by a second wall with air gap

1 Lageplan, 1:2000.
A dreigeschossiger Block, B viergeschossiger Block,
C Einfamilienreihenhäuser, D Garagen, E Spielplatz
2 Die Eingangsseite am viergeschossigen Block (B). Die Giebelwände und die Köpfe der tragenden Wände sind aus Backsteinmauerwerk, das zu den Wohnräumen hin durch eine Mauerschale mit Luftzwischenraum isoliert ist

Paris-Meudon, 1957–1959 · Hausgruppe in einem Park
Architekten: Henry Pottier und Jean Tessier

Unterhalb der vom Observatorium gekrönten großen Terrasse von Meudon sind in einem zwei Hektar großen Park die beiden Wohnblöcke gebaut, an die drei Einfamilienhäuser für die vorherigen Besitzer des Geländes angeschlossen wurden. Die Gebäude sind so gegliedert und in den Park eingefügt, daß die Geländeform weitgehend erhalten blieb. Das für die »luxury flats« in der Londoner Baulücke (Seite 95) Gesagte gilt sinngemäß auch hier. Zu der guten technischen Ausrüstung kommt in Meudon die Lage im Park hinzu. Besonders in den gestaffelten Häusern bieten die Wohnungen viele Vorteile des Einfamilienhauses. Die Garagen liegen außerhalb des Wohnbereichs. Die Zugangsseite der dreigeschossigen Blöcke offenbart in liebenswürdiger Weise eine Seite französischen Wesens, die in den »grands ensembles« der großen Neubaugebiete um Paris oft als Hypertrophie erscheint: die Freude am Spiel mit Konstruktionen. Man sagt nicht umsonst im Französischen statt bâtir (bauen) immer construire (konstruieren).

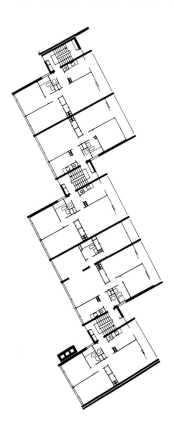

3   Part of floor plan in Block B, 1 in 500
4   Entrance side of Block A. Balustrades clad with decorative blue ceramic slabs; all woodwork and railings painted white

3   Grundrißausschnitt Block B, 1:500
4   Eingangsseite Block A. Brüstungen mit dekorativen Keramikplatten verkleidet, alles Holzwerk und die Geländer weiß gestrichen

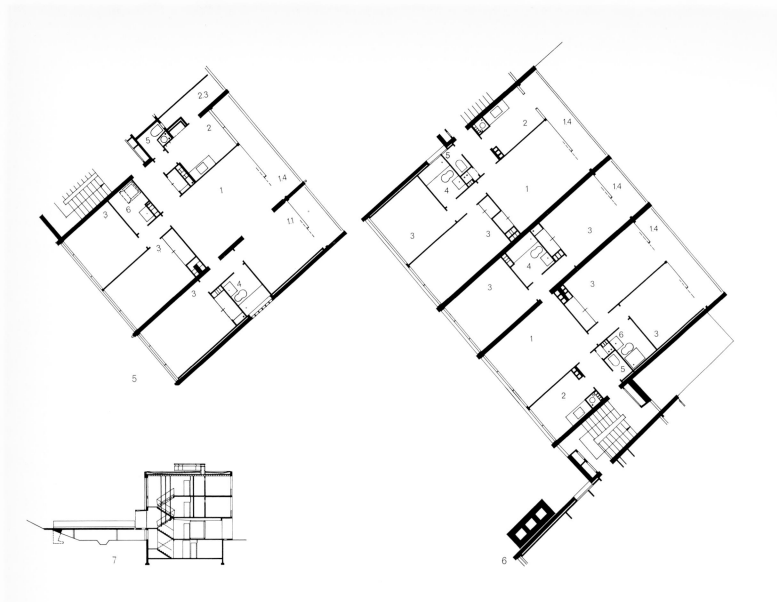

5 Plan of Block A, 1 in 200. The laundry room (6) of the five-room flats on the top floor has a hatch leading to the roof
6 Plan of Block B, 1 in 200. As with many Swedish flats the sitting room serves as a circulating area; two small intermediate corridors lead to the bedrooms, nurseries and bathrooms
7 Section of Block A, 1 in 500
8 A sitting room in the three-storey block (A)

5 Grundriß Block A, 1:200. Im 2. Obergeschoß ist bei den 5-Zimmer-Wohnungen im Waschraum (6) eine Dachluke angebracht
6 Grundriß Block B, 1:200. Der Wohnraum dient wie in vielen schwedischen Wohnungen als Verteiler; kleine Zwischenflure führen zu Schlafräumen, Kinderzimmern und Bädern
7 Schnitt durch Block A, 1:500
8 Ein Wohnraum im dreigeschossigen Block (A)

Competition project (Germany), 1962
Architects: Walter Schwagenscheidt and Tassilo Sittmann

The architects, whose project was awarded the First Prize, took the opportunity of a competition sponsored by the manufacturers of light-weight limestone concrete to formulate their ideas of an ideal grouping of low-height and multi-storey housing units. The detached houses form "nests" of their own. But the multi-family blocks with two to six storeys, which form a separate group, generally contain a single type of dwelling only. The differentiation of the blocks has therefore not yet led to an adequate differentiation of the dwelling sizes.

Wettbewerbsprojekt (Deutschland), 1962
Architekten: Walter Schwagenscheidt und Tassilo Sittmann

Den Wettbewerb eines Herstellers von Leichtkalkbeton nahmen die Architekten – ihr Entwurf erhielt den 1. Preis – zum Anlaß, ihre Vorstellung von einer idealen Gruppierung niedriger und hoher Wohneinheiten zu präzisieren. Die Einfamilienhäuser bilden »Nester« für sich. Die zwei- bis sechsgeschossigen Mehrfamilienhäuser, die eine Gruppe bilden, enthalten zumeist jedoch nur eine einzige Typenwohnung. Die Differenzierung der Baukörper hat also noch nicht zu einer adäquaten Differenzierung der Wohnungsgrößen geführt.

2

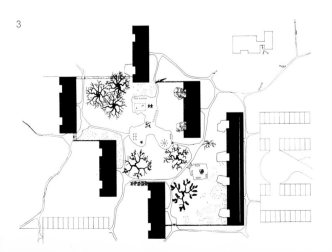

1

1 Isometric drawing of the multi-family houses, seen from south-west. In the south-western and south-eastern corners are clusters of single-family houses
2 Plan of a flat in the six-storey block, 1 in 200
3 Site plan, 1 in 2000
4 West elevation of the six-storey block, 1 in 500. On the roof, a drying room and a roof terrace are provided

1 Isometrie der Mehrfamilienhäuser, von SW gesehen. Im Südwesten und Südosten Einfamilienhaus-Gruppen
2 Grundriß einer Wohnung im 6-geschossigen Haus, 1:200
3 Lageplan, 1:2000
4 Ansicht des 6-geschossigen Hauses von Westen, 1:500. Auf dem Dach sind ein Trockenraum und eine Terrasse vorgesehen

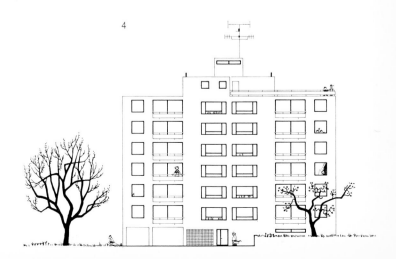

3

4

Blackheath, London, 1957 · The Priory housing scheme
Architect: Eric Lyons

In the garden of an old priory, two-storey and three-storey blocks have been placed in such a way that many of the old trees could be preserved. Here, as in the cases of Roehampton and Meudon, the quality of the site is enhanced by the existing trees. The principle underlying the site plan is simple. The double-U pattern formed by loosely connected blocks is also encountered in the older English garden cities. The garages are placed along the boundary on the north and south-west sides.
Despite consistent adherence to cross-wall construction, the types of flats are skilfully mixed; there are three-room, four-room, and five-room flats with kitchen, bathroom and well ventilated spare room at the staircase. With all types, the living room serves as a circulating area, with access even to the kitchen, which might have been given a direct access from the entrance hall without difficulty. A very favourable space utilisation is obtained by the corner-to-corner connection between living room and dining room in the five-room flat.
With the cross-wall system, the windows can be extended from wall to wall. The window breasts and lintels have a good thermal insulation and a simple but effective rain-protection consisting of asbestos cement facing or panels.

Blackheath bei London, 1957 · Siedlung »The Priory Blackheath«
Architekt: Eric Lyons

In einen alten Klostergarten sind zwei- und dreigeschossige Häuser so eingefügt, daß ein großer Teil der Bäume erhalten blieb. Hier wie in Roehampton oder Meudon ist die Qualität des Bauplatzes durch den vorhandenen Baumbestand bestimmt. Das Prinzip des Lageplanes ist einfach. Die Form des doppelten U, das aus lose aneinandergestellten Häusern besteht, findet sich schon in alten englischen Gartenstädten. Garagen liegen im Norden und Südwesten an der Grundstücksgrenze.
Trotz des starren Querwandsystems sind die Wohnungstypen in geschickter Weise gemischt: Drei-, Vier- und Fünf-Zimmer-Wohnungen mit Küche, Bad und einem gut belüfteten Abstellraum im Treppenhaus. Der Wohnraum ist bei allen Typen Durchgangszimmer, sogar zur Küche hin, die ohne weiteres direkt vom Eingangsflur zugänglich sein könnte. Räumlich sehr günstig ist die Übereckverbindung zwischen Wohn- und Eßraum in der Fünf-Zimmer-Wohnung.
Das Querwandsystem erlaubt es, von Wand zu Wand durchlaufende Fenster einzubauen. Die gut wärmegedämmten Fensterbrüstungen und -stürze sind auf einfache Weise durch Asbestzement-Schindeln oder -Platten gegen Schlagregen geschützt.

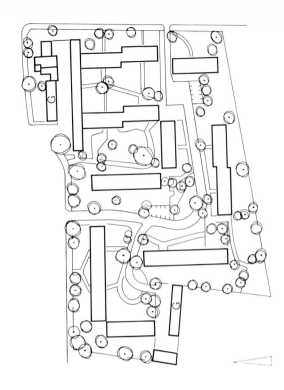

1 Site plan, 1 in 2000. G = Garages
2 The point at which the two garden courts meet
3 The inner garden court, bordered on three sides, opens up at ground floor level to the second court

1 Lageplan, 1:2000. G Garagen
2 Der Verbindungspunkt der beiden Höfe
3 Der innere, U-förmig umschlossene Gartenhof öffnet sich im Erdgeschoß zum zweiten Hof hin

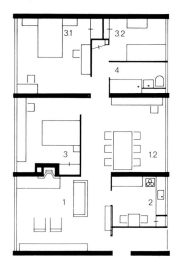

4 Plan of a five-room flat, 1 in 200
5 The eastern part of the garden court with the turning point in the foreground, bordered on the north side by the garage block facing the outside road

4 Grundriß einer Fünf-Zimmer-Wohnung, 1:200
5 Der östliche Teil des Gartenhofes mit der Wendeplatte im Vordergrund, nach Norden durch den nach außen geöffneten Garagentrakt abgeschlossen

6–8 Section, ground floor plan and upper floor plan of a block, 1 in 500

6–8 Schnitt, Erdgeschoß- und Obergeschoßgrundriß eines Hauses, 1:500

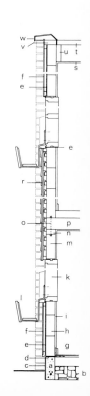

9 Facade cross-section, 1 in 50.
Key: a Concrete plinths resting on cross-wall foundations, b Hardcore, c Bitumen coating, d Metal core d.p.c. "Astos", e Bituminous felt, f "Eternit" asbestos facing, g Screed, skirting and two coats of "Synthaprufe", h 4″ "Thermalite" block, i Plaster, k Window frame, $5^1/_2″ \times 2″$, l Window box, m "Thermalite" block filling, n Window framing, carried up to underside of floor slab, o Bolts for fixing top of timber frame, p Concrete floor slab, r Asbestos cement tiles hanging on battens, s Plasterboard, t Roof insulation, u $7″ \times 2″$ joists, v Framing finished with $5″ \times 2″$ plate, w Pressed aluminium drip

9 Schnitt durch die Fassade, 1:50,
a auf Querwandfundamenten gelagerte Betonbalken, b Steinpackung, c Bitumenanstrich, d Metallfolie, e Bitumenpappe, f Eternitplatte, g Estrich, Eckisolierung, mit 2 Lagen »Synthapruf«, h »Thermalite«-Block 4″, i Putz, k Fensterrahmen $5^1/_2″ \times 2″$, l Blumenkasten, m Füllung: »Thermalite«-Block, n Fensterrahmen, an der Dekke angeschlagen, o Zargenbefestigung, p Betondecke, r Asbestzement-Schindeln auf Holzlattung, s Gipskartonplatte, t Dachisolierung, u Holzträger $7″ \times 2″$, v Fensterzarge, w Aluminium-Profilleiste

From Ground Plan to Plastic Design

Not so long ago, orderliness still used to be mistakenly equated with symmetry. This idea did not support the demand that the external appearance of a building should be developed from the conditions of the plan, i.e. from the interior. But the expressionistic revolution brought a change.

Just as, in Schinkel's time, the advent of the "English Garden" obliterated the formal language of the baroque, the inspirations derived from English low-height housing had a profound effect on the progressive forces in Europe.

The facades are freed from the restraints imposed by the central perspective; they are folded and staggered so as to ensure for the private zone of each individual dwelling a protected and quiet position. In England, the attempt has been made, even in multi-storey housing, to isolate the smaller units of the dwelling, or group of dwellings, and to create an intermediate zone between the wider space open to the public and the secluded, private space.

Vom Grundriß zur plastischen Form

Vertrug sich zunächst die Auffassung, daß Ordnung mit Symmetrie gleichzusetzen sei, nicht mit der Forderung, auch das Äußere eines Hauses aus den Bedingungen des Grundrisses, also des Innenraumes heraus zu entwickeln, so ist mit der expressionistischen Revolution ein Wandel eingetreten.

Ähnlich wie zu Schinkels Zeiten mit dem Englischen Garten die barocke Formensprache aufgehoben wurde, wirkten Anregungen des englischen Landhausbaues auf die fortschrittlichen Kräfte im europäischen Raum.

Die Front der Gebäude wird aus dem von der Zentralperspektive bestimmten Rahmen herausgelöst, gefaltet, gestaffelt, um der Privatzone jeder einzelnen Wohnung eine geschützte, ruhige Lage zu sichern. Selbst im Hochhausbau wird in England der Versuch unternommen, die kleineren Einheiten der Wohnung oder Wohnungsgruppe herauszusondern, einen Zwischenbereich zu schaffen, der zwischen offenem öffentlichem und geschlossenem privatem Raum liegt.

Not only flats but also vehicles are "built". The horse-drawn carriage, representing the culmination of a long development in which the purpose of the vehicle has played a decisive part, shows more clearly than housing architecture the significance of function. The materials, i.e. timber and iron fittings, are reduced to a minimum. Midway between the structural key-points, the cross-section is reduced, though still leaving sufficient margin for deliberate variations in the rhythm, e.g. of the foot-plate. This horse carriage, seen on the cheese market at Gouda (Holland), has even room for decorative features. Pleasure in dressing up and in playing are, in fact, equally functions of life; land, water and air are reflected in the contrast of water horse and dove

Nicht nur Häuser, auch Wagen werden »gebaut«. Deutlicher als die Architektur zeigt der Pferdewagen, der am Ende einer langen zweckbestimmten Entwicklungsreihe steht, was »Funktion« ist. Das Material, Holz und Eisenbeschläge, ist auf ein Minimum reduziert. Von den Knotenpunkten aus verringert sich der Querschnitt, wobei der Spielraum groß genug bleibt, z.B. beim Bodenbrett die Fase im gewollten Rhythmus abzuwandeln. An diesem Wagen auf dem Käsemarkt in Gouda (Holland) ist auch dem Schmuck Raum gelassen. Schmuck- und Spielbedürfnis sind eben auch Funktionen des Lebens; Land, Wasser- und Luft spiegeln sich wider im Gegenüber von Wogenpferdchen und Taube

Nippes, Cologne (Germany), 1959/60 · Low-rent housing
Architect: Oswald Mathias Ungers

Low-rent housing in Germany, known as "Social Housing", has developed in such a way that the term "social" has come to assume a derogatory meaning. That such derogation is not a necessary concomitant is illustrated by these houses in Cologne. But one drawback cannot be passed over. The architect adopted the minimum wall thickness permitted by the Codes of Practice; in the event, this was found to be inadequate so that it was, subsequently, necessary to improve the thermal insulation at relatively high costs. Because of this, the landscaping of the open spaces, which is of such importance to the total effect of the buildings, has been omitted so far. The unmitigated cubic shapes are reminiscent of the experiments of the nineteen-twenties. It is perhaps rather ominous to find that these houses, with their expressionistic design features, differ so greatly from normal present-day housing. This would seem to indicate that, whilst the experience gathered in Germany during the nineteen-thirties was exploited up to a point – and watered down in the process – it has not been taken as a point of departure for further research. In this context, the flash-back to the heritage of an earlier era is refreshing and encouraging.

Köln-Nippes (Deutschland), 1959/60 · Sozialer Wohnungsbau
Architekt: Oswald Mathias Ungers

Der deutsche Soziale Wohnungsbau hat sich zu einem Bild hin entwickelt, das dem Wort »sozial« einen abwertenden Beigeschmack eingetragen hat. Daß dieses Bild aus den Bedingungen heraus nicht zwangsläufig entstehen mußte, zeigen diese Häuser in Köln. Ein Nachteil sei nicht verschwiegen. Der Architekt wählte die minimal zulässige Wanddicke, die sich dann jedoch als unzureichend erwies, so daß nachträglich mit relativ hohen Kosten die Wärmedämmung verbessert werden mußte. Wegen dieser Kosten unterblieb bisher der für die plastische Wirkung der Häuser so sehr wichtige Ausbau der Freiflächen. Die harten, blockigen Formen erinnern an Experimente der zwanziger Jahre. Ist es nicht bedenklich, daß diese aus dem Expressionismus stammenden Gestaltungsmittel die Häuser erheblich vom gegenwärtigen Normalwohnungsbau abheben; wir also zugeben müssen, daß gemeinhin die Erfahrungen der dreißiger Jahre in Deutschland nur weiter ausgenutzt (und verwässert) wurden, nicht aber auf ihnen aufbauend die Forschung weitergetrieben wurde? So gesehen wirkt das Anknüpfen an das Erbe dieser Jahre erfrischend und aufmunternd.

1 Seen from north-west, Block B makes a rather fortress-like impression
2 Site plan, 1 in 2000. K Children's playground with 24 benches, 6 sandboxes, 23 duct pipes (measuring 3'3" × 2'7") 28 concrete pegs, 43 wooden pegs, 180 piles (not yet erected)

1 Von Nordwesten bietet der Block B einen recht festungsartigen Anblick
2 Lageplan, 1 : 2000. K Kinderspielplätze mit 24 Sitzbänken, 6 Sandkästen, 23 Kanalrohren 1,0 × 0,8 m, 28 Betonpflöcken, 43 Holzpflöcken, 180 Pfählen (noch nicht ausgeführt)

3 Block B seen from south-west: Kitchen, dining area
and living room face the "outdoor sitting room", i.e. the
balcony. As the flats are staggered in the plan, the balconies enjoy complete privacy, yet are open to the afternoon sun. On the top floor, the dining space is reduced in
height and a high-level window provides daylight for the
kitchen behind it
4/5 Plans and sections, 1 in 500. Left: Block A; right:
Block B

3 Block B von Südwesten gesehen. Küche, Eßplatz und
Wohnraum sind auf den Freiluftraum, den Balkon, bezogen.
Durch die Staffelung der Grundrisse ist dieser Balkon der
Einsicht der Nachbarn entzogen und öffnet sich dennoch
nach der Seite der Nachmittagssonne. Im Obergeschoß
ist der Eßplatz niedriger und ein hochliegendes Fenster
erhellt die dahinterliegende Küche
4/5 Grundrisse und Schnitte, 1:500. Links Block A, rechts
Block B

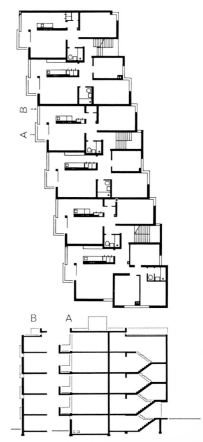

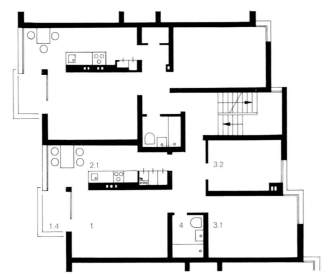

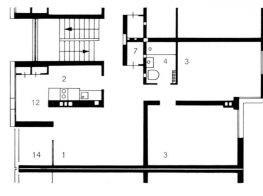

6　Plan of two flats in Block B, 1 in 200
7　Plan of a standard type flat in Block C, 1 in 200
8　The blocks, seen from north-west; in the foreground on the right the two point blocks A; in the centre, Block B

6　Grundriß zweier Wohnungen im Block B, 1:200
7　Grundriß einer Normalwohnung im Block C, 1:200
8　Die Baugruppen von Nordwesten gesehen. Vorne rechts die beiden Punkthäuser A, in der Mitte Block B

Pforzheim (Germany), 1962 · North-slope block
Architect: Karl-Heinz Stocker

On a narrow site with a steep fall towards north-east, the block is staggered in height and width so that each flat has a sunny nook on the south-east side, protected from over-looking, and against the wind. The site adjoins a stretch of woodland which, in this way, has become part of the residential zone.

Pforzheim (Deutschland), 1962 · Haus am Nordhang
Architekt: Karl-Heinz Stocker

Auf einem schmalen, nach Nordosten stark geneigten Hanggrundstück wird durch Staffelung des Hauskörpers in Höhe und Breite erreicht, daß jede Wohnung einen sonnigen, gegen Sicht und Wind geschützten Winkel an der Südostseite der Wohnung erhält. Das Grundstück grenzt hier an ein Waldstück, das auf diese Weise in den Wohnbereich einbezogen wird.

1 View of the hillside block
2 Plan of a top floor flat, 1 in 200
3 Ground floor and top floor plans, 1 in 500

1 Ansicht des Hanghauses
2 Grundriß einer Obergeschoßwohnung, 1:200
3 Grundrisse des Erd- und Obergeschosses, 1:500

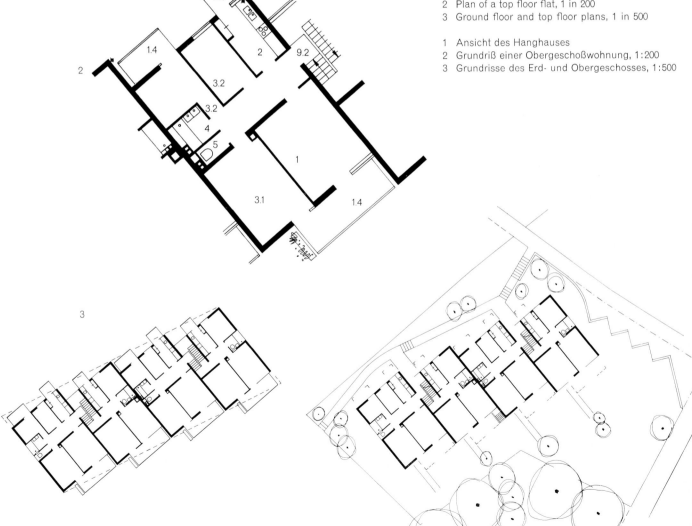

Lauttasaari, Helsinki, 1961 · Park-side block of flats
Architects: Toivo Korhonen and Sakari Halonen

A small site was reserved, in the development plan, for a four-storey point block. It was only on the east side that an adjoining park permitted a congenial view and a somewhat quieter position, whilst the south side is taken up by the road and the west side by closely adjacent conventional three-storey blocks, also usual in Finland. Owing to the staggering of the east side, all the balconies enjoy the south position, yet share the view on the park. The mixture of flats of different sizes also helps to remove the feeling of envy from chance meetings on the stair landing, which often occurs among people of the same income group.
The building is erected in reinforced concrete. The outer walls have a rockwool insulation and a cladding of sand-lime bricks.
On the ground floor are the garages, the sauna and other jointly used premises.

Helsinki-Lauttasaari, 1961 · Haus neben einem Park
Architekten: Toivo Korhonen und Sakari Halonen

Auf dem kleinen Grundstück sah die Stadtplanung ein viergeschossiges Punkthaus vor. Nur nach Osten war durch einen Park die Aussicht ins Grüne und eine ruhigere Wohnlage möglich, im Süden führt die Straße vorbei und im Westen rückt die auch in Finnland übliche, dreigeschossige Bebauung nahe an das Grundstück heran.
Durch die Staffelung der Ostseite liegen alle Balkone in der Südsonne und haben dennoch teil an der Sicht auf den Park. Die Mischung der Wohnungsgrößen trägt dazu bei, den Begegnungen auf dem Treppenabsatz jene neidvolle Schärfe zu nehmen, die unter Gleichgestellten oft zu beobachten ist.
Das Haus ist in Stahlbeton konstruiert. Die Außenwände sind mit Steinwolle isoliert und mit Kalksandsteinen verkleidet.
Im Erdgeschoß liegen die Garagen, die Sauna und andere gemeinsame Räume.

1 In contrast to the sand-lime brick claddings, the concrete faces of the balcony balustrades are kept in white whilst the woodwork of windows and doors is painted black
2 View from the south, with the east side staggered to permit a view of the park

1 Im Kontrast zu den Kalksandstein-Vermauerungen sind die Betonflächen der Balkonbrüstungen weiß. Das Holzwerk der Fenster und Türen ist schwarz gestrichen
2 Ansicht von Süden mit der zum Park hin aufgefalteten Ostseite

3 View from the east
4 Plan and section, 1 in 500
5 Interior, with an open fireplace on the right

3 Ostansicht
4 Grundriß und Schnitt, 1:500
5 Innenansicht, rechts ein offener Kamin

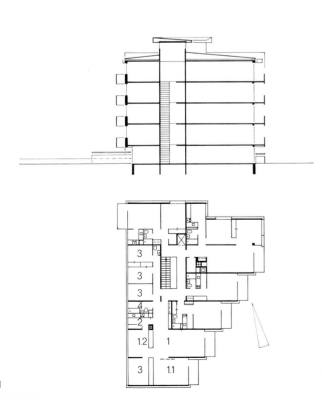

Oberhausen (Germany), 1961 · Flat in Kurze Strasse
Architect: Theo Scholten

Our generation will not live to see the necessary fundamental renewal of many German and other European cities. Resignedly, we can in many cases do nothing but fill the gaps in the building lines. In the old streets, the tenement house dating back to the early age of industrialisation is of little use, mainly because the function of the street has changed completely. Where, formerly, people took an interest in street life, i.e. in those passing on foot or in horse carriages, our generation has turned its back to the street and tries to hide behind thick walls against the noise and smell of motor vehicles whose passengers would in any case not be recognisable from the window. Because of air pollution, the noise-protection-walls consist of unplastered brickwork (as, for example, in the case of the Park Hill Redevelopment Scheme at Sheffield, pages 191 ff.). Despite the legal restrictions on low-rent housing, the flats show differences in design. A two-level living room with gallery links the ground floor flat with the garden; one half of the large hall on the second floor forms a loggia whilst the study behind it is connected by an internal flight of stairs with the floor above.

Oberhausen (Deutschland), 1961 · Haus in der Kurzen Straße
Architekt: Theo Scholten

Die notwendige grundsätzliche Neuordnung deutscher und ebenso vieler europäischer Städte wird unsere Generation nicht mehr erleben. Resignierend bleibt ihr in vielen Fällen nur übrig, Baulücken zu füllen. In den alten Straßen ist das Haus aus den Gründerjahren so schlecht zu gebrauchen, weil sich vor allem die Funktion der Straße, der es sich zuwendet, völlig gewandelt hat. Wollte man einst teilhaben am Leben der zu Fuß oder auch mit der Kutsche Vorbeikommenden, so kann man sich heute nur noch abwenden und sich mit dicken Mauern gegen den Lärm und die Abgase der Benzinfahrzeuge schützen, deren Insassen vom Fenster aus ohnehin nicht mehr zu erkennen wären. Die »Lärmabwehrwände« sind wegen der Luftverschmutzung aus unverputztem Ziegelmauerwerk (wie Park-Hill-Redevelopment in Sheffield, Seite 191 ff.). Trotz der Einschränkungen, die das Gesetz dem »Sozialen Wohnungsbau« auferlegt, sind die Wohnungen unterschiedlich angelegt. Ein zweigeschossiger Wohnraum mit Galerie verbindet die Erdgeschoßwohnung mit dem Gartensitzplatz; die große Wohndiele ist im zweiten Obergeschoß zur Hälfte Loggia, das dahinterliegende Studio ist durch eine interne Treppe mit dem darüberliegenden Geschoß verbunden.

1

1 South side with arbour in front of the two-level living room
2 Site plan, 1 in 2000. The site plan conveys a miniature picture of the disorderliness characteristic for the five-million conurbation in the Ruhr district. A motley collection of five-storey tenement houses lining the streets, contiguous to the new building; detached houses, some of them with sheds along the rear boundary, and small terrace houses
3 Ground floor plan with the gallery in the two-level living room, and a third-floor plan, 1 in 200
4 Section of living rooms and kitchens, 1 in 500
5 Street frontage with noise-protection-walls
6 On the third floor, a loggia is separated from the hall by a glass partition

1 Südansicht mit Gartensitzplatz vor dem hohen Wohnraum
2 Lageplan, 1:2000. Der Lageplan zeigt im kleinen die im 5-Millionen-Einwohner-Konglomerat des Ruhrgebiets herrschende Unordnung: Fünfgeschossige Block-Randbebauung, an die das neue Haus anschließt, Einzelhäuser, zum Teil mit Schuppen an der rückwärtigen Grundstücksgrenze, und schmale Einfamilien-Reihenhäuser
3 Grundrisse des Erdgeschosses mit der Galerie im zweigeschossigen Wohnraum, sowie des 2. Obergeschosses, 1:200
4 Schnitt durch Wohnräume und Küchen, 1:500
5 Straßenseite mit den »Mauern gegen den Lärm«
6 Im dritten Obergeschoß ist durch eine Glaswand eine Loggia von der Wohndiele abgetrennt

2

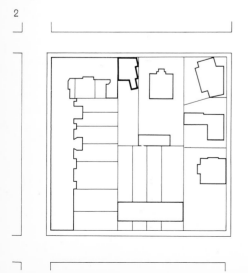

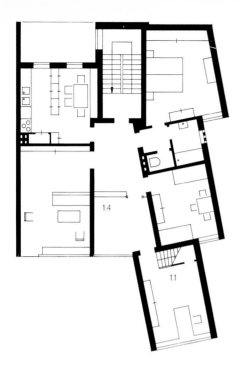

1.4

1.1

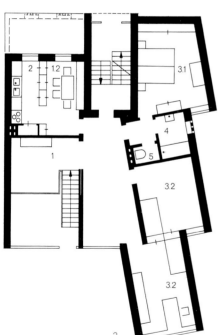

2   1.2

1

4

5

3.1

3.2

3.2

3

4

5

6

Boston, Massachusetts (USA), 1960 · Apartment house

Architects: Hugh Stubbins & Associates, assisted by Norman Paterson, Douglas Cole Smith, John Wacker
Structural engineers: Goldberg, Le Messurier & Associates

Up to now, the quest for the low-height flats of suburbia has been so strong that, e.g. in Boston, no apartment houses had been built for 27 years. But, like all exaggerations motivated by social prestige rather than necessities, the mania for suburbia is now fading. A town flat is no longer regarded as inferior, and the advantages of a short journey to work and to the shops are appreciated more. The privately financed apartment house of the 330 Beacon Street Corporation contains 81 flats, some offices, and a three-storey parking garage (see section). The reinforced concrete frame permits a differentiation between flats of different sizes on each floor. Access is provided by three vertical communication centres. On every third floor, the staircases are linked by escape corridors. Apart from the flats on the two lower floors which lie behind the garage, all the apartments share the view across Charles River with the Massachusetts Institute of Technology on the other side, and on the north-western part of the town. As is usually the case in the United States, the view is regarded as more important than the orientation (north-west); all the living rooms are concentrated on this side. The bedrooms face the quiet Beacon Street whilst, on the living room side, the block is separated from the river-side gardens by an expressway.

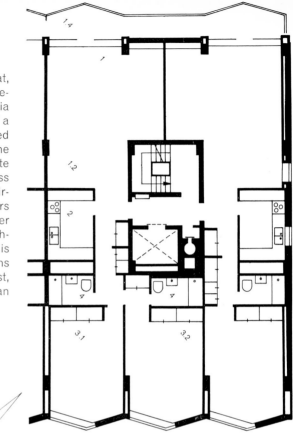

1 Plan of two apartments, 1 in 200
2 Air photograph of the City of Boston. The black arrow indicates the site; the Charles River appears as a bright spot on this stretch
3 River-side front with the garage roof featured by a multi-coloured gravel cover

1 Grundriß zweier Wohnungen, 1:200
2 Luftaufnahme der Stadt Boston. Der schwarze Pfeil weist auf den Bauplatz. Der Charles River zeichnet sich an dieser Stelle hell ab
3 Die Wasserseite mit dem durch verschiedenfarbige Kiesschüttung verzierten Garagendach

114

Boston, Massachusetts (USA), 1960 · Appartementhaus

Architekten: Hugh Stubbins & Ass., Mitarbeiter: Norman Paterson,
Douglas Cole Smith, John Wacker
Ingenieure: Goldberg, Le Messurier & Ass.

Der Drang in die Einfamilienhauslandschaft der Vorstädte war bisher so stark, daß
beispielsweise in Boston 27 Jahre lang kein Appartementhaus mehr gebaut wurde.
Wie alle Übertreibungen, die mehr von sozialem Prestige als von Notwendigkeiten
bestimmt sind, ebbt die »Suburb-Welle« jetzt ab. Man gilt mit einer Stadtwohnung
nicht mehr als deklassiert und weiß die Vorteile der kurzen Wege zu Arbeitsplatz
und Geschäften zu schätzen. Im frei finanzierten Haus der »330 Beacon Street
Corporation« finden sich 81 Wohnungen, einige Geschäftsräume und eine dreigeschossige Sammelgarage (siehe Schnitt). Die Stützenkonstruktion aus Stahlbeton erlaubt eine Differenzierung der Wohnungsgrößen in den einzelnen Geschossen. Drei vertikale »Verkehrsknoten« erschließen das Haus. In jedem dritten Geschoß
sind die Treppenhäuser als Fluchtwege miteinander verbunden. Außer den Appartements in den unteren beiden Geschossen, denen die Garage vorgelagert ist, haben
alle Wohnungen teil am Blick auf den Charles River, an dessen jenseitigem Ufer
das Massachusetts Institute of Technology liegt, und auf den Nordwestteil der Stadt.
Die Aussicht zählt hier, wie allgemein in den USA, mehr als die Himmelsrichtung:
alle Wohnräume liegen an der Nordwestseite. Die Schlafräume sind zur ruhigeren
Beacon-Straße hin orientiert; an der Wohnseite trennt eine Schnellstraße das Haus
von der Grünanlage am Flußufer.

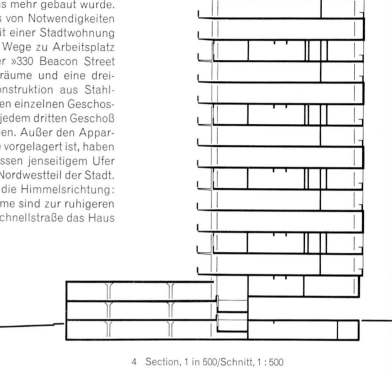

4   Section, 1 in 500/Schnitt, 1 : 500

5   A bedroom on the south-east side with a view on the
old buildings in Beacon Street; the worst that could happen
to this apartment house would be the demolition of all the
old buildings in the neighbourhood and the construction
of a number of similar apartment houses
6   Living room side of the house which offers a wide view
across the Charles River. Projecting towards the expressway is the three-level garage

5   Ein Schlafraum an der Südostseite mit dem Blick auf
die Häuser der Beacon Street. Das Schlimmste, was diesem Appartementhaus widerfahren könnte, wäre der Ab-
bruch aller alten Häuser in der Nachbarschaft und der
Bau lauter gleichartiger Appartementblöcke
6   Wohnzimmer. Vom Fenster bietet sich eine weite Aussicht über den Charles River hinweg

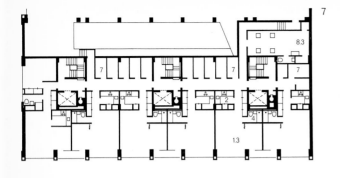

7

8.3

7

7

7

2

4

1.3

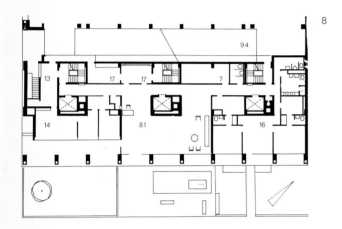

8

9.4

13

17

17

7

14

8.1

16

7/8 First floor and ground floor plans, 1 in 500
9–12 Plans, 1 in 500.
A two-room flat (where the livingcum-dining room and possibly the study are reckoned as one room), B Three-room flat, C Four-room flat, D Five-room flat
9 Plan of the floors below the corridor storey (3rd, 6th, 9th, 12th, 15th floor)
10 Plan of corridor storeys (4th, 7th, 10th, 13th, 16th floor)
11 Plan of the floors above the corridor storey (5th, 8th, 11th, 14th floor)
12 Roof storey

7/8 Erdgeschoß und 1. Obergeschoß, 1:500
9–12 Grundrisse, 1:500.
A 2-Zimmer-Wohnung (Wohn-Eßraum und eventuell Studio als ein Zimmer gerechnet), B Drei-Zimmer-Wohnung,
C Vier-Zimmer-Wohnung, D1 und D2 Fünf-Zimmer-Wohnung
9 Unter dem Korridorgeschoß (3., 6., 9., 12., 15.)
10 Korridorgeschoß (4., 7., 10., 13., 16.)
11 Über dem Korridorgeschoß (5., 8., 11., 14.)
12 Dachgeschoß

13 The new block thrives on the contrast with the motley collection of old buildings

13 Das neue Haus lebt vom Gegensatz zu der vielgestaltigen alten Bebauung

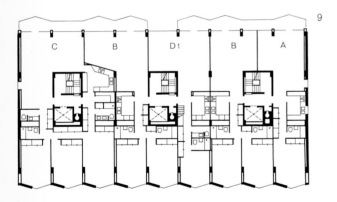

9

C B D1 B A

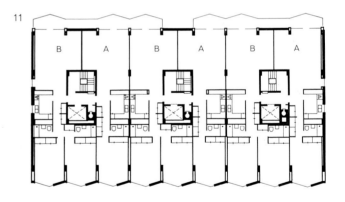

11

B A B A B A

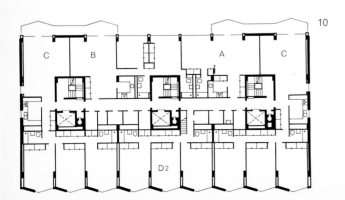

10

C B A C

D2

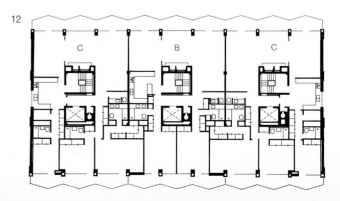

12

C B C

Bethnal Green, London, 1960 · Tower blocks of flats at Claredale Street
Architect: Denys Lasdun

In English cities, and particularly in London, industrialisation gave rise to the development of enormous areas with small-scale housing, mostly built by speculators for the working class population streaming into the towns. Large areas of this kind in the north and east of London are now ripe for redevelopment. This fact should be taken to heart by all those in other countries who believe that the construction of terrace houses can solve all the problems of a metropolitan city.
In the Claredale Street tower block, 75 per cent. of all tenants can reach their entrance door without passing the doors of other flats. The platforms created at the separate stair and lift tower take the place of the courtyard of the old tenement houses. Here is space for laundry drying, a small roof garden, and rooms for hobbies or pets. The bearing structure of the tower blocks consists of cross-walls with one pair of stanchions between each of them. The structural floors are of concrete; the intermediate floors of the maisonettes are of timber because of the lesser load. Structurally, the cross-walls of the towers provide a mutual bracing. The two adjacent six-storey blocks (containing three maisonettes, one above the other) brought the financial compensation required for financing the tower block scheme. With 160 flats, a nett density of 150 persons per acre was obtained.

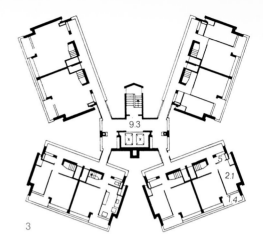

3

London, Bethnal Green, 1960 · Turmhäuser in der Claredale Street
Architekt: Denys Lasdun

In den englischen Städten, vor allem in London, entstanden mit der Industrialisierung riesige Einfamilien-Reihenhausgebiete, die meist von spekulativ denkenden Bauunternehmern für die in die Stadt strömende Arbeiterbevölkerung angelegt wurden. Große in dieser Art bebaute Gebiete im Norden und Osten Londons sind heute »sanierungsreif«. Das sollte allen zu denken geben, die in anderen Ländern glauben, mit dem Bau von Einfamilien-Reihenhäusern alle Probleme der Großstadt lösen zu können.
Im Claredale-Street-Turmhaus können 75 Prozent der Mieter ihre Wohnungstür erreichen, ohne andere Wohnungstüren zu passieren. Die Plattformen am herausgelösten Treppen- und Aufzugselement ersetzen den Hofbereich der alten Bebauungsform. Hier ist Raum für Wäschetrockenplätze, für kleinere Dachgärten, Handwerkerräume, kleine Kioske oder Haustierhaltung. Die Türme sind im Querwandsystem mit jeweils einem dazwischengestellten Stützenpaar konstruiert. Die Wohnungstrenndecken sind aus Beton, die Maisonette-Zwischendecken der geringeren Last wegen aus Holz. Statisch sind die Querwände der Türme gegenseitig zur Aussteifung herangezogen. Die beiden benachbarten sechsgeschossigen Zeilen (drei Maisonettes übereinander) brachten den für die Finanzierung des Turmes notwendigen Ausgleich. Bei 160 Wohnungen wurde eine Dichte von 380 Personen pro Hektar (netto) erreicht.

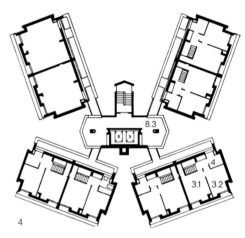

4

3–6 Plans, 1 in 500
3 Ground floor plan
4 Plan of fifth-floor flats
5 Plan of the entrance floor of the maisonettes
6 Plan of the upper maisonette floors

3–6 Grundrisse, 1:500
3 Erdgeschoß
4 Eingeschossige Wohnungen im fünften Obergeschoß
5 Eingangsgeschosse der Maisonettewohnungen
6 Obergeschosse der Maisonettewohnungen

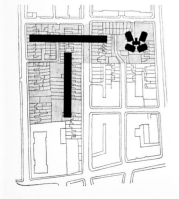 

1 Site plan, 1 in 5000. North is at top. The hatched area indicates the redevelopment site, where the previous buildings and former boundaries are marked
2 Section of a wing of the tower block, 1 in 1000

1 Lageplan, 1:5000. Die Rasterfläche bezeichnet das Baugebiet, auf dem die vorherige Bebauung und die alten Grenzen eingezeichnet sind
2 Schnitt durch einen Flügel des Turmhauses, 1:1000

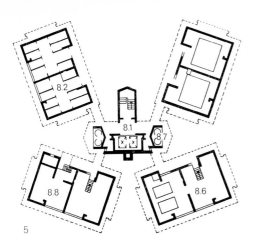

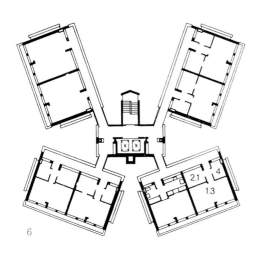

5

6

7 The tower blocks seen from the west. On the right, one
of the six-storey blocks containing three maisonettes, one
above the other. The cornices of this block correspond, at
the tower block, with the fifth-floor flat and the gap in the
wall cladding
8 Air view, taken from south-east, of the redevelopment
area in Bethnal Green. The Claredale Street area is on
the left

7 Das Turmhaus von Westen gesehen. Rechts schließt
sich die »Flat«-Zeile mit drei Maisonettes übereinander
an, deren Höhe im Turmhaus durch die eingeschossige
Wohnung und die Unterbrechung der Platten an den Stein-
wänden markiert ist
8 Luftbild des Sanierungsgebietes in Bethnal Green von
Südosten. Links die Baugruppe an der Claredale Street

9 As the building volume is dissolved into four tower blocks of flats which hang like a cluster of grapes on the fifth tower containing the stairs and lift, there is a multiple inter-relation between the flats and their environment. On the right, an access gallery; on the left, the cross-wall of the adjacent tower block

9 Die Auflösung der Hausmasse in vier Wohntürme, die traubenartig am fünften Turm, dem Verkehrselement, hängen, verknüpft in vielfältiger Weise den Außenraum mit dem Haus. Rechts ein Laubengang, links die Querwandscheibe des benachbarten Wohnturmes

10 The approach is impersonal and designed to stand up to wear. Visible between the access galleries which converge on the stair and lift tower from either side are the screens of the laundry drying platforms
11 Maisonettes in the six-storey blocks. Plans, 1 in 500

10 Der Eingangshof ist unpersönlich und möglichst unverwüstlich gehalten. Zwischen den Laubengängen, die beiderseits auf den Treppenturm zustreben, ist die Verkleidung der Plattformen zu sehen, die als Wäschetrockenplatz genutzt werden
11 Maisonettes in den sechsgeschossigen Zeilen. Grundrisse, 1:500

Hutchesontown, Gorbals, Glasgow (Scotland), 1962–1965 · Maisonette blocks in The Gorbals

Architects: Basil Spence & Partners
Consulting engineers: Ove Arup & Partners

With 29 comprehensive development area projects, the City of Glasgow is to be rebuilt and renewed within the next 20 years. The first urban renewal scheme of the Corporation of Glasgow has materialised in a former slum area with four-storey tenement houses where the population density is in fact to be increased still further in order to permit a better provision of schools and other community facilities.

After the reconstruction, about 10,000 of the present population of 20,000 can be rehoused in an area of 62 acres. In the case of the tower block, which occupies a site of about 15 acres, the population density will be about 150 per acre.

The total floor area of the maisonettes, 336,000 sq.ft., compares with 169,000 sq.ft. for the garden balconies. The maisonettes are flanked by continuous terraces and garden balconies and contain four apartments, with all the living rooms facing south-west and all the bedrooms north-east. Bathrooms and kitchens receive their daylight and air from the terrace side. The tenants must, however, do without the conventional fireplaces; instead, an electric under-floor heating system has been provided which, because of favourable electricity charges, is economic. The tower block will have a population of about 1300 people.

The 400 dwellings are divided as follows: 140 three-room dwellings (each with kitchen and bath) with a floor area of about 720 sq.ft. 160 three-room dwellings (each with kitchen and bath) with a floor area of about 650 sq.ft. 40 four-room dwellings (each with kitchen and bath) with a floor area of about 915 sq.ft. 60 flatlets (with bed-sitting room) with a floor area of about 360 sq.ft. The in-situ cast concrete cross-walls, pillars and slabs are supplemented by non-bearing precast concrete wall panels measuring 20 × 9 ft. These panels were produced in Edinburgh.

Glasgow-Hutchesontown (Schottland), 1962–1965 · Maisonette-Türme in den Gorbals

Architekt: Basil Spence und Partner
Ingenieure: Ove Arup und Partner

Glasgow will mit 29 großen Bauprojekten die Stadt in den kommenden zwanzig Jahren umbauen und erneuern. Das erste Projekt der »Corporation of the City of Glasgow« liegt in einem der verrufenen Gebiete mit viergeschossiger Randbebauung, deren Bevölkerungsdichte noch erhöht werden soll, um eine bessere Versorgung mit Schulen und allen öffentlichen Einrichtungen zu ermöglichen.

10000 der etwa 20000 Bewohner des gesamten Gebietes sollen nach dem Umbau auf einer Fläche von 25 Hektar wohnen. Bei dem Hochhaus rechnet man bei einem 6 Hektar großen Grundstück mit 375 Einwohnern auf den Hektar.

Das Verhältnis der Maisonettefläche zur Terrassenfläche beträgt etwa 31 200 m² zu 15 700 m². Die von durchgehenden Terrassendecken und Freilufträumen begrenzten »Häuschen« enthalten jeweils vier Wohnungen, deren Wohnräume alle nach Südwesten und deren Schlafräume alle nach Nordosten orientiert sind. Bäder und Küche sind von der Terrassenseite her belichtet und belüftet. Auf die traditionellen offenen Kamine müssen die Bewohner allerdings verzichten; es ist eine bei den günstigen englischen Stromtarifen (unter 4 Pfennig/kWh) wirtschaftliche elektrische Fußboden-Raumheizung eingebaut. Das Gebäude wird etwa 1300 Bewohner haben.

Die 400 Wohnungen sind folgendermaßen aufgeteilt: 140 Drei-Zimmer-Wohnungen (jeweils mit Küche und Bad) mit etwa 67 m² Fläche, 160-Drei-Zimmer-Wohnungen (jeweils mit Küche und Bad) mit etwa 60 m² Fläche, 40 Vier-Zimmer-Wohnungen (jeweils mit Bad und Küche) mit 85 m² Fläche, 60 Einraumwohnungen (Wohnschlafraum) mit etwa 34 m² Fläche. Die Ortbetonkonstruktion der Querwände, Pfeiler und Decken wird durch vorgefertigte, 6,0 × 2,7 m große Betonplatten für die nichttragenden Außenwände ergänzt. Diese Platten werden in Edinburgh hergestellt.

1 This photograph of the building site clearly shows the splayed concrete legs which are tapered up to the eighth floor and will then continue vertically upwards. These concrete legs are provided at every third of the bearing cross-walls

1 Auf dem Baustellenfoto ist die Pfeilerkonstruktion gut zu erkennen, die sich bis zum achten Geschoß verjüngt und dann vertikal nach oben steigen wird. In jeder dritten Achse der tragenden Innenwände ist ein Pfeiler angeordnet

2 Together with the shopping centre, the tower blocks occupy the central site of the entire slum clearance area in The Gorbals. The facilities include: forty shops, three pubs, two cafes, doctors' surgeries, a bank, post office, police station, bowling alley, various kinds of offices and garages

2 Die Wohntürme bilden mit dem Geschäftszentrum den Mittelpunkt des gesamten Sanierungsgebietes in den Gorbals. Als Dienste sind vorgesehen: 40 Läden, 3 »Pubs«, 2 Cafés, Arztpraxen, Bank, Post, Polizeistation, Bowling-Bahn, verschiedenartige Büros und Sammelgaragen

2

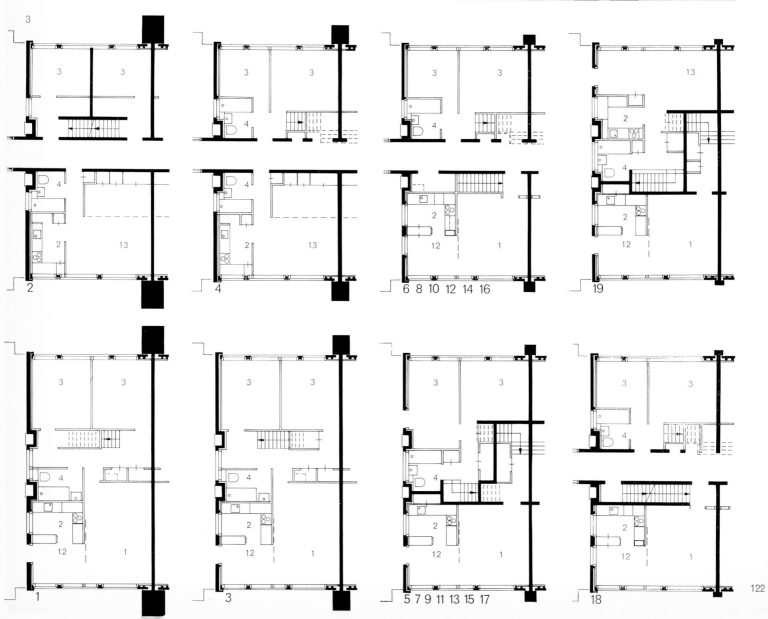

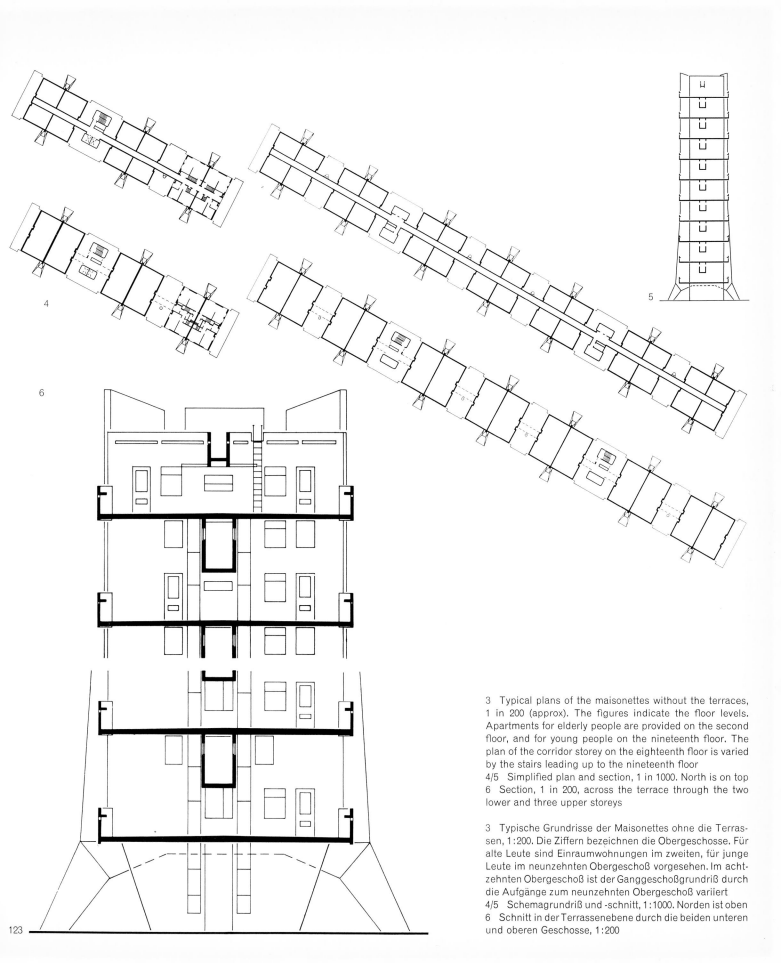

3 Typical plans of the maisonettes without the terraces, 1 in 200 (approx). The figures indicate the floor levels. Apartments for elderly people are provided on the second floor, and for young people on the nineteenth floor. The plan of the corridor storey on the eighteenth floor is varied by the stairs leading up to the nineteenth floor
4/5 Simplified plan and section, 1 in 1000. North is on top
6 Section, 1 in 200, across the terrace through the two lower and three upper storeys

3 Typische Grundrisse der Maisonettes ohne die Terrassen, 1:200. Die Ziffern bezeichnen die Obergeschosse. Für alte Leute sind Einraumwohnungen im zweiten, für junge Leute im neunzehnten Obergeschoß vorgesehen. Im achtzehnten Obergeschoß ist der Ganggeschoßgrundriß durch die Aufgänge zum neunzehnten Obergeschoß variiert
4/5 Schemagrundriß und -schnitt, 1:1000. Norden ist oben
6 Schnitt in der Terrassenebene durch die beiden unteren und oberen Geschosse, 1:200

Staggered and Terraced Building Volumes

The staggering of the facade in the plan was followed by terracing, i.e. the arrangement of building volumes in steps on a slope. This only became possible when the builders had learned to produce waterproof terraces at a reasonable cost. As with any technical innovation, it took several decades before the theoretical knowledge was translated into general practice. Unpredictable concomitant features – the teething troubles of any invention – must be overcome before a product can be described as satisfactory. Flat roof and roof terrace have been through these stages, and now, defects are no longer intrinsic, but due to lack of skill in design or workmanship.

This has made it possible to overcome one drawback of many urban dwellings, viz the lack of an outdoor living space, and to enliven the barren townscape with miniature meadows.

Auffaltungen und Abtreppungen

Der Auffaltung der Fassade folgte die Abtreppung in der Höhenentwicklung, die Staffelung der Wohneinheiten am Hang. Voraussetzung war die Kenntnis in der Technik, wasserdichte Terrassenflächen ohne übermäßige Kosten herzustellen. Wie bei jeder technischen Neuerung war auch hier ein Zeitraum von mehreren Jahrzehnten notwendig, um die theoretische Kenntnis in allgemein gebrauchsfähige Erzeugnisse umzusetzen. Nicht vorausgesehene Nebenerscheinungen – die Kinderkrankheiten jeder Erfindung – müssen durchgestanden sein, ehe ein Produkt als »empfehlenswert« bezeichnet werden kann. Flachdach und Dachterrasse haben diese Entwicklungsstufen inzwischen durchlaufen. Fehler sind nicht mehr grundsätzlicher Art, sie entspringen dem mehr oder weniger großen Können der Entwerfenden und Ausführenden.

Damit ist die Möglichkeit gegeben, einen Nachteil städtischen Wohnens, das Fehlen einer zum Himmel offenen Wohnfläche, für eine große Zahl von Wohnungen zu beseitigen und die Karstlandschaft der Wohngebirge durch winzige grüne Matten zu kultivieren.

A factor contributing greatly to the quality of any dwelling is its immediate environment, the view from the window. In towns, even a paved courtyard with a few trees and plants will provide relaxation and recreation to the eye. In England, the provision and maintenance of such semi-public spaces is facilitated by a long-standing tradition for paying attention to these ancillary aspects of housing (courtyard of flats in London, see page 95)

Die Qualität der Wohnung wird mitbestimmt durch den Außenraum, den Blick aus dem Fenster der Wohnung. Im Stadtbereich bietet auch ein gepflasterter Hof mit wenigen Bäumen und Pflanzen dem Auge Entspannung und Erholung. Jahrzehntelange Übung, auch diesen Nebendingen des Bauens Beachtung zu schenken, erleichtert in England Anlage und Pflege dieses halböffentlichen Bereichs (Hof eines Hauses in London, siehe Seite 95)

Zürich, 1959/60 · Flats in Hegibachstrasse
Architect: Ernst Gisel

With imagination and good will urban building sites may carry residential buildings which differ from conventional routine. In the case of this privately financed block of flats in Zürich, the horizontal and vertical staggering ensures a very good utilisation and a high degree of privacy (balconies) as well as a sensitive adaptation to the existing character of the street without slavish acceptance of conventional designs. The simple yet flexible layout plans were of particular interest to a circle of tenants who know how to make use, by suitable furnishing, of the possibilities of non-conventional room arrangements. Among the thirty tenants are seven architects and two photographers.

Outer walls of insulating stone material with light-grey high-quality plaster, left unpainted; rough-cast inner walls painted white; floors covered with linoleum or close carpeting; radiation heating in the ceilings.

A number of lock-up garages and terrace houses to be erected in the south-eastern part of the building site will be provided with green roofs and roof terraces which will blend with the splendid garden.

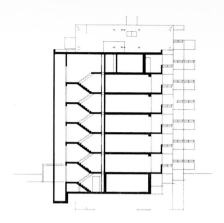

1   Cross-section, 1 in 500/Schnitt, 1 : 500

Zürich, 1959/60 · Haus Hegibachstraße
Architekt: Ernst Gisel

Auch innerstädtische Bauplätze können mit Phantasie und gutem Willen Wohnbauten tragen, die vom Schematismus der Denkfaulheit abweichen. Die Staffelung in der Horizontalen und Vertikalen bietet bei diesem privat finanzierten Haus in Zürich den Mietern eine sehr gute Nutzung und Distanzierung vom Nachbarn (Balkone) wie auch eine feinfühlige Anpassung an das vorhandene Straßenbild ohne Übernahme der äußeren Formen. Für die einfachen, dennoch offenen Grundrisse interessierte sich vor allem ein Kreis von Mietern, der durch entsprechende Möblierung die Möglichkeiten einer unkonventionellen Raumverbindung zu nutzen weiß. – In den dreißig Wohnungen wohnen unter anderem sieben Architekten und zwei Fotografen.

Außenwände aus Isolierstein, mit hellgrauem ungestrichenem Edelputz; Innenwände mit Gipsabrieb, weiß gestrichen; Böden mit Linoleum oder Spannteppichen belegt; Deckenstrahlungsheizung.

Eine geplante Reihe von Garagen und Einfamilienreihenhäusern im Südosten des Bauplatzes soll in Ergänzung der ausgezeichneten Gartenanlagen mit grünen Dächern und Dachterrassen ausgestattet werden.

2   Much skill is apparent in the design of the playground. A fenced-in corner offers additional protection against wind and trespassers

2   Mit viel Geschick ist der Spielplatz angelegt. Eine palisadenumzäunte Ecke bietet zusätzlich Wind- und Blickschutz

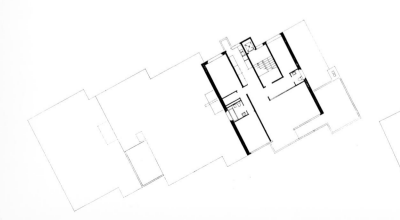

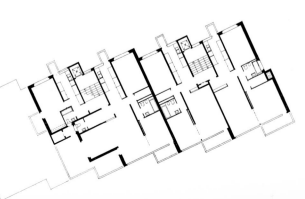

3 Garden frontage, seen from the south
4 Plans, 1 in 500. From left to right: 6th floor, 5th floor, 1st
to 3rd floor, ground floor with entrance (A–A Line of cross-
section)

3 Die Gartenseite von Süden gesehen
4 Grundrisse, 1:500. Von links nach rechts: 6. Obergeschoß, 5. Obergeschoß, 1.–3. Obergeschoß, Untergeschoß
mit Eingang (A–A Schnittebene)

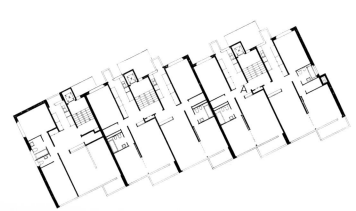
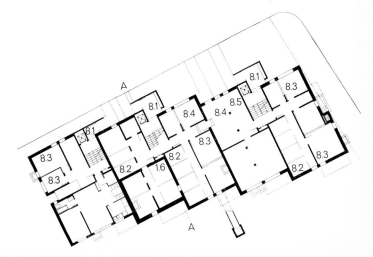

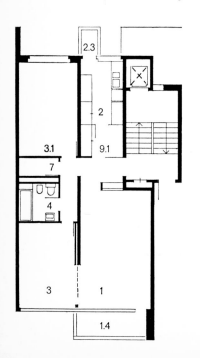

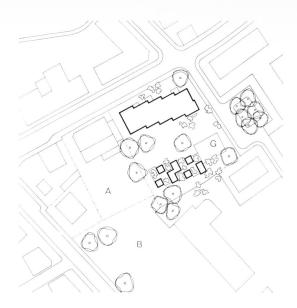

6 Site plan, 1 in 2000. The two-storey flats next to the garages (G) have not yet been built. A Green house, B Open space adjoining the school

6 Lageplan, 1:2000. Die zweigeschossigen Einfamilienhäuser neben den Garagen (G) sind noch nicht gebaut. A Gärtnerei, B Grünfläche bei der Schule

5/8 Staggered garden and road frontage, respectively
7 Plan, 1 in 200 (corresponding to A on the 1st, 2nd and 3rd floor)

5/8 Die gestaffelte Hausfront an der Garten- und Straßenseite
7 Grundriß, 1:200 (A im 1.–3. Obergeschoß)

9 The two spacious rooms facing south-east are connected by a large sliding door
10 View from the window and balcony wall into the living room which is in open connection with the entrance hall. In the background the kitchen

9 Die beiden großen Räume an der Südostseite sind durch eine Schiebetür miteinander verbunden
10 Blick von der Fenster- und Balkonwand in den Wohnraum, der offen in den Eingangsbereich übergeht. Im Hintergrund die Küche

Berlin, 1961 · ADAC Building
Architect: Willi Kreuer

If only because of the ambitious facade treatment, such an office block with several residential floors cannot be regarded as an example of low-rent housing. The block is distinguished from the great number of others merely designed to fill a gap in the building line by the manner in which the architect has made the best of a difficult site, with some of the old tenement houses still standing further north. The offices of the Automobile Club (ADAC) make full use of the space hemmed in by the building lines. The upper floors with the flats are completely retracted. Because of the large car park on the west side, it was possible to apply the plastic facade treatment to three sides of the block. There is no longer any rear elevation but merely a transition from the street space of the main traffic artery (Bundesallee) to that of the side street joining it at right angles.

Bundesallee, which carries a great part of the traffic between the commercial districts around the Zoo and the southern districts of Berlin is far from being an ideal, quiet residential street. In a metropolitan city, however, there is always a demand for small, luxury-type flats in the vicinity of the town centre.

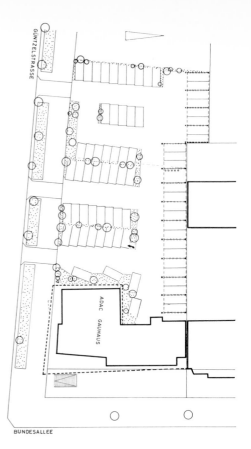

2 View from the south. The two lower floors are occupied by offices

2 Südansicht, unten zwei Bürogeschosse

1 Site plan, 1 in 1000/Lageplan, 1:1000

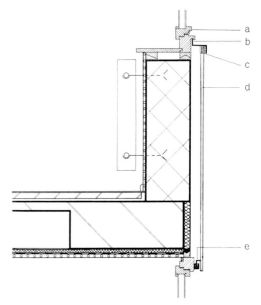

3 Section of window wall of a flat, 1 in 10.
a Wooden window frame, b Hot-galvanized iron fitting, c Neoprene sliding buffers, d Three-edged anodically coated aluminium bar, e Two chamfers for each panel

3 Schnitt durch die Fensterwand eines Appartements, 1:10.
a Holzfenster, b feuerverzinkte Eisenkonstruktion, c Neopren-Gleitpuffer, d eloxiertes Aluminium, dreiseitig abgekantet, e zwei Abkantungen pro Platte

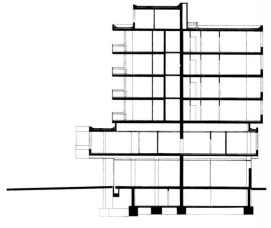

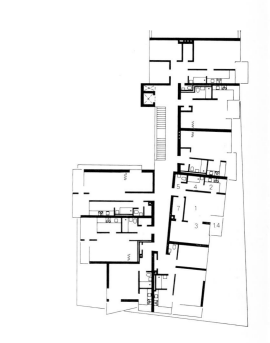

Berlin, 1961 · ADAC-Haus
Architekt: Willi Kreuer

Ein derartiges Geschäftshaus mit mehreren Appartementgeschossen kann, schon wegen der aufwendigen Fassadengestaltung, kein Musterbeispiel des Sozialen Wohnungsbaus sein. Das Ausnutzen der schwierigen städtebaulichen Situation unter Anlehnung an die Reste der alten Blockbebauung im Norden hebt dieses Haus aus der Masse der »Baulückenfüller« heraus. Die Büroräume des Automobilclubs (ADAC) nutzen den von Baufluchten begrenzten Raum. Die Appartementgeschosse treten dann völlig zurück. Dank des großen, im Westen liegenden Parkplatzes kann sich der Bau in seiner plastischen Gliederung nach drei Seiten entfalten. Es gibt keine Rückfront mehr, sondern ein Überleiten vom Straßenraum der Hauptverkehrsstraße (Bundesallee) in den rechtwinklig einmündenden der Nebenstraße.

Die Bundesallee, die einen großen Teil des Verkehrs aufnimmt, der das Geschäftsviertel am Zoo mit den südlichen Bezirken Berlins verbindet, ist keine lärmgeschützte, ideale Wohnstraße. In einer Millionenstadt ist jedoch immer Bedarf an kleinen, sehr gut ausgestatteten Appartements in der Nähe der City.

4 View from south along Bundesallee before the trees had to be felled for the construction of the Underground railway
5 Section and plan of an upper floor, 1 in 500

4 Ansicht entlang der Bundesallee, bevor die Bäume dem U-Bahn-Bau zum Opfer fielen
5 Schnitt und Grundriß Obergeschoß, 1:500

Ullernaasen, Oslo, 1964 · Terraced flats
Architects: Anne Tinne Friis and Mogens Friis

The site has a steep, 45° eastward slope and is studded with a number of old fir and pine trees. All the dwellings have a magnificent view eastwards towards Oslo and southwards on the Oslo Fjord. Access to the site is on three levels. To each dwelling belongs a lock-up garage or car port.

The flats are 66 ft. wide and have a plan module of 4 metres (13'1½''). In this way, depending on the topography of the slope, there are some 22 different types of dwellings with floor areas ranging from 2000 to 4300 sq.ft.; but all the dwellings are variants of the standard type with a floor area of 2300 sq.ft., shown on a scale of 1 in 200. The larger dwellings have a sauna of their own. The outer terrace covers an area of approx. 860 sq.ft. and is, in the direction of the slope, protected against view from above by an overhanging roof or by the large flower boxes which cover an area of nearly 200 sq.ft. For cold spring and autumn days, infra-red heating has been built into the terrace roof. The dwellings are heated by electric wall panel heaters, the flues are connected by a blower with an inclined chimney.

Bearing parts are of reinforced concrete, non-bearing parts and facade units of timber insulated with mineral wool. The outdoor stairs are equipped with built-in electric heating cables to keep them free from ice in winter. One drawback of the dwellings at medium level is the need for walking up long flights of stairs, which is not quite in keeping with the otherwise comfortable appointments. An inclined lift might have been called for.

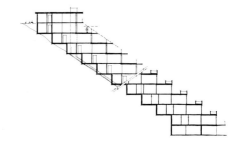

1/2   Standard plan (see Fig. 12) and section, 1 in 500

1/2   Grundriß (Normaltyp Bild 12) und Schnitt, 1:500

Oslo-Ullernaasen, 1964 · Terrassenhäuser
Architekten: Anne-Tinne Friis und Mogens Friis

Der Bauplatz fällt mit 45° Neigung steil nach Osten ab und ist vorwiegend mit alten Rottannen und Kiefern bewachsen. Alle Wohnungen haben eine wunderbare Aussicht nach Osten auf Oslo und nach Süden auf den Oslofjord. Das Grundstück wird in drei Ebenen erschlossen. Zu jeder Wohnung gehört eine Garage oder ein Einstellplatz.

Die Häuser sind 20 m breit und in der Horizontalen nach einem 4-m-Modul gestuft. Auf diese Weise ergeben sich je nach der Form des Hanges etwa 22 verschieden große Wohnungstypen von 190 bis 400 m² Wohnfläche, die jedoch alle Abwandlungen des im Maßstab 1:200 gezeigten Normaltyps (215 m² Wohnfläche) sind. Große Appartements haben eine eigene Sauna. Die Außenterrasse ist etwa 80 m² groß und in Hangrichtung durch ein Vordach oder die etwa 18 m² großen Pflanzentröge gegen Einblick von oben geschützt. Für den kalten Frühling und Herbst sind Infrarotheizungen im Terrassendach eingebaut. Die Wohnungen werden mit elektrischen Wandpaneelen beheizt, die Kamine sind mit einem Gebläse an einen schrägen Schornstein angeschlossen.

Tragende Teile sind aus Stahlbeton, nichttragende Teile und Fassadenelemente aus Holz, isoliert mit Mineralwolle. In die Außentreppen sind elektrische Heizkabel eingelegt, um sie im Winter eisfrei zu halten. Das Treppensteigen ist für die mittleren Wohnungen allerdings ein Nachteil, der nicht ganz mit der komfortablen Ausstattung übereinstimmt.

3   Northside of House E. The stairs are electrically heated during the winter

3   Nordseite Haus E. Die Treppen werden im Winter elektrisch beheizt

4 North side, flat B. The concrete is kept white, the woodwork is painted black-brown, all the glazing consists of thermopane

4 Nordseite Haus B. Der Beton ist weiß, die Holzteile sind schwarzbraun gestrichen, alle Glasflächen sind aus Thermopane

5 Site plan, 1 in 2000.
G Garages, E Car ports, P Car parks

5 Lageplan, 1:2000.
133 G Garagen, E Einstellplätze, P Parkieren

6   View from the south-east. At the time when this photograph was taken, some of the wooden parts had not yet been painted dark. There are, on the slope, six groups of houses with 54 terrace dwellings. Care was taken to preserve the existing trees between the buildings; for this reason, the building materials were conveyed by means of three aerial cableways

7   South side of Block E. An admitted disadvantage is that toddlers cannot be left without supervision as the balustrades may tempt them into dangerous climbing expeditions

6   Südostansicht. Die Holzteile sind zum Teil auf dieser Aufnahme noch nicht dunkel gestrichen. Am Hang liegen in 6 Hausgruppen 54 Terrassenwohnungen. Die vorhandenen Bäume zwischen den Bauten wurden sorgfältig erhalten und das Baumaterial deshalb mit 3 Seilbahnen befördert

7   Die Südseite der Hausgruppe E. Kleinkinder brauchen allerdings eine Aufsicht, da die horizontal geschichtete Terrassenbrüstung zu gefährlichen Kletterspielen verleitet   134

8 View towards Oslo, with Block A in the foreground
9 From the northernmost Block C, the view ranges across the adjacent Blocks B and A southwards over the Oslo Fjord
10/11 Living room and fireplace
12 Standard plan, 1 in 200

8 Blick auf Oslo, im Vordergrund Haus A
9 Vom am weitesten nördlich gelegenen Haus C aus schweift der Blick über die benachbarten Terrassenhäuser B und A nach Süden zum Oslofjord
10/11 Wohnraum und Kaminplatz
12 Grundriß des Normaltyps, 1:200

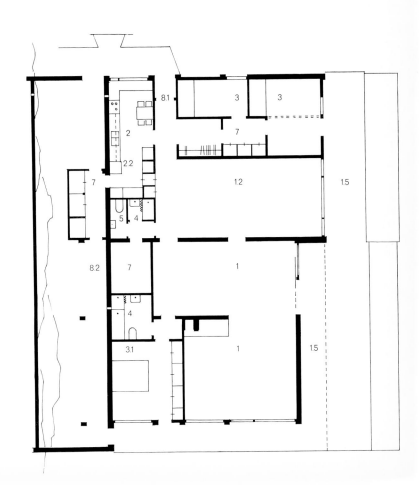

Zug (Switzerland), 1957–1962 · Terraced flats
Architects: Fritz Stucky and Rudolf Meuli

In Switzerland, good building sites in towns with low local rates have become so scarce that they are now confined to unfavourable positions and steep slopes such as on this north-west slope at Zug. Owing to the progressive attitude of the local authorities (regarded by the architects as exceptional among Swiss towns), it was possible to try out an unconventional solution. The flats are supported, as it were, by a number of "stringboards" which, in their turn, are supported by the heavy garage block. The loads transmitted to the slope are thus virtually confined to vertical forces. The different floors rest, like steps of a flight of stairs, on the concrete stringers so that they are not in contact with the grown soil. The terrace balustrades consist of prefabricated units. The dwellings are protected against view from outside by their skew position and the built-in flower boxes. In these terrace gardens, the noise level is in fact lower than in the private gardens of conventional terrace houses. The best possible sound insulation of the floors has been ensured, inter alia, by providing each house with separate mains connections so that the floors have no recesses or apertures.

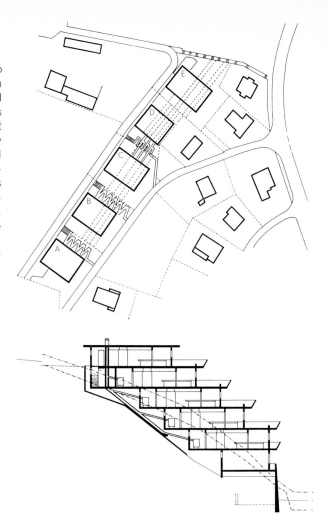

Zug (Schweiz), 1957–1962 · Terrassenhäuser
Architekten: Fritz Stucky und Rudolf Meuli

Gutes Bauland in Gemeinden mit niedrigen Steuersätzen ist in der Schweiz so selten geworden, daß nur noch ungünstige Lagen und steile Hänge übriggeblieben sind, wie der Nordwesthang in Zug. Die Aufgeschlossenheit aller örtlichen Behörden – die Architekten bezeichnen das als Ausnahmefall für die meisten Schweizer Orte – machte die Erprobung einer unkonventionellen Lösung möglich. Die Häuser ruhen gleichermaßen auf einer Reihe von »Treppenwangen«, die sich unten auf dem schweren Garagenblock abstützen. Praktisch wirken so nur senkrechte Kräfte auf den Hang. Die einzelnen Stockwerke sitzen, ohne mit den Decken den gewachsenen Boden zu berühren, wie Treppenstufen auf den Betonwangen. Die Terrassenbrüstungen bestehen aus vorgefertigten Teilen. Die Schrägstellung und die festeingebauten Blumenbänke verhindern den Einblick. Akustische Störungen sind in den Terrassengärten sogar geringer als in den Privatgärten üblicher Reihen-Einfamilienhäuser. Für eine möglichst gute Schalldämmung der Wohnungsdecken ist unter anderem dadurch gesorgt, daß jedes Terrassenhaus gesonderte Leitungsanschlüsse besitzt, die Decken also ohne Aussparungen und Durchbrüche sind.

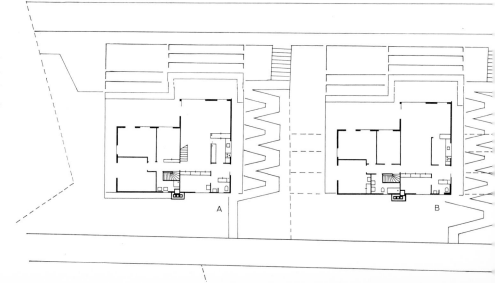

4 Plan of the fifth terrace, 1 in 500. At the time of construction, flat ownership was not permissible under Swiss law, whilst the erection of buildings above another owner's ground was allowed. Some of the terraced flats therefore occupy sites of no more than 8½ ft. width. Owners of no more than, say, 500 sq. ft. of land are thus able to claim the ownership of a bungalow with a floor area of, say, 1500 sq.ft. and a terrace of 600 sq.ft., and can obtain corresponding mortgages

4 Lageplan mit den Grundrissen der fünften Terrasse, 1:500. Die Schweizer Gesetze, die seinerzeit kein Stockwerkseigentum zuließen, erlaubten jedoch die Überbauung fremden Eigentums. Die Terrassenhäuser stehen also auf zum Teil nur 2,50 m breiten Grundstücken. Besitzer von nur 50 m² Land können so eingeschossige Häuser von 150 m² Grundfläche zuzüglich 60 m² Terrassenfläche im Grundbuch eintragen lassen und beleihen

1 Site plan, 1 in 2000
2 Section of House E, 1 in 500
3 View from the west

1 Lageplan, 1:2000
2 Schnitt durch Haus E, 1:500
3 Ansicht von Westen

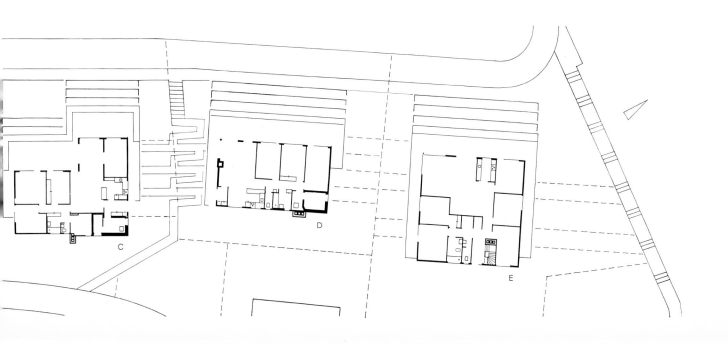

5 The privacy of the dwelling is also safeguarded on the road side
6 View from the north on the groups of terraced flats. In the background on the right a glimpse of the Lake of Zug. Such terraced flats must be regarded as equivalent to detached houses with private gardens. Windows can be provided on three sides

5 Die Straßenseite wahrt das Privatissimum der Wohnung
6 Blick von Norden auf die Terrassenhausgruppen. Im Hintergrund rechts der Zuger See. Derartige Terrassenhäuser sind Einfamilienhäusern mit Privatgärten gleichzusetzen. Nach drei Himmelsrichtungen können Fenster vorgesehen werden

7 View on the Lake of Zug and the mountains from the living room of one of the upper terrace levels

7 Ausblick auf Zuger See und Berge vom Wohnraum eines obersten Terrassengeschosses aus

8

8–10 Typical plans, 1 in 200, of flats on the second terrace level. 8 House D; 9 House B, 10 House E

8–10 Typengrundrisse, 1:200, jeweils im zweiten Terrassengeschoß; 8 Flat D, 9 Flat B, 10 Flat E

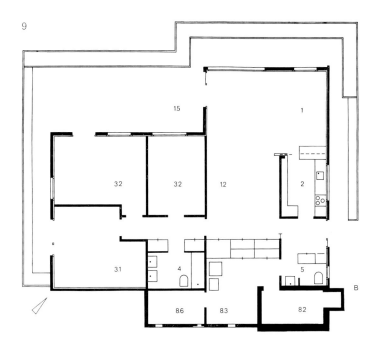

9

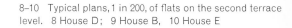

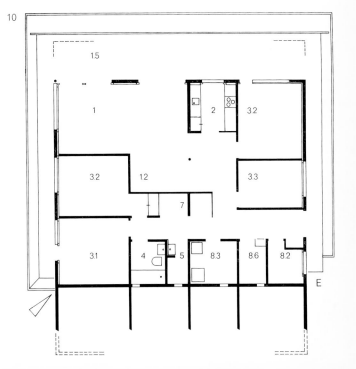

10

Skönstavik, Stockholm, 1959/60 · Terraced flats
Architect: Axel Kandell

The terraced flats at Skönstavik were planned in 1957. The rocky south-east slope has an angle of about 20°. From the flats, there is a magnificent view across the woods onto Lake Dreviken. Three internal corridors give access to 32 flats, each with four rooms, kitchen, bathroom, W.C. and basement. In addition, each dwelling has a terrace of nearly 200 sq.ft., which is roofed at one end. In each case, one terrace level is directly accessible from the corridor whilst the next level is reached via a hall and the stairs. The top flats have an additional direct access from the hilltop and a studio with north light.

Stockholm-Skönstavik, 1959/60 · Terrassenhäuser
Architekt: Axel Kandell

Die Terrassenhäuser in Skönstavik wurden 1957 geplant. Der felsige Südosthang hat etwa 20° Neigung. Von den Häusern aus hat man einen herrlichen Ausblick über den Laubwald auf den See Dreviken. An drei Innenkorridoren liegen 32 Wohnungen mit je vier Zimmern, Küche, Bad, WC und Keller sowie einer 18 m² großen Terrasse, deren eine Schmalseite überdacht ist. Jeweils eine Terrassenstufe ist direkt vom Korridor aus zugänglich, die nächste wird über einen Eingangsraum und die Treppe erreicht. Die oberste Wohnreihe besitzt von der Bergseite aus einen weiteren direkten Zugang und ein Atelier mit Nordlicht.

1 North side with one of the five spacious studios
2 The terraces, seen from the east

1 Die Nordseite mit einem der fünf geräumigen Ateliers
2 Die Terrassen von Osten gesehen

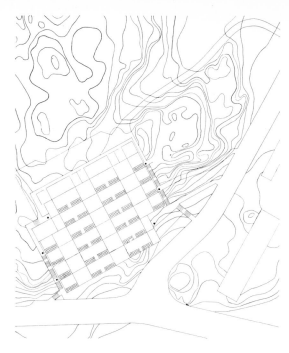

3 Site plan, 1 in 2000. North is at top

3 Lageplan, 1:2000, Norden ist oben

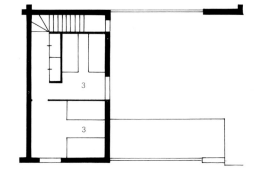

4 Ground floor and top floor plan, 1 in 200

4 Erd- und Obergeschoßgrundriß, 1:200

140

5 View from the south
6 Plans of the upper and lower floors, and section, 1 in 500.
A Flat with studio, B Terrace, C Bedrooms of the lower
flat, K Corridor

5 Südansicht
6 Grundrisse des oberen und unteren Wohngeschosses
und Schnitt, 1:500.
A Wohnung mit Atelier, B Terrasse, C Schlafräume der
unteren Wohnung, K Korridor

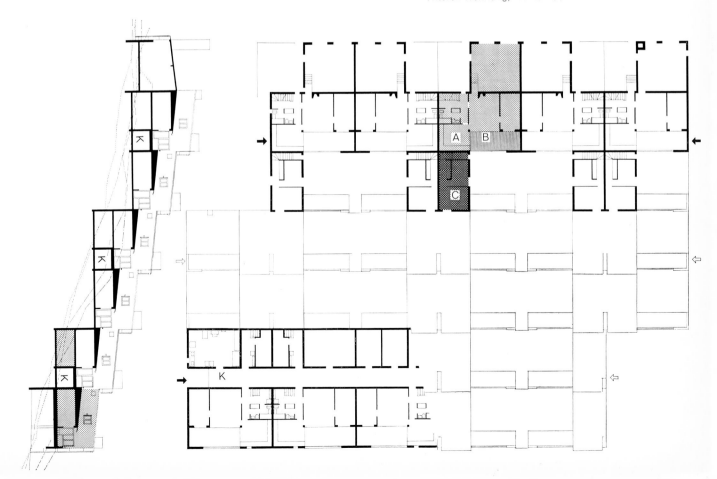

Bogota (Colombia), 1962 · "Los Cerros" project for a terraced block
Architect: Rogelio Salmona

Bogota, the capital of Colombia, is situated in the Andes at an altitude of 8500 ft. and has an annual mean temperature of 57°F. During the colonial era, the favourable climate of the high plateau attracted the Spaniards so that, even to-day, except for Argentina and Brazil, Colombia has the highest percentage (25 pC) of 'white' population. The City of Bogota, founded in 1538 on a favourable site with ample water supply, lies at the western edge of a plateau known as Sabana, leaning against a wooded range of hills of up to 1000 ft. in height. Following the foot of the mountain range, the plateau extends mainly northwards and was protected by the topographical conditions from being engulfed by a system of ring roads. Up to now, it was mainly the difficulties of water supply which prevented an expansion of the town up the slope. Now, however, it is intended to open up the lower slopes, which offer a magnificent view on the mountain-framed Sabana, as a rationally planned residential district. One of the first attempts at solving the special problems of this position is the Los Cerros project. The design of the building is adapted to the skyline of the mountain range. The high concentration is necessary in order to preserve the open spaces of the slope between adjacent groups of houses and to retain, for the upper floors, a view on the landscape even when the lower sites are built up.

The owners, all of whom belong to the free professions and require a study at home, have pooled their resources to finance the project. 13 houses are horizontally and vertically staggered in such a way that each has its own entrance and a private garden at ground floor level, a terrace with a view westwards across the Sabana, and a bedroom with a view on the mountain range in the east and north (or, in some cases, south). The S-shaped plan corresponds to the division of the dwelling into five levels, a–e. This rise of the dwelling levels in the direction opposite to that of the slope was already a feature of the terraced block at Wiedikon, Zürich, designed by Paillard and Leemann; in that case, however, the variation in level was confined, by the layout plan, to *one* direction. In the case of Los Cerros, this westward direction is supplemented, in the plans, by a northward swing which is completely neutralized by giving the bedrooms daylight access from the east. A spiral stair between the upper group of bedrooms and the study provides a connection with the garden which can be used without passing through the living room.

1 Perspective of the group of terrace flats, seen from the west. To each dwelling belongs a balcony, covered by a roof terrace, and a roof terrace above the next level lower down
2 View from the entrance yard. The garages are in the bottom left corner. This view shows even more clearly the interlacing of the dwellings. The roof terraces have a window in the side wall facing south. The balcony in front of this side-wall, at a slightly lower level, belongs to the same dwelling whilst the entrance below belongs to the next house

1 Perspektive der Terrassenhausgruppe von Westen aus gesehen. Jeweils ein von einer »Dachterrasse« überdeckter Balkon und eine im nächsten, abwärts gestaffelten Abschnitt gelegene »Dachterrasse« gehören zu einer Wohnung
2 Ansicht vom Eingangshof aus. Links unten die Garagen. Hier läßt sich das Ineinanderschachteln noch besser ablesen. Die »Dachterrassen« haben in der Seitenwand nach Süden ein Fenster. Der Balkon vor dieser Seitenwand, etwas tiefer gelegen, gehört zur gleichen Wohnung, der darunterliegende Eingang zum nächsten Haus

Bogota (Kolumbien), 1962 · Terrassenhausprojekt »Los Cerros«
Architekt: Rogelio Salmona

Bogota, die Hauptstadt Kolumbiens, liegt in den Anden in 2600 m Höhe und hat im Jahresmittel eine Temperatur von + 14°C. Das für Europäer günstige Klima der Hochebene zog in der Kolonialzeit die Spanier an, so daß Kolumbien noch heute, nach Argentinien und Brasilien, mit 25% den drittgrößten »weißen« Bevölkerungsanteil in Südamerika hat. Die 1538 an einer günstigen, wasserreichen Stelle gegründete Stadt Bogota liegt am Westrand einer Hochebene, der »Sabana«, angelehnt an eine mehrere hundert Meter hohe bewaldete Bergkette. Dem Fuß der Berge folgend, dehnte sie sich hauptsächlich nach Norden hin aus und wurde durch die natürlichen Gegebenheiten davor bewahrt, in ein Ringstraßensystem gepreßt zu werden. Vor allem die Schwierigkeiten der Wasserversorgung verhinderten bisher die Ausdehnung der Stadt die Hänge hinauf. Die unteren Hänge sollen nun wegen ihrer herrlichen Aussicht auf die von Bergen eingefaßte Sabana in rationeller Weise als Wohngebiet erschlossen werden. Einer der ersten Versuche, die besonderen Probleme dieser Wohnlage zu lösen, ist das Projekt »Los Cerros«. Die Gebäudeform ist den Bergsilhouetten angepaßt. Die Konzentration ist erforderlich, um das Grün der Hänge zwischen den benachbarten Hausgruppen noch durchfließen zu lassen und um von den Obergeschossen aus den Blick auf die Landschaft zu behalten, wenn die unterhalb gelegenen Grundstücke bebaut werden.
Die Eigentümer, die alle freiberuflich tätig sind und einen Arbeitsplatz zu Hause brauchen, haben sich zur Finanzierung des Baues zu einer »Cooperative« zusammengetan. 13 Häuser sind so neben und übereinander gestaffelt, daß jedes einen eigenen Eingang und einen Privatgarten im Erdgeschoß, eine Terrasse mit Blick nach Westen auf die Sabana und Schlafräume mit dem Blick auf die Berge im Osten und Norden (beziehungsweise Süden) hat. Der S-förmigen Grundrißordnung entspricht die Gliederung der Wohnung in fünf Ebenen (a–e). Schon das Terrassenhaus in Zürich-Wiedikon, von Paillard und Leemann, zeigt dieses Ansteigen der Wohnebene entgegengesetzt zur Hangneigung, das jedoch durch die Grundrißform auf eine Bewegungsrichtung festgelegt ist. Bei »Los Cerros« wird diese nach Westen gerichtete Bewegung in den Grundrissen ergänzt durch das Ausschwingen nach Norden, das durch die Lichtführung von Osten her in den Schlafräumen völlig aufgefangen wird. Eine Wendeltreppe stellt zwischen der oberen Schlafraumgruppe und dem Studio eine Verbindung mit dem Garten her, die ohne Störung des Wohnraumes benutzt werden kann.

3–5 Section and plans of a dwelling within the staggered sequence, 1 in 200. From the entrance level b, some steps lead down to the conservatory and study (a). The spiral stairs connect this part of the dwelling with the bedroom and the fireplace corner on level d which are, in each case, above the entrance zone (b) of the next dwelling further down on the left. Each dwelling has a floor area of 2250 sq.ft., not counting the terrace and balcony

3–5 Schnitt und Grundrisse einer Wohnung innerhalb der gestaffelten Reihe, 1:200. Von der Eingangsebene (b) führen einige Stufen hinunter in das Gartenzimmer und das Studio (a). Die Wendeltreppe verbindet diesen Wohnteil mit dem Schlafraum und der Kaminecke der Ebene d, unter der dann jeweils wieder der Eingangsteil (b) der links abwärts folgenden Wohnung liegt. Die Wohnung ist ohne Terrasse und Balkon 210 m² groß

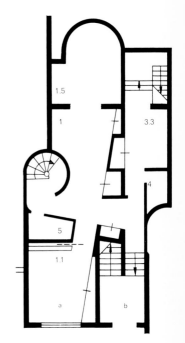

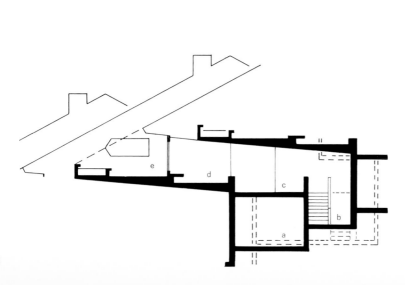

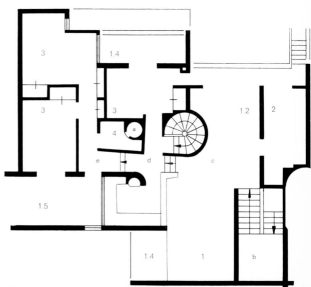

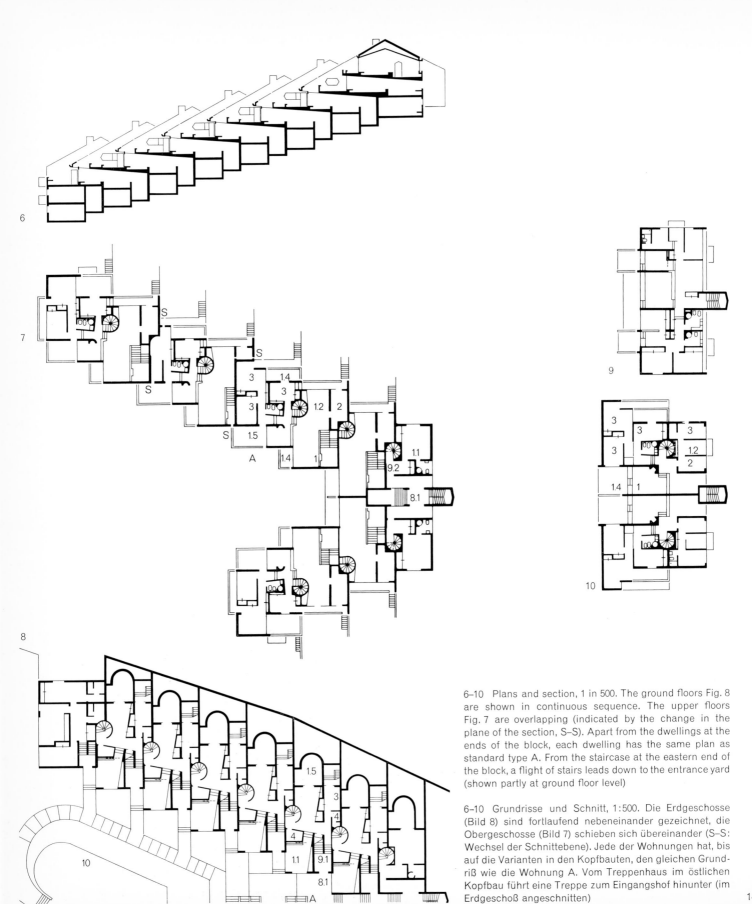

6–10 Plans and section, 1 in 500. The ground floors Fig. 8 are shown in continuous sequence. The upper floors Fig. 7 are overlapping (indicated by the change in the plane of the section, S–S). Apart from the dwellings at the ends of the block, each dwelling has the same plan as standard type A. From the staircase at the eastern end of the block, a flight of stairs leads down to the entrance yard (shown partly at ground floor level)

6–10 Grundrisse und Schnitt, 1:500. Die Erdgeschosse (Bild 8) sind fortlaufend nebeneinander gezeichnet, die Obergeschosse (Bild 7) schieben sich übereinander (S–S: Wechsel der Schnittebene). Jede der Wohnungen hat, bis auf die Varianten in den Kopfbauten, den gleichen Grundriß wie die Wohnung A. Vom Treppenhaus im östlichen Kopfbau führt eine Treppe zum Eingangshof hinunter (im Erdgeschoß angeschnitten)

Projects for terraced flats (Germany), 1959–1963
Architects: Hermann Schröder, Roland Frey
Structural engineer: Walter Pieckert

With this project for clusters of flats named Sonnenhügel – Sunny Hills – the architect intended to combine the main advantages of the single-family house with the requirements of multi-family housing. In contrast to conventional blocks with central corridors, the east and west orientation of the terraced sides enables the dwellings to receive the sun from the south throughout the year. The module spacing of the structure is 3.37 metres (11′1″). Party walls, floors and flower boxes are mounted as prefabricated units. Inside the building, the frame girder of the garage roof absorbs the loads so that no stanchions are required. The garage floor has a separate foundation.

Terrassenhausprojekte (Deutschland), 1959–1963
Architekten: Hermann Schröder, Roland Frey
Ingenieur: Walter Pieckert

Wesentliche Vorteile des Einfamilienhauses mit den Notwendigkeiten des Mehrfamilienhauses in Einklang zu bringen war Ausgangspunkt für die Planung der »Sonnenhügel«. Im Gegensatz zu üblichen Mittelganghäusern fällt bei einer Orientierung der Terrassenseiten nach Osten und Westen auch die Südsonne das ganze Jahr in die Wohnungen. Das Achsmaß der Konstruktion beträgt 3,37 m. Wohnungstrennwände, Decken und Blumentröge werden als Fertigteile eingesetzt. Der Rahmenträger der Garagendecke nimmt im Gebäudeinnern die Lasten auf, so daß eine stützenfreie Konstruktion möglich ist. Der Garagenboden wird getrennt fundiert.

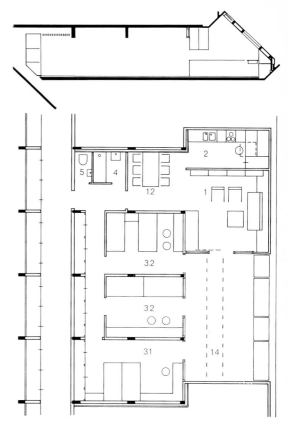

1 Plan and section of a flat, 1 in 200
2 Model of the Stuttgart-Neugereut housing estate; competition project awarded the First Prize.

1 Grundriß und Schnitt einer Etagenwohnung, 1:200
2 Modell der Siedlung Stuttgart-Neugereut, Wettbewerbsprojekt (1. Preis).

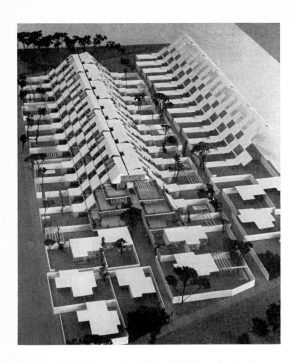

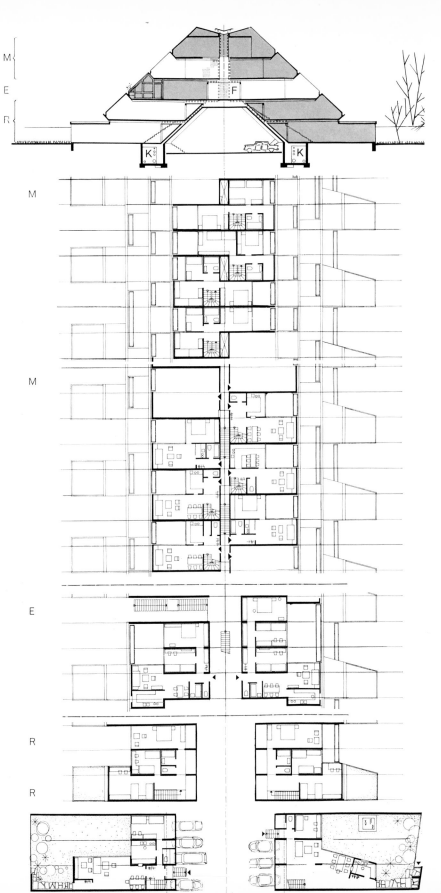

3/4 Model photographs of two "hills" and of a terrace serving as outdoor living room on the east side of the block
5/6 Section and plans, 1 in 500. Each "hill" contains about 95 dwelling units, viz. 12 with two rooms, 38 with three rooms, 12 with four rooms, and 4 with five rooms; there are also 30 detached houses with five or six rooms plus kitchen and bathroom.
R Terraced flat with garden, E Flat with terrace,
M Maisonette with terrace and two balconies, F Hall,
K Installation duct

3/4 Modellbilder zweier Wohnhügel und einer Wohnterrasse an der Ostseite des Hauses
5/6 Schnitt und Grundrisse, 1:500. Ein Wohnhügel enthält etwa 95 Wohnungen: 12 Zwei-, 38 Drei-, 12 Vier- und 4 Fünf-Zimmer-Wohnungen; sowie 30 »Einfamilienhäuser« mit 5–6 Zimmern (jeweils mit Küche und Bad).
R Reihenhaus mit Garten, E Etagenwohnung mit Wohnterrasse, M Maisonette mit Wohnterrasse und zwei Balkonen, F Flur, K Installationskanal

Breaking with the Parallel Systems

Unfettered freedom is anarchy. Building without any constraints is impracticable; the designer's imagination is restricted by the geographical position, by the materials and their intrinsic properties, by the people who erect the building.

In many cases, however, constraints are still imposed which merely aim at the appearance of uniformity: – uniformity of building lines; uniformity of cornice levels and roof shapes; parallelism of walls; equal distances. Freedom is merely conceived within a so-called orderliness of bureaucratic regulations which remove the need for making decisions even from those who do not require such relief. It is not difficult to demonstrate that it is this orderliness which is the cause of the barrenness and inhospitality of our cities, as it leaves the essential features un-ordered and precludes excellence yet fails to dam the dull flood of near-mediocrity.

What we plead for is not complete lack of order but an orderliness which leaves the greatest possible degree of freedom in expressing the aspirations of progressive contemporaries – aspirations which are just as much opposed to unscrupulous exploitation as to unimaginative directivism, and which recognize the diversity of a free democratic society.

Building creates the new metropolis. In it, there is no room for freedom if the necessary orderliness is regimented into formal rules. The right of the stronger, if practised in building, creates lack of freedom. Yet the modern notion of building is the vision of a free human society.

Aufbrechen der Parallelsysteme

Freiheit ohne Bindung ist Anarchie. Bauen ohne jede Bindung ist unmöglich; der gegebene Ort, die Materialien und ihre Gesetzmäßigkeiten, die Menschen, die den Bau aufrichten, setzen dem ungebundenen Geist Schranken.

Jedoch werden oft noch Bindungen auferlegt, die nur äußerliche Gleichheit bezwecken: Gleichheit der Bauflucht, Gleichheit der Traufhöhe und Dachform, Parallelität der Wände, Gleichheit der Abstände. Freiheit wird nur gedacht innerhalb einer sogenannten »Ordnung« bürokratischer Reglementierungen, die auch dem Unbedarften jegliche Entscheidungsnöte abnehmen. Daß diese »Ordnung« schuld ist an der Öde und Unwirtlichkeit unserer Städte, weil sie das Wesentliche ungeordnet läßt und Spitzenleistungen verhindert, die trübe Flut des fast noch Mittelmäßigen aber nicht eindämmt, läßt sich unschwer beweisen.

Nicht völliger Unordnung soll das Wort geredet werden, sondern einer Ordnung, die uns ein größtmögliches Maß an Freiheit läßt, Ausdrucksformen für den die Gegenwart bejahenden Menschen zu finden; Formen einer Gegenwart, die rücksichtslose Ausnutzung ebenso verhindert wie phantasielosen Dirigismus, die vielmehr die Mannigfaltigkeit einer freien demokratischen Gesellschaft anerkennt.

Durch Bauen entsteht die neue »Polis«. Es gibt in ihr keine Freiheit, wenn die notwendige Ordnung des Bauens in formalen Regeln erstarrt. Das Recht des Stärkeren, im Bauen praktiziert, schafft Unfreiheit. Neues Bauen dagegen beruht auf der Vision einer freien menschlichen Gesellschaft.

Krefeld (Germany), 1962 · Low-rent housing
Architect: Friedrich Mebes

In 1960, a design competition for standard types of dwellings was sponsored for a prescribed site plan (sic!). Despite the adoption of standard components such as sanitary units, it has been possible to attain a high degree of diversity in the layout of the dwellings. At the ends of the blocks are large flats with four or five rooms. The three-dimensional treatment of the west side ensures wind protection and privacy for the balconies and, by widening the field of vision, relieves the occupiers of the rigidity of a dwelling hemmed in within such a block.

Unfortunately, interference by the sponsors of this "demonstration programme" has had nothing but detrimental results: – there are four instead of three storeys; there is a lean-to roof instead of a flat roof; there are individual heaters instead of hot-air heating from a central stove; there are symmetric plans; on the other hand, the bath-tub under the window and the single-bowl kitchen sinks were accepted without protest. The floor areas of the flats, from north to south, are approximately as follows: 910 sq.ft., 730 sq.ft., 720 sq.ft., 730 sq.ft., 720 sq.ft., 730 sq.ft., 725 sq.ft., 1200 sq.ft.

Krefeld (Deutschland), 1962 · Sozialer Wohnungsbau
Architekt: Friedrich Mebes

Bei gegebenem Lageplan(!) wurde 1960 ein Wettbewerb für Wohnungstypen ausgeschrieben. Obwohl Installationseinheiten und andere Bauteile gleich sind, ist eine möglichst große Verschiedenheit des Zuschnitts aller Wohnungen erreicht. An den Hausenden liegen größere Wohnungen mit vier und fünf Zimmern. Die Auffaltung der Westfassade gibt den Balkonen Wind- und Blickschutz und löst durch die Erweiterung des Blickwinkels die Bewohner aus der Starrheit einer in die Zeile eingeklemmten Wohnung.

Die Eingriffe der Betreuer dieses »Demonstrativ-Programms« haben leider nur Verschlechterungen gebracht: vier- statt dreigeschossig, Drempel- statt Flachdach, Einzelöfen statt Kachelofen-Warmluftheizung, spiegelbildliche Grundrisse; während man die Badewanne unter dem Fenster und die einteiligen Spülbecken ruhig hinnahm. Die Wohnungen haben von Norden nach Süden folgende Wohnflächen: 85,58 m², 67,75 m², 66,97 m², 67,75 m², 66,97 m², 67,75 m², 67,20 m², 110,69 m².

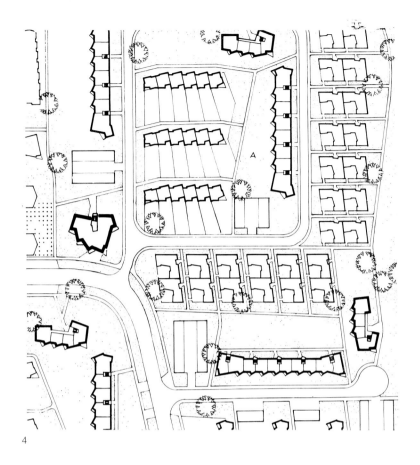

4

5

1 The balconies have a south-west orientation, open to the afternoon sun. At the ends of the block are the larger flats. They provide a distinct terminal feature for the otherwise more or less indifferent block
2 Plan of the five-room flat at the south end of the block already built, 1 in 200
3 Part of the floor plan of the competition project, 1 in 200, which was unfortunately reduced in quality by misplaced attempts at economy by the sponsors (see Fig. 5): entrance doors "eye to eye"; sanitary units arranged symmetrically on either side of the staircase so that the nursery in the flat on the right is smaller; individual heating units in each room

4 Site plan for the competition project, 1 in 2000. The block featured here is marked "A"
5 Plan of the block as actually built, 1 in 500
6 View from north-west

4 Lageplan des Wettbewerbsprojekts, 1:2000. A bezeichnet den hier dargestellten Bau
5 Grundriß des ausgeführten Projektes, 1:500
6 Blick von Nordwesten

1 Nach Südwesten öffnen sich die Balkone zur Nachmittagssonne hin. An den Kopfenden liegen die größeren Wohnungen. Damit wird ein sichtbarer Abschluß der sonst meist indifferenten Zeile erreicht
2 Grundriß der Fünf-Zimmer-Wohnung am Südende des gebauten Hauses, 1:200
3 Grundriß des Wettbewerbsprojekts, Ausschnitt, 1:200, das durch sogenannte Rationalisierungsversuche der am Demonstrativprogramm Beteiligten leider verschlechtert wurde (siehe Bild 5): Flurtüren »Auge in Auge«, Installationsräume beiderseits des Treppenhauses symmetrisch gereiht und dadurch in der rechten Wohnung ein kleineres Kinderzimmer, Einzelofenheizung in jedem Zimmer, ferner Badewanne unter dem Fenster, einteilige Spülbecken und anderes mehr

6

Bogota (Colombia), 1962 · "Polo" blocks of maisonettes
Architect: Rogelio Salmona

With the "Polo" blocks of maisonettes, too, the position of the living rooms in the two differently orientated blocks was governed by the north view towards the mountains and the west view over the plateau. In the lower maisonettes, the living rooms are therefore placed on the upper floor. The bedrooms at ground floor level are protected against noise by a belt of ancillary rooms whilst, towards the road, a covered car port is provided.

In the upper maisonettes, the height of the living rooms increases with the rising roof. A corner of the bedroom, used as a study, has a window on the living room.

The floor area of each dwelling is approx. 1900 sq. ft. including the car port and the share of the stairs. The price is about 100,000 Pesos, i.e. approx. 10,000 US Dollars. 25 per cent. of this amount must be paid when the agreement is signed, the remainder must be paid off over a period of 20 years. The project is sponsored by a Bogota bank.

All the firm believers in standard types will here be able to see how a layout plan can be modified within the standard series and how certain design components, confined to certain positions such as the access galleries with their stairs, can be ingeniously used to counter the rigidity of the standard block.

A surprising feature is the high standard of workmanship which gives the lie to all preconceived ideas of South-American laissez-faire.

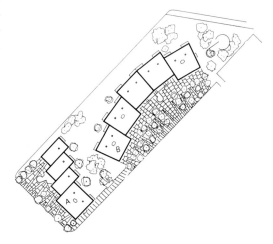

1 Site plan, 1 in 2000/Lageplan 1:2000

Bogota (Kolumbien), 1962 · Maisonette-Gruppe »Polo«
Architekt: Rogelio Salmona

Die Aussicht nach Norden auf die Berge und nach Westen auf die Hochebene bestimmte auch bei der Hausgruppe »Polo« die Lage der Wohnräume in den beiden verschieden orientierten Zeilen. Bei den unteren Maisonette-Typen liegt daher das Wohngeschoß im oberen Teil der Wohnung. Die ebenerdigen Schlafräume sind durch eine Zone von Nebenräumen gegen Lärm geschützt, an der Straßenseite ist der gedeckte Wagenabstellplatz vorgelagert.

In den oberen Maisonettes weitet sich der Wohnbereich mit dem ansteigenden Dach nach oben. Der Arbeitsplatz im Schlafraum ist durch ein Fenster mit dem Wohnraum verbunden.

Eine Wohnung ist ungefähr 175 m² groß, wobei Wagenabstellplatz und Treppenanteile mitgerechnet sind, und kostet etwa 100000 Pesos, das entspricht etwa 10000 US-Dollar. 25% der Summe sind anzuzahlen, der Rest wird in 20 Jahren getilgt. Bauherr ist eine Bank in Bogota.

Allen »Typen-Gläubigen« wird hier gezeigt, wie ein Grundriß innerhalb der Typenreihe sich abwandeln läßt und wie gewisse, aus der Situation heraus einmalige Bauteile, wie die Laubengänge mit ihrem Treppenhaus, durch eine sinnvolle Anordnung die Starrheit des Typenhauses lockern.

Überraschend ist die handwerkliche Präzision, die alle Vorurteile gegenüber südamerikanischer Lässigkeit Lügen straft.

2 Upper maisonette of the access gallery type (Block B); plans, 1 in 200

2 Obere Maisonettewohnung, Laubengangtyp (Block B), Grundrisse, 1:200

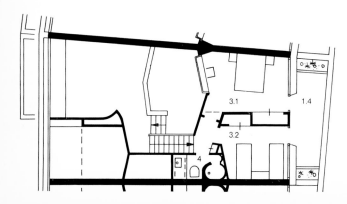

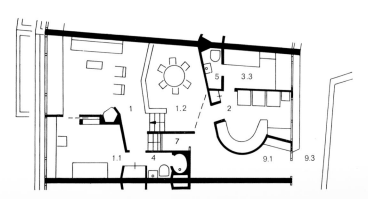

3 View from north-east of the road-side frontage of Block B. The paved entrance yard will later be shaded by trees. Owing to the stagger of the blocks and the curvature imposed by the plan, the courtyard space does not form a barren area between building and road

3 Blick von Nordosten auf die Straßenseite des Blockes B. Der gepflasterte »Eingangshof« wird später von Bäumen beschattet sein. Das Versetzen der Häuser und die sich aus dem Grundriß ergebende Schwingung formt aus dem Hof einen Raum, der nicht als tote Fläche zwischen Haus und Straße in Erscheinung tritt

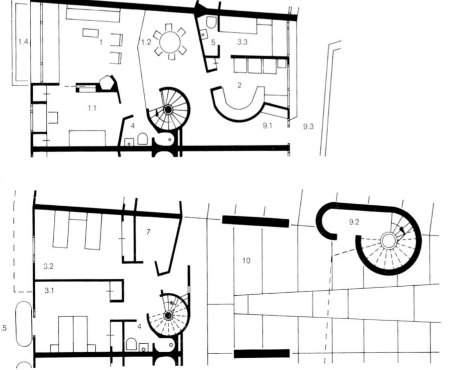

4 Lower maisonette, access gallery type; plans, 1 in 200. The walls separating the maisonettes are not parallel, the living room (in Block B) widens out westwards

4 Untere Maisonettewohnung, Laubengangtyp, Grundrisse, 1:200. Die Wohnungstrennwände sind nicht parallel, der Wohnraum weitet sich (bei Block B) nach Westen

5 View from the north, along Block B, on the living room side of Block A. The terrace in front of the bedrooms of the lower maisonettes is bordered by a low earth mound of about 1'8" height and is thus segregated from the slope. All the bearing and outer walls consist of brick, the floors of prefabricated concrete units, windows and doors of oakwood, the roofing of asbestos cement tiles

6 Access gallery type, Block A; Section, 1 in 200

7 Upper maisonette of the internal stairs type at the south end of Block B, 1 in 200 (O = skylight)

5 Blick von Norden entlang Block B auf die Wohnblockseite des Blockes A. Die Terrasse vor den Schlafräumen der unteren Maisonettes ist durch einen kleinen, kaum 50 cm hohen Erdwall begrenzt und so als Raumform von dem fallenden Hang abgesondert. Alle tragenden und Außenmauern sind aus Backsteinen, die Decken aus vorfabrizierten Betonteilen, Fenster und Türen aus Eiche, das Dach ist mit Asbestzementplatten gedeckt

6 Laubengangtyp Block A, Schnitt, 1:200

7 Obere Maisonettewohnung, Innentreppentyp am Südende von Block B, 1:200 (O Oberlicht)

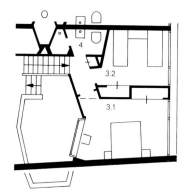

6
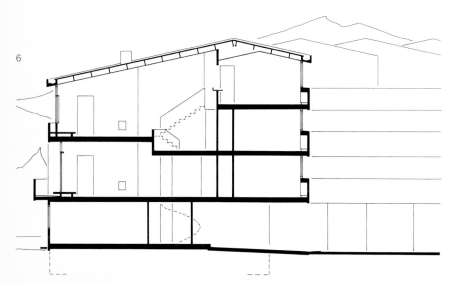

7
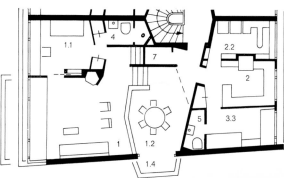

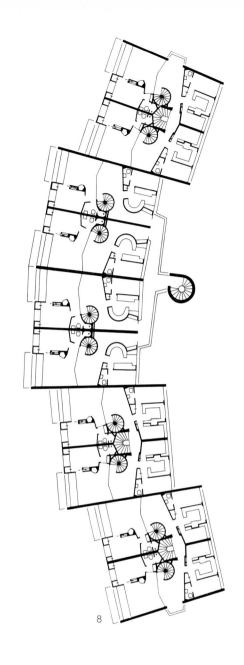

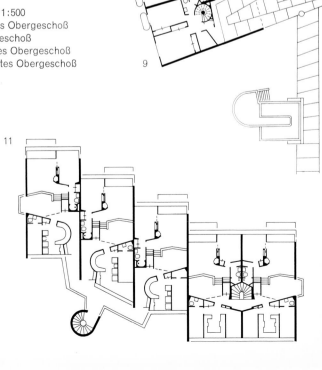

8–11 Plans, 1 in 500
  8 Block B, first floor
  9 Block B, ground floor
 10 Block A, third floor
 11 Block A, second floor

8–11 Grundrisse, 1:500
  8 Block B, erstes Obergeschoß
  9 Block B, Erdgeschoß
 10 Block A, drittes Obergeschoß
 11 Block A, zweites Obergeschoß

8

9

10

11

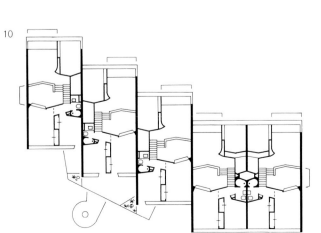

Basle, 1963/64 · Tower blocks at Hechtliacker
Architects: Otto Senn and Walter Senn

The design of the three Hechtliacker tower blocks at Basle has benefited from experience gathered at the Hansa District in Berlin in 1957. A point block without definite orientation can be more easily integrated with the organism of an old town than an oblong block which can only be logically justified as part of a (generally non-existent) overall development plan or regional plan. There is no longer any playing about with shapes of the kind still encountered at the Hansa District where the point blocks are lined up along the railway. At Basle, the townscape has been enriched by the free composition of the three tower blocks on a wooded ridge. Situated in a park and placed at a considerable distance from each other, the point blocks offer the advantages of a free position and wide view for all flats. With the adoption of the polygonal principle, the zone forming the field of vision of each flat and without being disturbed by neighbours is of maximum size and permits, in spite of differences in the specifications and in the size of the flats, the provision of identical and inter-related forms of dwellings. In this way, the disadvantages inherent in the arrangement of several flats on one floor are greatly reduced, and all the flats have windows and views in two or three directions.

Basel, 1963/64 · Turmhäuser auf dem Hechtliacker
Architekten: Otto Senn und Walter Senn

Bei den drei Hechtliacker-Hochhäusern in Basel werden die im Hansaviertel in Berlin 1957 gewonnenen Erfahrungen ausgewertet. Das nicht richtungsbetonte Punkthaus ist leichter in den Organismus einer alten Stadt einzuordnen als ein Scheibenhochhaus, das nur im Rahmen einer (meist fehlenden) Gesamtplanung der Stadt und Region sinnvoll ist. Statt der Formspielereien, wie sie noch das Hansaviertel mit der Aufreihung der Turmhäuser entlang eines Bahnstranges aufweist, ist mit der freien Komposition der drei Baseler Türme auf einem bewaldeten Höhenrücken das Stadtbild bereichert. Die Lage im Park und der große Abstand der Türme untereinander bietet allen Wohnungen die Vorteile der freien Lage und der weiten Sicht. Das polygonale Prinzip weitet den von der einzelnen Wohnung aus wahrnehmbaren, vom Nachbarn ungestörten Bereich auf das größtmögliche Maß und läßt trotz verschiedenartiger Bauprogramme und Wohnungsgrößen die Anordnung ähnlicher, aufeinander bezogener Hausformen zu. Die Nachteile der Vielspännertypen werden durch die Grundrißform stark reduziert; alle Wohnungen haben Fenster und Ausblick nach zwei oder drei Himmelsrichtungen.

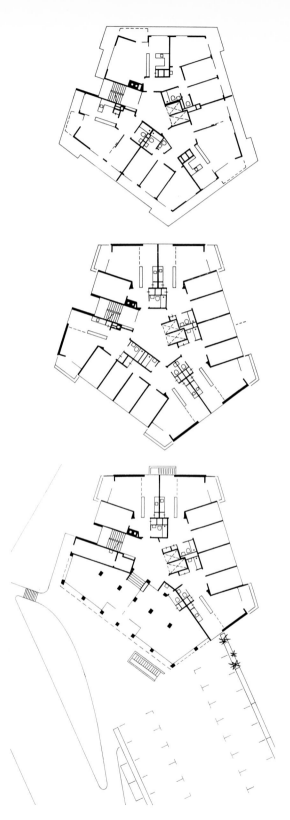

1 Perspective drawing/Perspektivzeichnung

2–4 Floor plans, Block C, 1 in 500. Bottom to top: Entrance floor, standard floor, roof storey

2–4 Grundrisse Haus C, 1:500. Von unten nach oben Eingangsgeschoß, Normalgeschoß, Dachgeschoß 154

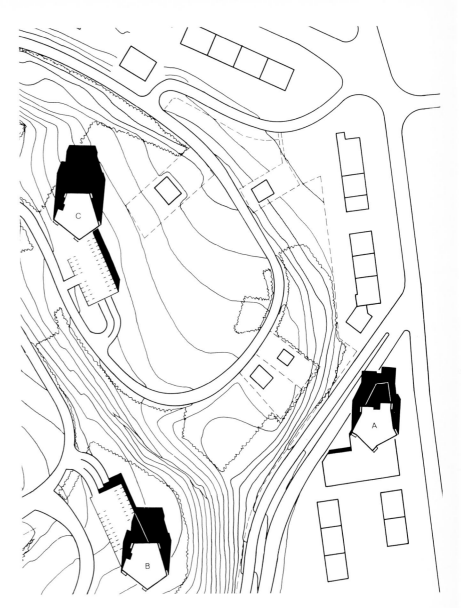

6 Standard floor plan, Block A, 1 in 500. The specifications for this block broadly correspond to normal German low-rent housing standards

6 Grundriß eines Normalgeschosses im Haus A, 1:500. Das Bauprogramm dieses Hauses entspricht etwa dem des Sozialen Wohnungsbaus in Deutschland

7 Model of the three tower blocks, seen from the north

7 Modellansicht der drei Turmhäuser, von Norden gesehen

8 Standard plan of flats in Blocks B and C, 1 in 200

8 Wohnung in einem Normalgeschoß der Häuser B und C,
1 : 200

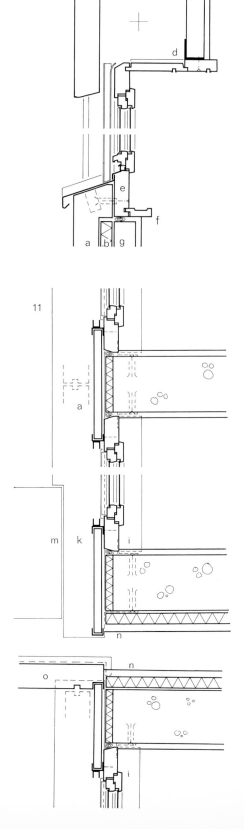

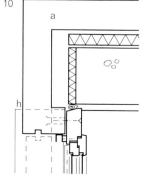

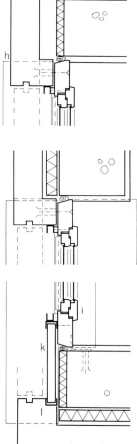

9–11 Sections of details, 1 in 10, showing the assembly of
windows and prefabricated facade panels: 9 vertical,
10/11 horizontal.
a Prefabricated concrete units, b Glued cork, 3 cm (1.3/16″),
c Cork inserted in the formwork 2 cm (3/4″), d Angle iron,
suspended; Oris boards 5 cm (2″), e Putty, f Silk braid-
ing, g Cellular clay, 6 cm (2.3/8″), h Metal sheet, bent
upwards at the edges, i Window stop with angle iron,
k Asbestos cement board, l Precast concrete profile,
m Flower box connection, n Balcony side wall, o Balcony side slab

9–11 Detailschnitte, 1 : 10. Anschlüsse der Fenster und der
vorgefertigten Fassadenplatten: 9 vertikal, 10/11 horizontal.
a vorfabrizierte Betonelemente, b aufgeklebter Kork, 3 cm,
c in die Schalung eingelegter Kork, 2 cm, d L-Eisen, auf-
gehängt, Orisplatten, 5 cm, e Kitt, f Seidenzöpfe, g Zell-
ton, 6 cm, h Blech, an den Rändern hochgezogen, i Fen-
steranschlag mit Eisenwinkel, k Eternitplatte, l U-Profil in
vorfabriziertem Betonelement, m Anschluß der Blumenbank, n Balkonseitenwand, o Seitenplatte am Balkon

12 In the Hansa District, Otto Senn was only able to try out his tower block ideas on a small-scale model. An enquiry among the tenants showed that, apart from the fixed windows which are unusual for Berlin and were not in accordance with the architect's suggestions, the advantages of this type of dwelling were appreciated
13 View from the living room of the Interbau building in Berlin towards the dining area which can be separated by a folding partition
14 The view in the opposite direction shows the skilfully arranged juxtaposition of the three zones of kitchen, dining area and living room

12 Im Hansaviertel konnte Otto Senn seine Turmhaus-Überlegungen nur an einem »Stumpfmodell« erproben. Eine Mieterbefragung ergab, daß die Bewohner die Vorteile dieser Wohnform (bis auf die in Berlin ungewohnten und nicht nach den Vorschlägen des Architekten eingebauten Fenster) zu schätzen wissen
13 Blick aus dem Wohnraum des Interbau-Hauses in Berlin auf den durch eine Faltwand abtrennbaren Eßplatz
14 Der Blick in der umgekehrten Richtung läßt die geschickte Verbindung der drei Bereiche Küche, Eßplatz und Wohnraum erkennen

1 South-west view of a cluster of three fan-type blocks (model)
2 Part of site plan of blocks of flats, 1 in 10,000

1 Südwestansicht einer Gruppe von drei Fächerhäusern im Modell
2 Lageplanausschnitt der Appartementhausgruppen, 1:10000

Copenhagen, 1959 · Project for blocks of flats
Architects: Jean-Jacques Baruël and Paul Niepoort

The housing development along the edges of a park which forms the boundary between two Copenhagen suburbs was the subject of an architectural competition. The programme called for 4000 dwelling units in informally arranged blocks of flats, terraced houses, patio-type houses and detached houses. The valley with its little lakes and clusters of old trees was to be preserved.
To emphasize the topography of the ground with its, by Danish standards, steep south-west slope, the project envisaged a chain of informally arranged blocks of flats. In the Danish climate, the sun is very welcome, and sun protection is not required. The desire to catch as much sunshine as possible is reflected in the layout plans of the dwellings as well as in the design of the blocks. The flats have 1, 1½ or 2 rooms; all the larger dwellings are reserved for the other types of housing. For these small apartments, the fan-shaped plan is particularly well suited; with parallel side walls, the relatively small area of the bed-sitting room often conveys the impression of restrictiveness and narrowness. With the fan-shaped layout, the ancillary rooms recede, and greater emphasis is placed on the window wall with the balcony, serving as a link between public and private outdoor space.

Kopenhagen, 1959 · Appartementhaus-Projekt
Architekten: Jean-Jacques Baruël und Paul Niepoort

Für die Bebauung der Ränder eines Parkgeländes, das zwei Kopenhagener Vororte trennt, war ein Wettbewerb ausgeschrieben. Für 4000 Wohnungen waren in offener Bebauung Appartementhäuser, Reihenhäuser, Gartenhofhäuser und »Villen« zu planen. Nicht bebaut werden durfte das Tal mit seinen kleinen Seen und alten Baumgruppen.
Um die Kontur des Geländes mit dem für dänische Verhältnisse »steilen« Südwesthang zu unterstreichen, wurde eine Kette locker gruppierter Appartementhäuser entworfen. Im dänischen Klima ist der Sonnenhunger groß, Sonnenschutz ist kaum erforderlich. Die Wohnungsgrundrisse wie die Hausform kennzeichnen diesen Wunsch, möglichst viel Sonnenschein einzufangen. Die Appartements haben einen, eineinhalb oder zwei Räume, alle größeren Wohnungen sind auf die anderen Haustypen verteilt. Für diese kleinen Appartements eignet sich der Fächergrundriß besonders gut; die relativ kleine Fläche des Wohnschlafraumes wirkt bei parallel stehenden Seitenwänden oft bedrückend und eng. Der Fächer läßt die Nebenräume zurücktreten und betont die Fensterwand mit dem Verbindungsglied zwischen öffentlichem und privatem Freiraum, dem Balkon.

3 Model of a cluster of three fan-type blocks. Apart from the advantageous type of plan, the design has permitted a felicitous arrangement of the 14 fan clusters on the hilltop slope and a type of building of well balanced proportions. Unfortunately, not even one of these blocks has been built so far

4/5 Layout plan of a cluster of three blocks, and section, 1 in 500

3

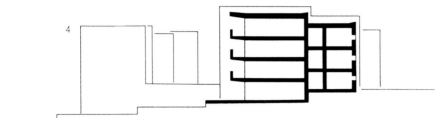

4

3 Modellfoto der Fächerhausgruppe. Außer der vorteilhaften Grundrißform wurde eine geschickte Gliederung der 13 Fächerabschnitte am Hang der Hügelkuppe und eine im Maßstab gut abgestimmte Hausform gefunden. Es ist bedauerlich, daß bisher nicht wenigstens eine dieser Hausgruppen gebaut werden konnte

4/5 Grundriß einer Gruppe von drei Häusern und Schnitt, 1:500

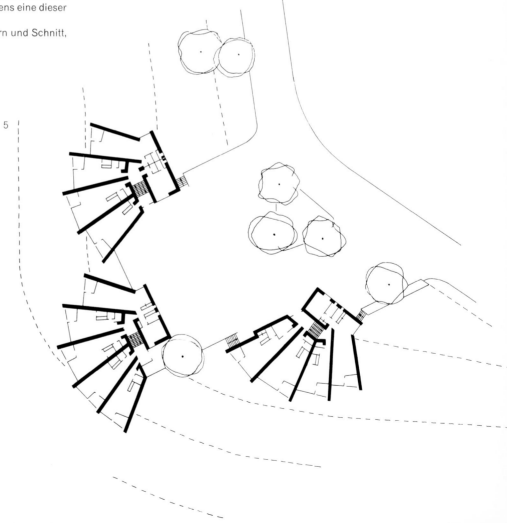

5

Neue Vahr, Bremen (Germany), 1962 · Multi-storey block of flats
Architect: Alvar Aalto

The construction of 10,000 dwelling units in the Neue Vahr district in the south-eastern part of Bremen was begun, in 1957, in accordance with plans drawn up by Ernst May, Max Säume, Günter Hafemann, Hans-Bernhard Reichow and Wolfgang Bilau.

It was intended to mark the position of the shopping centre in the heart of this low-rent housing estate by a building with outstanding features. The Finnish architect Alvar Aalto was asked to design a 22-storey block, taking into account the specific requirements of single people and childless couples going to work. All the flats face the evening sun in the west and south-west and are separated from the possibly noisy corridors by cupboard rooms, bathrooms and halls. At the southern end of each corridor, a club room is provided for the joint use of all the residents on the floor, offering a view over the shopping centre and the two neighbourhood units further east, centred on two artificial lakes. The north-west side has been treated as completely indifferent. This block, conceived as a dominating feature, is wholly designed to "put its best foot forward" – that is, to let the undulated south-west facade with its acute-angled ends have its full effect on the onlooker.

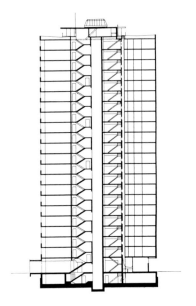

1 Section of north-east wing, 1 in 1000
2–4 Ground floor plan, typical floor plan, and roof storey plan, 1 in 500

1 Schnitt durch den Nordwestteil des Hochhauses, 1:1000
2–4 Grundrisse des Erd-, Normal- und Dachgeschosses, 1:500

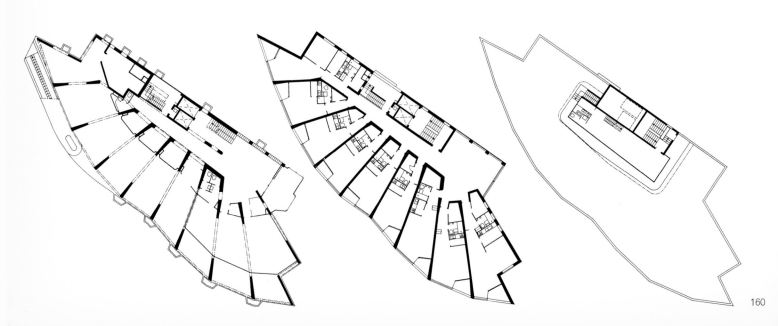

5 View from south-west / Ansicht von Südwesten

Bremen-Neue Vahr (Deutschland), 1962 · Hochhausscheibe
Architekt: Alvar Aalto

Mit dem Bau der 10000 Wohnungen umfassenden Neuen Vahr im Südosten der Stadt Bremen wurde 1957 nach den Plänen von Ernst May, Max Säume, Günter Hafemann, Hans-Bernhard Reichow und Wolfgang Bilau begonnen.
Die Lage des Ladenviertels im Mittelpunkt dieser im Sozialen Wohnungsbau errichteten Siedlung sollte durch einen sich deutlich abhebenden Bau hervorgehoben werden. Man übertrug dem Finnen Alvar Aalto den Auftrag, den besonderen Gewohnheiten der Alleinstehenden und der berufstätigen Ehepaare mit einem zweiundzwanziggeschossigen Hochhaus Rechnung zu tragen. Er richtete alle Wohnungen zur Feierabendseite nach Westen und Südwesten, trennte sie durch Abstellräume Bäder und Eingangsflure vom eventuell geräuschvollen Flur und richtete einen für alle Geschoßbewohner gemeinsam zu nutzenden Klubraum an jedem südlichen Gangende ein, der den Blick auf das Ladenzentrum und die an zwei künstliche Seen angelehnten örtlichen »Nachbarschaften« bietet. Im übrigen ist die Nordwestseite als völlig nebensächlich behandelt. Das als Dominante gedachte Haus ist ganz darauf angelegt, mit seiner »schönen Seite«, der gewellten Südwestfassade mit ihren spitzwinkligen Endungen, auf den Betrachter zu wirken.

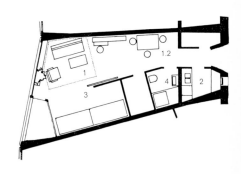

6 Layout plan of a flat, 1 in 200. Instead of showers, bath tubs have been provided. The sliding doors for the sleeping recesses have unfortunately been omitted

6 Grundriß einer Wohnung, 1:200. Statt der Brausen sind Badewannen eingebaut worden. Auf die Schiebetüren vor den Schlafnischen wurde leider verzichtet

Rot, Stuttgart (Germany), 1956–1959 · "Romeo" and "Juliet" tower blocks
Architects: Hans Scharoun, Wilhelm Frank
Structural Engineers: Hybl and Lehrle

The first two tower blocks, designed by Hans Scharoun to disprove the conventional thesis that, to be economic, the layout plan of such buildings had to be based on a rectangular pattern, were erected at Stuttgart where post-war reconstruction and expansion was marked by an odd mixture of bold progressiveness and nervous narrowmindedness. Even so, it was possible, in this atmosphere, to pursue an experiment right up to the finished building, which would elsewhere have been stifled at an early stage by overwhelming forces of mediocrity. The two tower blocks with their freehold flats, forming a bizarre contrast to the pre-existing housing in the area, have endowed the urban district of Rot not only with a valuable sociological compensation but also with a prominent feature as the site lies at the escarp of the slope rising up from Zuffenhausen. The Romeo block contains 104 flats whilst the Juliet block, where the number of storeys is graduated from eleven to four, contains 82 flats. Several shops, a restaurant and a pub in the lower floors of the Romeo block obviate the impression of lifelessness often encountered with tower blocks containing flats only.

Stuttgart-Rot (Deutschland), 1956–1959 · Hochhausgruppe »Romeo« und »Julia«
Architekten: Hans Scharoun, Wilhelm Frank
Ingenieure: Hybl und Lehrle

Die ersten beiden Wohnhochhäuser, mit denen Scharoun das bislang für derartige Häuser allein für wirtschaftlich vertretbar angesehene rechtwinklige Grundriß- und Formschema widerlegte, entstanden in Stuttgart, dessen Aufbau und Ausdehnung nach dem Krieg in einer merkwürdigen Mischung von weit vorausgreifendem Wagemut und ängstlicher Engstirnigkeit vor sich ging. Immerhin konnte in dieser Atmosphäre ein Experiment bis hin zum fertigen Bau durchgestanden werden, das andernorts im frühen Stadium vom Übergewicht des Mittelmäßigen bereits erstickt worden wäre. Der Stadtteil Rot erhielt durch die beiden im Gegensatz zur übrigen Bebauung bizarr anmutenden Hochhäuser mit seinen Eigentumswohnungen sowohl eine wertvolle soziologische Ergänzung als auch ein ausgeprägtes Gesicht, denn das Grundstück liegt an der Bruchkante des von Zuffenhausen her ansteigenden Hanges. »Romeo« enthält insgesamt 104 Wohnungen; »Julia«, deren Geschoßzahl stufenweise von elf auf vier sinkt, enthält 82 Wohnungen. Mehrere Läden, ein Restaurant und ein Bierlokal in den unteren Geschossen des »Romeo« nehmen dem Haus die leblose Starre, die reinen Wohnhochhäusern oft anhaftet.

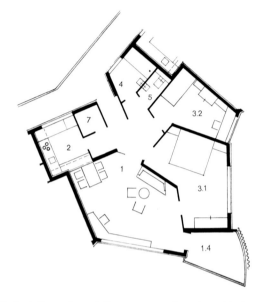

1 Typical floor plan of the access gallery type block, Juliet, 1 in 200. Removed from the rigidity of rectangular patterns, the different rooms are related to each other and have a relaxing as well as inspiring effect on those who are capable of responding

1 Typischer Wohnungsgrundriß im Laubenganghaus »Julia«, 1:200. Herausgelöst aus der Starre rechtwinkliger Umgrenzungen nehmen die Räume aufeinander Bezug und wirken auf die, die ansprechbar sind, entspannend wie auch anregend

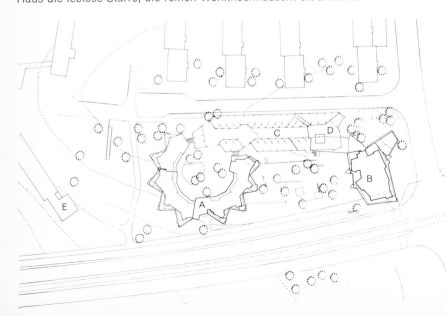

2 Site plan, 1 in 2000.
A Juliet, B Romeo, C single-storey lock-up garages, D cafe, E school building further down the slope

2 Lageplan, 1:2000.
A »Julia«, B »Romeo«, C eingeschossiger Garagenhof, D Café, E hangabwärts im Westen die Silcherschule

3 View from the studio terrace of the Romeo block westwards across the adjacent block, then under construction, and a new school building (Architect Günter Wilhelm) towards the district of Zuffenhausen. Unfortunately, the new road – not strictly necessary in this position – severs the connection with the orchard slope on the south side and disturbs both school and dwellings by its traffic noise

3 Blick von der Atelierterrasse des »Romeo« nach Westen auf das seinerzeit im Bau befindliche Nachbarhochhaus, die Silcherschule (Architekt Günter Wilhelm) und Zuffenhausen. Leider zerschneidet die an dieser Stelle nicht notwendige, neu angelegte Straße den Zusammenhang mit dem südlich vorgelagerten Obstbaumhang und stört Schule wie Wohnungen durch den Verkehrslärm

4/5 Typical floor plans of the Juliet block (left) and the Romeo block, 1 in 500

4/5 Normalgeschoßgrundrisse »Julia« (links) und »Romeo«, 1:500

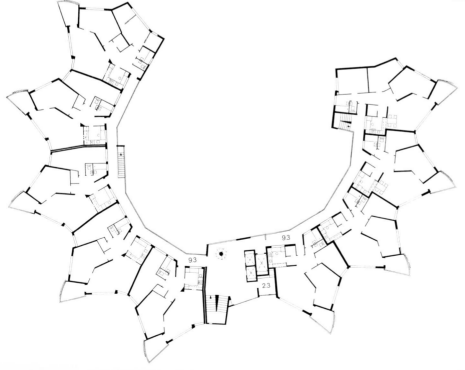

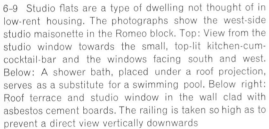

6–9 Studio flats are a type of dwelling not thought of in low-rent housing. The photographs show the west-side studio maisonette in the Romeo block. Top: View from the studio window towards the small, top-lit kitchen-cum-cocktail-bar and the windows facing south and west. Below: A shower bath, placed under a roof projection, serves as a substitute for a swimming pool. Below right: Roof terrace and studio window in the wall clad with asbestos cement boards. The railing is taken so high as to prevent a direct view vertically downwards

6–9 Atelierwohnungen sind ein vom Sozialen Wohnungsbau vergessener Wohnungstyp. Die Bilder zeigen die westliche Atelierwohnung im Hochhaus »Romeo«. Oben der Blick vom Atelierfenster auf die kleine mit einem Oberlicht versehene Barküche und die sich nach Süden und Westen anschließende Fensterwand. Unten die unter einem Dachvorsprung angelegte Duschecke und die Dachterrasse mit dem Atelierfenster in der mit Eternitschindeln verkleideten Wand. Das Geländer ist so angelegt, daß der Blick am Haus hinab verwehrt wird

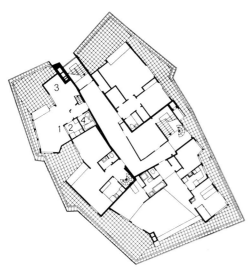

10 View of both blocks from south-west
11 Roof storey plan of the Romeo block, 1 in 500. In the studio maisonette on the west side, a flight of stairs leads further up to another bedroom
12 Juliet block, seen from the south

10 Ansicht der beiden Hochhäuser von Südwesten
11 Dachgeschoßgrundriß »Romeo«, 1:500. Von der westlichen Atelierwohnung führt eine Treppe hinauf in eine Schlafkammer

12 Das Hochhaus »Julia« von Süden gesehen

Stuttgart-West (Germany), 1962 · Hillside apartments
Architect: Chen Kuen Lee, assisted by Kurt Storm
Landscape gardener: Hermann Mattern

In Stuttgart, sites for detached houses in the vicinity of the central area are at a premium. A lucky coincidence brought together four clients, a derelict site, and an architect who designed, for each of these clients, a dwelling to individual specifi- cations, directly connected with a private garden on a western slope. The contours of the buildings fit in well with the old buildings in the neighbourhood. Those familiar with present-day conditions in Germany will not be surprised to find that the construction of the house, though privately financed, met with great opposition on the part of the authorities. That is was built speaks for the tenacity of the sponsors. Walking up the hill, then passing through the main entrance door embedded in the slope and through a corridor at basement level, one takes the lift or mounts the stairs in the projecting glass enclosed staircase to reach the doors of the individual dwellings. Most of the furniture has been designed by the architect. Even such a tiny room as the flatlet for guests on the top floor (Photographs, page 166) still con- veys the impression of luxury and freedom which is characteristic of the plans. To include the garden, however small, in the living space of a dwelling is a basic

feature of Chinese housing, and came naturally to the architect. The town is not regarded as a hostile element that must be excluded; it makes itself felt in the dwelling which is wide open towards south-west, and is spread before one's eyes as one stands on the terrace.

Stuttgart-West (Deutschland), 1962 · Hangwohnhaus
Architekt: Chen Kuen Lee, Mitarbeiter: Kurt Storm
Gartengestaltung: Hermann Mattern

In Stuttgart zählen stadtnahe Einfamilienhaus-Grundstücke zu den größten Kostbarkeiten. Wenn vier Baulustige sich auf einem Ruinengrundstück zusammenfinden und auf einen Architekten treffen, der jedem von ihnen eine Wohnung nach individuellen Wünschen mit jeweils einem Stück direkt erreichbaren Gartens an einem Westhang komponiert, zählen sie zu den vom Glück Begünstigten. Daß ein solches Haus, dessen Konturen sich ohne Zwang in die alte Nachbarbebauung einfügen, trotz freier Finanzierung den Behörden abgerungen werden muß, nimmt die Kenner der Verhältnisse in Deutschland nicht wunder; daß es dennoch gebaut werden konnte, spricht für die Zähigkeit der Stuttgarter Bauherren.
Den Berg hinansteigend, trifft man auf die in den Hang gebettete Hauseingangstür, gelangt durch einen Gang im Untergeschoß des Hauses zum Aufzug oder steigt durch das verglaste, aus dem Hauskörper ragende Treppenhaus zu den Wohnungstüren. Die Wohnungen wurden zum größten Teil vom Architekten möbliert. Selbst bei einem so winzigen Raum wie dem Gästeappartement im obersten Geschoß (Bilder Seite 166) bleibt die großzügige und befreiende Wirkung erhalten, die für die Grundrisse charakteristisch ist.
Das Wohnen im Garten und mit dem Garten ist als Grundthema chinesischen Wohnbaues dem Architekten Selbstverständlichkeit. Die Stadt ist nicht als feindlich ausgeschlossen, sie wird durch die Öffnung nach Südwesten spürbar im Raume und breitet sich beim Blick von der Terrasse vor den Augen aus.

1 Westward view along the south side of the house
2–4 Single-room apartment on the third floor, as seen from the sleeping gallery, from the desk, and from the sitting corner (see also the plan on page 171)
5 West-side balconies

1 Blick nach Westen entlang der Südseite des Hauses
2–4 Die Einraumwohnung im dritten Obergeschoß, von der Schlafgalerie, vom Schreibplatz und vom Sitzplatz her gesehen (siehe auch Grundriß auf Seite 171)
5 Die Balkone auf der Westseite

6 The western escarp with the terraced house. In the centre of the photograph are the two tower blocks of Stuttgart Technical University and, at the bottom of the valley, the New Palace which is within 15 minutes' walking distance
7 Layout plan, 1 in 500. The plan level is indicated in the Section. B bridge
8 Section, 1 in 500
a Entrance level
b Basement level
c Ground floor level
d First floor level
e Second floor level
f Third floor level
g Gallery level

6 Der steile Westhang mit dem Terrassenhaus. In der Bildmitte die beiden Hochhäuser der Technischen Hochschule Stuttgart und das Neue Schloß im Mittelpunkt des Talkessels, der in 15 Minuten zu Fuß erreicht werden kann
7 Lageplan, 1:500. Rasterplan siehe Schnitt. B Brücke
8 Schnitt, 1:500
a Eingangsebene
b Erstes Untergeschoß
c Erdgeschoß
d Erstes Obergeschoß
e Zweites Obergeschoß
f Drittes Obergeschoß
g Galeriegeschoß

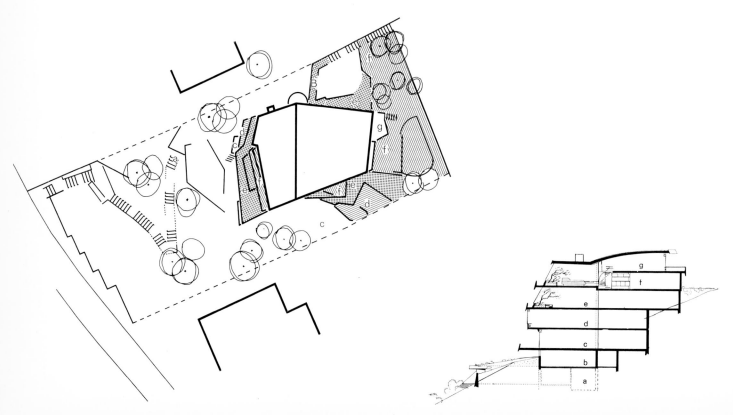

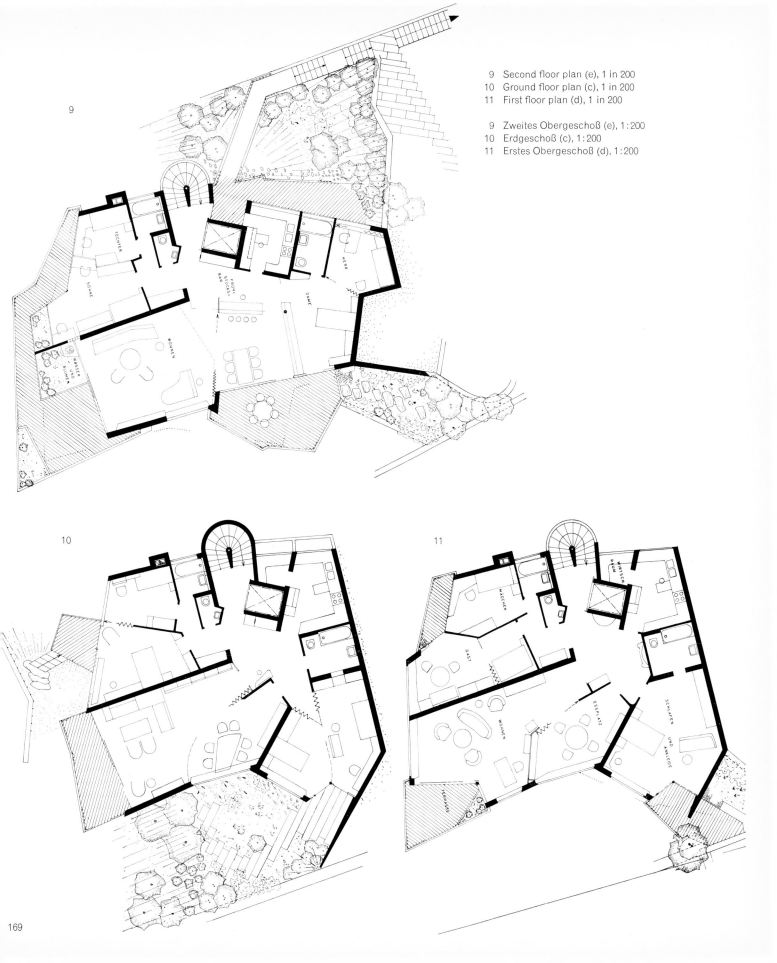

9   Second floor plan (e), 1 in 200
10 Ground floor plan (c), 1 in 200
11 First floor plan (d), 1 in 200

9   Zweites Obergeschoß (e), 1:200
10 Erdgeschoß (c), 1:200
11 Erstes Obergeschoß (d), 1:200

12 Third floor apartment. Below the gallery from which the studio can be separated by a folding partition is the dining area which is separated by a sideboard (and cocktail bar) from the son's bedroom and study, The dining area itself can be curtained off against the living room

13 From the gallery, balustraded by book shelves, there is a view across the living room and the terrace westwards over the roofs of one of Stuttgart's dales

14 View from the dressing room across the gallery to the living room

12 Die Wohnung im dritten Obergeschoß. Unter der Empore, von der das Studio mit einer Faltwand abgeschlossen werden kann, der Eßplatz, der durch eine Anrichte (und Hausbar) getrennt ist vom Zugang zum Zimmer des Sohnes und zu einem Arbeitszimmer. Der Eßplatz kann durch einen Vorhang vom Wohnraum abgeteilt werden

13 Von der Empore aus, die mit Bücherregalen abgeschrankt ist, blickt man über den Wohnraum und die Terrasse hinweg nach Westen auf die Dächer dieses Stuttgarter Seitentales

14 Blick von der Ankleide über die Empore in den Wohnraum

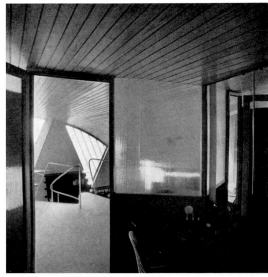

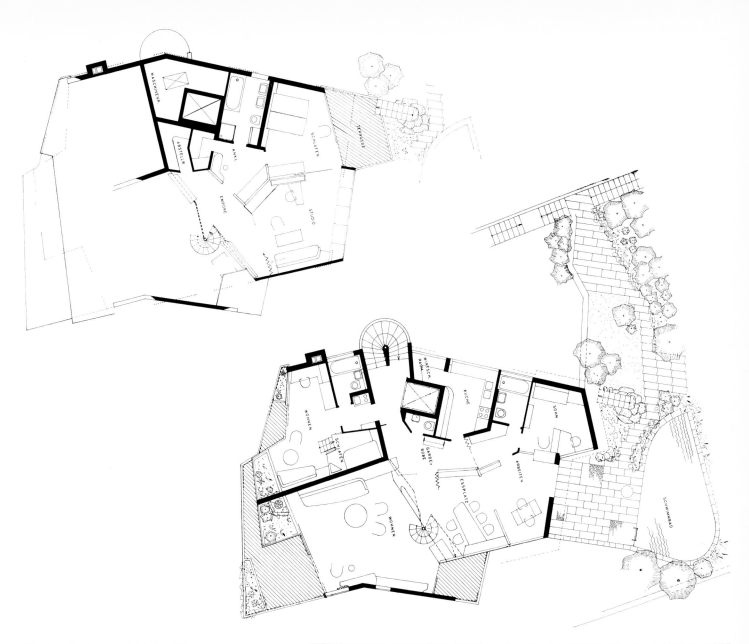

15 Plan of gallery level (g), 1 in 200
16 Third floor plan (f), 1 in 200
17 East and north sides of the building

15 Galeriegeschoß (g), 1:200
16 Drittes Obergeschoß (f), 1:200
17 Die Ost- und Nordseite des Hauses

Urban Units

The vision of the new town, the town without precedent, is not one that comes easily, even to the genius. When Le Corbusier sketched his first visionary pictures of a modern town, he was unable to shake off the convention of symmetrical systems with central perspectives: Space is partitioned by multi-storey blocks, and between them a network of low buildings sited among trees and grass covers the ground of a town freed from through traffic.

True, the axial views have disappeared from the creations of those who emulate Le Corbusier's ideas; but even now, we have hardly succeeded in freeing ourselves from formal conceptions. First attempts, made in the United States, at overcoming the chaos of completely uninhibited freedom of building construction are guided by a formalism, imported from Europe. But self-contained forms are unsuitable for the open community of our cities. The picture of urban development designed for Hook New Town shows most clearly the possible trend of development.

Stadtquartiere

Das Bild der neuen Stadt, das ohne Vor-Bild ist, enthüllt sich auch dem Genie nicht von heute auf morgen. Le Corbusier konnte sich nicht aus den Fesseln symmetrisch auf Perspektivachsen aufgebauter Systeme befreien, als er seine ersten Zukunftsbilder einer modernen Stadt entwarf, in denen Hochhäuser den großen Raum gliedern und ein Netz in Grün gebetteter niedriger Bauten den Boden der vom Durchgangsverkehr befreiten Stadt bedeckt.

Aus den Realisationen derer, die von Le Corbusiers Ideen zehren, sind die Achsen zwar verschwunden, aber die Befreiung von formalen Vorstellungen ist bisher kaum gelungen. Erste Versuche in den USA, das Chaos völlig ungebundener, von Rücksichtslosigkeit gekennzeichneter Baufreiheit zu überwinden, orientieren sich an einem aus Europa importierten Formalismus. In sich geschlossene Formen sind jedoch für die offene Gesellschaft unserer Städte unbrauchbar. Das für Hook gezeichnete Bild städtischer Bauformen zeigt am ehesten die mögliche Entwicklungsrichtung.

Townscape, viewed with the distance-shrinking eye of the telescopic lens. The images, consecutive in reality, are superimposed and symbolize a motion: the street with its furniture; outdated forms of buildings; the urban railway above street level with its elegant viaduct making us more conscious of the crudeness of some of the more recent concrete structures of roads and railways; behind them the many strata of the housing mountain in the new part of Siemensstadt, Berlin (cf. pages 204 ff.)

Stadtlandschaft, gesehen mit dem die Entfernungen zusammenraffenden Auge des Teleobjektivs. Die in Wirklichkeit hintereinander liegenden Bildebenen sind damit übereinanderkopiert und spiegeln einen Bewegungsablauf: Die Straße mit ihrem technischen Mobiliar, Hausformen einer vergangenen Zeit, die Schnellbahn in der zweiten Ebene, deren elegante Brückenformen erst durch die ungeschlachten Betonkonstruktionen späterer Verkehrsbauten ins Bewußtsein rücken, dahinter die Vielschichtigkeit der Wohngebirge im neuen Teil von Siemensstadt (siehe Seite 204 ff.)

Lake Meadows, Chicago (USA), 1950–1960 · Housing scheme for medium-income residents
Architects: Skidmore, Owings & Merrill

A typical American redevelopment scheme: the solution consists in razing everything to the ground and replacing it by bigger and more profitable blocks, placed at hygienic distances. The gaps will mainly be filled by the coloured metal of parked cars, against which a few poor young trees will compete in vain.
A vigorous protest against this "ghetto" production was written by a courageous woman architect who contrasts these outsize villages, frequently separated from their surroundings by fences and hedges, with the advantages of a continual process of urban regeneration (Jane Jacobs, "Death and Life of Great American Cities").

Chikago-Lake Meadows (USA), 1950–1960 · Siedlung für Bewohner mit mittleren Einkommen
Architekten: Skidmore, Owings & Merrill

Eines der typischen amerikanischen »Sanierungs«-Unternehmen: Die »Heilung« besteht in einer *tabula rasa* und dem Aufbau hoher, größere Rendite einbringender Klötze in hygienischen Abständen. Die Lücken werden vorwiegend mit farbigem Blech verziert sein, gegen das einige kümmerliche junge Baumstämmchen vergebens ankämpfen.
Der flammende Protest gegen diese »Ghetto«-Produktion blieb einer Architektenfrau vorbehalten, die diesen häufig mit Palisaden und Drahtzäunen von der Umwelt abgeschirmten Massendörfern die Vorteile sich fortlaufend regenerierender Stadtteile gegenüberstellt (Jane Jacobs, »Tod und Leben großer amerikanischer Städte«).

1 Typical apartment furniture

1 Typische Wohnungseinrichtung, die den architektonischen Vorstellungen der Architekten entspricht

3 Site plan, 1 in 5000. North is at top
Key to site plan:
A 21 storeys
B 13 storeys (see plan)
C 12 storeys
D Club house
E School
F Shopping centre, offices, bank
4 Typical floor plan, 1 in 500, of the 13-storey
block close to the club house. A north orientation is not regarded as detrimental if it is
compensated by the view, if the air-condition-
ing plant works well, and if the technical
equipment is up-to-date: fully equipped
kitchen; two bathrooms in the larger flats

3 Lageplan, 1:5000. Norden ist entgegen der
Schattenkonstruktion oben
Legende zum Lageplan:
A 21 Geschosse
B 13 Geschosse (siehe Grundriß)
C 12 Geschosse
D Klubhaus
E Schule
F Einkaufszentrum, Büros, Bank
4 Normalgrundriß des 13-geschossigen
Hochhauses neben dem Klubgebäude, 1:500.
Reine Nordlage wird nicht als Nachteil
empfunden, wenn dafür Aussicht geboten
wird, die Klimaanlage funktioniert und der
technische Standard zeitgemäß ist: voll ein-
gerichtete Küche, bei größeren Wohnungen
zwei Bäder

◀ 2 Aerial view from the south. In the foreground, the old buildings and planting
destined for demolition and one of the more
conventional rehousing schemes from which
the Lake Meadows Scheme (in the centre
of the photograph) is distinguished by a
higher architectural quality

2 Luftaufnahme von Süden. Im Vordergrund die alte, der Vernichtung anheimfal-
lende Bebauung und Bepflanzung, sowie
eines der üblichen Sanierungsquartiere, gegen das sich die Lake-Meadows-Siedlung
(Bildmitte) durch die architektonisch bessere Qualität abhebt

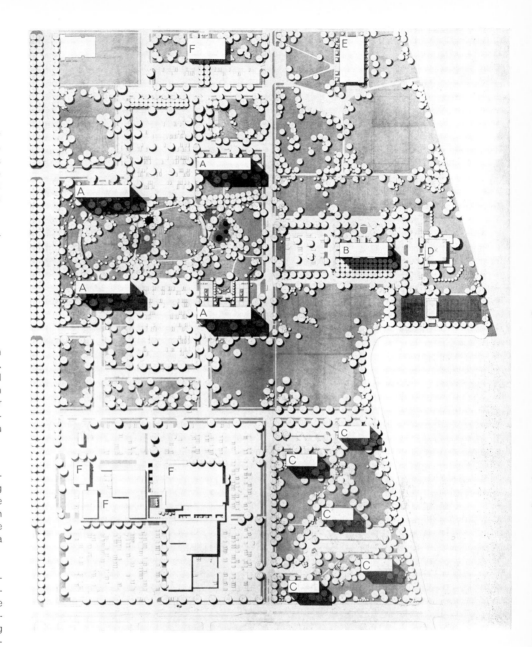

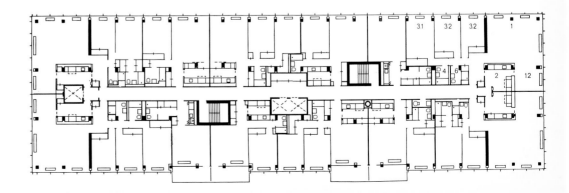

Rio de Janeiro, 1948 · Pedregulho district

Architect: Affonso Eduardo Reidy
Structural Engineers: Sydney Santos and David Astrachan

In contrast to other multi-storey housing schemes in South America based on Le Corbusier's ideas, this scheme, begun in 1947, for municipal employees in the low income groups offers a picture of orderly life.

The rent, which is deducted from salary, includes laundry costs for a certain quantity per head. The flats are inspected at intervals by officials of the Municipal Worker's Housing Board. On the basis of sociological surveys, the size of the flats has been varied over a wide range, from the single-room flatlet to the five-room flat with bathroom and kitchen.

Rio de Janeiro, 1948 · Quartier Pedregulho

Architekt: Affonso Eduardo Reidy
Ingenieure: Sydney Santos und David Astrachan

Das 1947 begonnene Wohnquartier für städtische Angestellte mit kleinem Einkommen bietet im Gegensatz zu anderen in Verfolgung der Idee Le Corbusiers entstandenen südamerikanischen Hochhausgruppen ein Bild geordneten Lebens.

In die vom Gehalt abgezogene Miete sind Wäschereinigungskosten für eine bestimmte Menge pro Kopf einbezogen. Die Wohnungen werden gelegentlich von Beamten des städtischen Arbeitersiedlungswerks besichtigt. Auf Grund soziologischer Untersuchungen sind die Wohnungsgrößen von der Einraumwohnung bis zur Fünf-Zimmer-Wohnung (mit Bad und Küche) variiert.

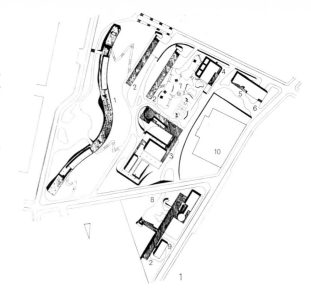

2 Aerial view of the site, which covers 12 acres. The westward fall is over 160 ft.

2 Luftaufnahme des 5 Hektar großen Baugeländes. Nach Westen 50 m Gefälle

3   4

1 Site plan, 1 in 5000. North, the sunny side, is at the bottom.
1 Block A with the kindergartens at access level; 2 Blocks of flats; 3 Elementary schools, gymnastic hall and swimming pool; 4 Clinic; 5 Laundry; 6 Shops; 7 Playground; 8 Pedestrian subway; 9 Creche; 10 Existing workshops
3 View from the west. In the foreground, left, the school and on the right, the clinic. The gardens are landscaped by Roberto Burle-Marx
4 The long block, adapted to the contour lines, seen from the hill side. The hollow brick walls screen the access galleries against the sun. The open floors ensure effective air circulation

1 Lageplan, 1:5000. Norden, als Sonnenseite, ist unten.
1 Block A mit den Kindergärten im Zugangs- oder Luft-Geschoß, 2 Wohnblöcke, 3 Volksschulen, Turnhalle und Schwimmbad, 4 Gesundheitszentrum, 5 Wäscherei, 6 Läden, 7 Spielplatz, 8 Fußgänger-Unterführung, 9 Kinderhort, 10 bestehende Werkstätten
3 Westansicht. Links im Vordergrund die Schule, rechts das Gesundheitszentrum. Die Gärten sind von Roberto Burle-Marx angelegt
4 Der lange, der Hügelform angepaßte Block von der Bergseite aus gesehen. Hohlziegelwände schirmen die Sonne an den Laubengängen ab. Die Stützengeschosse sorgen für eine gute Luftzirkulation

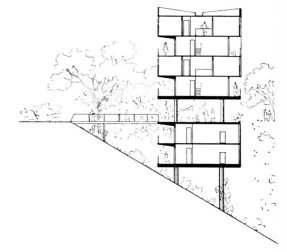

5 Section of Block A. As the street level coincides with the third floor, there is no need for lifts

5 Schnitt durch Block A. Durch den Zugang ins dritte Geschoß werden Aufzüge erspart

6 Plans, 1 in 200
First and second floor
Fourth and sixth floor
Fifth and seventh floor

6 Grundrisse, 1:200
Erstes und zweites Geschoß
Viertes und sechstes Geschoß
Fünftes und siebentes Geschoß

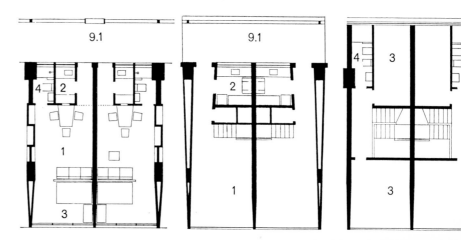

Alkmaar in North-Kennemerland (Netherlands), 1957/58
Urban development scheme
Architects: J. H. van den Broek and Jacob B. Bakema, assisted by J. M. Stokla

The conurbation of Dutch cities stretching from Rotterdam to Amsterdam hardly offers any further expansion facilities of the kind still available in Kennemerland, north of Amsterdam. To prevent a more or less unplanned sprawl in this area, it is intended to channel the expansion of the different communities into linear settlements. Identical basic units consisting of building volumes of different height and different orientation are composed in a rectangular pattern and connected in clusters to an 'activity strip' in the centre of the development area. Between the clusters, embedded in green, run the drainage canals indispensable in this reclamation area. The basic units of these residential districts are to comprise all types of dwellings. Experiments with smaller basic units, carried out at Pendrecht near Rotterdam, had not proved satisfactory.
The creation of a new urban district should show whether the schematic geometrical pattern offers the flexibility indispensable to urban life, especially if it were to be left to an architectural bureau to plan the townscape on uniform lines, down to the last detail.

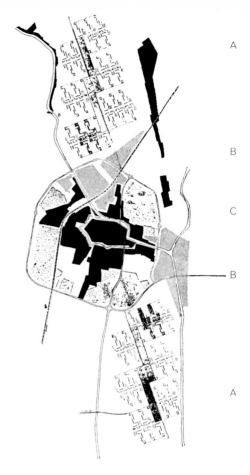

A

B

C

B

A

Alkmaar in Nord-Kennemerland (Niederlande), 1957/58 · Stadterweiterungsprojekt
Architekten: J.H. van den Broek und Jakob B. Bakema, Mitarbeiter: J.M.Stokla

Die »Randstadt Holland« zwischen Rotterdam und Amsterdam bietet kaum noch Erweiterungsmöglichkeiten, wie sie im Kennemerland nördlich von Amsterdam vorhanden sind. Um ein allmähliches, mehr oder weniger planloses Zuwachsen dieses Gebietes zu vermeiden, entstand der Plan, die Ausdehnungsbestrebungen der Gemeinden mit linearen Stadtvierteln aufzufangen. Gleichartige Grundelemente aus verschieden hohen und verschieden orientierten Baukörpern werden im rektangulären System zusammengestellt und gruppenweise an einen Aktivitätsstreifen in der Mitte des Erweiterungsgebietes angeschlossen. Zwischen den Gruppen liegen in Grünstreifen die im Polderland notwendigen Entwässerungskanäle. Die Grundelemente dieser Wohnquartiere sollen alle Wohnformen umfassen. Versuche mit kleineren Grundeinheiten in Rotterdam-Pendrecht hatten nicht befriedigt.
Der Bau eines Stadtviertels müßte erweisen, ob das schematisch geometrische Ordnungsschema die Variationsbreite zuläßt, die für ein städtisches Leben unumgänglich ist, besonders wenn ein Großbüro es unternehmen wollte, das Gesicht dieser Stadt bis zum letzten Detail einheitlich zu prägen.

A Linear city / Lineare Stadt
B Industry / Industrie
C Old city surrounded by a green belt / Altstadt mit Grüngürtel

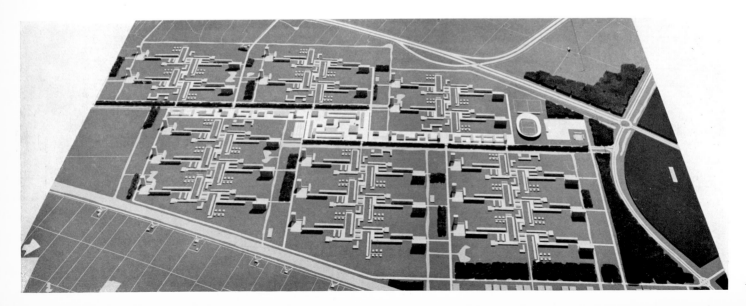

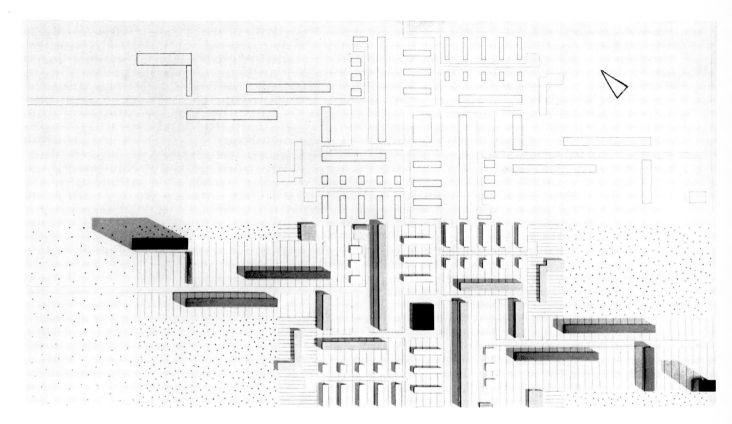

3 Part of site plan, 1 in 5000. Each unit is planned to contain 252 flats in the tower block, 568 flats or maisonettes in the other multi-storey blocks, and 134 single-family houses
4 Isometric view of a unit, seen from the west

3 Lageplanausschnitt, 1:5000. Vorgesehen in jeder Einheit sind 252 Wohnungen im Hochhaus, 568 Geschoßwohnungen und Maisonettes und 134 Einfamilienhäuser
4 Isometrie einer Grundeinheit, von Westen gesehen

◀1 Plan of Alkmaar, 1 in 10000
2 Model of the development area planned to the south of Alkmaar (A). The old city is at the right edge of the model. In the foreground, on the right, is an industrial estate. The central strip, standing out clearly, will contain the linear shopping centre

1 Situationsplan von Alkmaar, 1:10000
2 Modellfoto des südlich von Alkmaar geplanten Stadtviertels (A). Die Altstadt liegt rechts am Modellrand. Rechts im Vordergrund schließt sich ein Industriegelände an. Im heller angelegten Mittelstreifen ist das lineare Geschäftszentrum projektiert

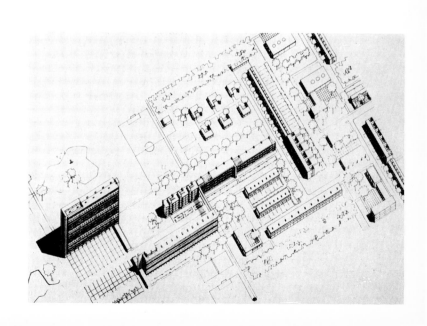

Cologne-New Town (Germany), 1962 · Competition project
Architect: Oswald Mathias Ungers

The competition programme called for different types of dwellings suitable for low-rent housing, and comprised an existing development plan which the architects were free to adapt to the types of dwellings chosen by them. In his effort to emphasize the plastic overall shape of the town, the architect placed a closely spaced cluster of tower blocks in the centre, matched by a ribbon-shaped block with pronounced three-dimensional treatment on the side of the housing estate which, like a wall, screens the estate against the traffic noise of the road running along the northeastern side. The multi-storey blocks consists of towers, each containing one or two rooms of a flat, arranged so that the free space in the centre may accommodate the sitting room, or that the core of the block may contain the staircase. The height of the towers containing these rooms differs so that both the layout plan and the size of the dwellings are varied. It is less fortunate that, in many cases, this part of the dwelling also serves as a passage to all the bedrooms and that, because of the many doors and sidelights, the room makes a somewhat unsettled impression.

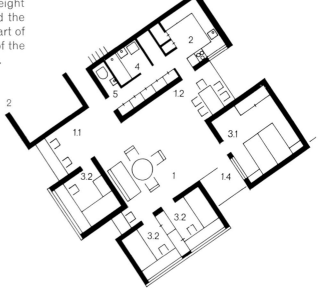

1 Site plan, 1 in 5000
A Tower block clusters, B Long wall, C Trading estate, D Shopping centre, E School, F Protestant community centre, G Roman Catholic church and kindergarten, H Garages

1 Lageplan, 1:5000
A Hochhausgruppen, B Lange Mauer, C Gewerbegebiet, D Ladenzentrum, E Schule, F Evangelisches Gemeindezentrum, G Katholische Kirche und Kindergarten, H Garagen

2 Plan of flat D (fig. 4), 1 in 200
3 Model of the tower block clusters, without the decks and glass partitions to be inserted between the towers
4 Part of the tower blocks cluster with different floor plans basement and ground floor on bottom; a top floor with roof terrace in the centre, and a typical floor plan on top
5 Plans of the "Long Wall" flats, 1 in 500

2 Grundriß der Wohnung D in Bild 4, 1:200
3 Modell der Turmhausgruppen, ohne die zwischen den Zimmertürmen eingebauten Geschoßdecken und Fensterwände
4 Ein Teil der Hochhausgruppe mit verschiedenen Geschoßgrundrissen; unten Keller und Erdgeschoß, in der Mitte ein Obergeschoß mit Dachterrasse und darüber ein Normalgeschoß
5 Grundrisse der Wohnungen an der langen Mauer, 1:500

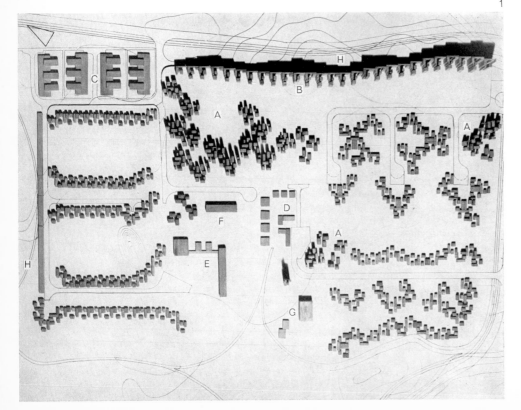

Köln-Neue Stadt (Deutschland), 1962 · Wettbewerbsprojekt
Architekt: Oswald Mathias Ungers

Bei dieser Wettbewerbsausschreibung wurden verschiedene Wohnungstypen gesucht, die für den Sozialen Wohnungsbau geeignet sind, wobei ein Bebauungsplan
vorgegeben war, der jedoch den entworfenen Typen angepaßt werden durfte. Der
Architekt hat in seinem Bestreben, die Stadt als plastische Großform sichtbar zu
machen, im Zentrum eine sehr dichte Hochhausgruppe angeordnet, die korrespon-
diert mit einem bandartigen, zur Siedlung hin stark gefalteten Hauskörper, der als
geschlossene Mauer den Lärm der im Nordosten verlaufenden Straße abschirmt.
Die Hochhäuser bestehen aus Türmen, die jeweils einen oder zwei Räume der
Wohnung beinhalten und die so aneinandergeschoben werden, daß im freibleiben-
den Mittelraum das Wohnzimmer oder, im Kern des Hauskörpers, das Treppenhaus
Platz finden. Die Zimmertürme enden in verschiedenen Geschoßhöhen, wodurch
Varianten in der Grundrißform und der Wohnungsgröße entstehen. Störend ist in
vielen Fällen, daß dieser Wohnteil zugleich Durchgangsraum zu sämtlichen Schlafräumen ist, und daß die vielen Türen und Lichtschlitze den Raum sehr unruhig
machen.

3

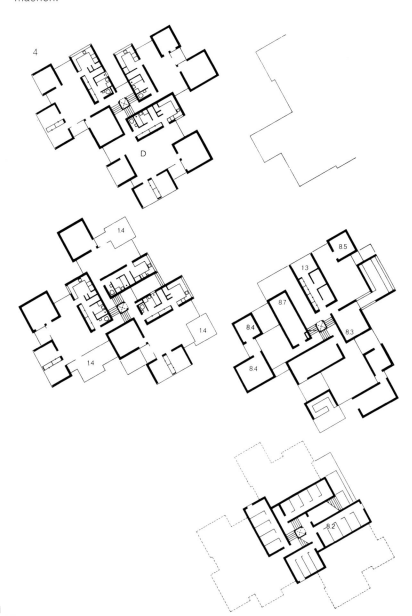

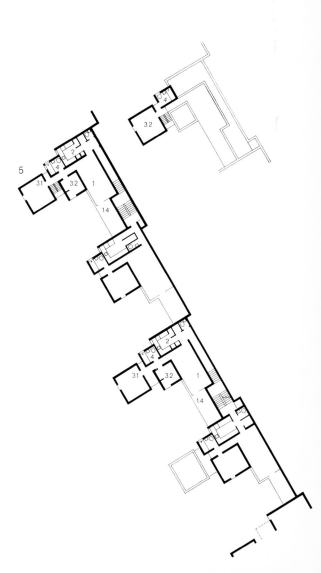

Project for Hook New Town (Britain), 1960/61
Architects: London County Council

The total sum of experience acquired from the building of earlier New Towns in Britain was to be put to good use in the development of Hook. Unfortunately this project, worked out with great attention to detail, for a New Town with a population of 100,000 has not been realised.

The most important conclusions drawn from the earlier New Towns were as follows:

The radial system is suitable neither for road traffic nor for a phased development of the town; on the other hand, a linear city can be built in stages, together with the central services required at any time.

The housing density in the inner areas must be at least 100 persons per acre to provide an adequate basis for the economic life of the centre.

The age composition should, as far as possible, be adapted to the national average so as to ensure a continual utilisation of public services, schools, etc.

The types of dwellings available must, from the outset, avoid the monotony of sociologically homogeneous housing schemes.

The industrial areas on the two short sides of the New Town ensure a better utilisation of the public transport services.

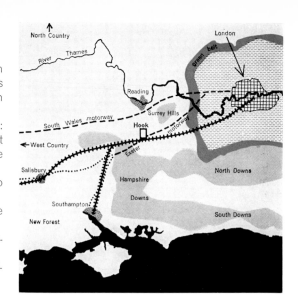

Projekt für die Stadt Hook (Großbritannien), 1960/61
Architekt: London County Council

Alle beim Bau der bisher in England und Schottland neu angelegten Städte gewonnenen Erfahrungen sollten beim Bau von Hook ausgewertet werden. Leider wurde diese mit großer Sorgfalt auf allen Teilgebieten erarbeitete Lösung einer Stadt für 100000 Einwohner nicht verwirklicht.

Die wichtigsten Erkenntnisse aus den ersten »New Towns« waren:

Das Radialsystem eignet sich weder für den Straßenverkehr, noch für den schrittweisen Aufbau der Stadt; eine lineare Stadt kann in Etappen einschließlich der jeweils erforderlichen zentralen Dienste gebaut werden.

Die Wohndichte in den inneren Stadtgebieten muß mindestens 250 Einwohner/ha betragen, um eine Basis für das wirtschaftliche Leben des Zentrums zu geben.

Die Alterszusammensetzung muß soweit wie möglich dem Landesdurchschnitt angepaßt werden, um eine kontinuierliche Benutzung der öffentlichen Dienste, Schulen usw. zu gewährleisten.

Das Wohnungsangebot muß von Anfang an die Monotonie soziologisch einseitig belegter Siedlungen vermeiden.

Industriegebiete an beiden Schmalseiten der neuen Stadt sorgen für gleichmäßige Auslastung der öffentlichen Verkehrsmittel.

1 Hook, once intended to be the last of the "New Towns", was planned at a point half-way between London and Southampton with good connection with the traffic arteries leading westwards from London, and at the northern edge of the recreational area of the North, South and Hampshire Downs

2 Section of the innermost residential zone adjoining the shopping centre (left), with a density of 100 persons per acre. The arrows indicate footbridges to the platform which covers all roads in the central area of the town

1 Hook, als letzte der New Towns, wurde auf halbem Wege nach Southampton mit Anschluß an die von London nach Westen führenden Strecken und am Nordrand der Erholungslandschaft »North-, South- und Hampshire-Downs« geplant

2 Schnitt durch das innerste, an das Geschäftsviertel (links) anschließende Wohngebiete mit einer Dichte von 250 Einwohnern je Hektar. Pfeilrichtung: Fußgängerüberwege zu der Plattform, die alle Straßen im mittleren Bereich der Stadt überdeckt

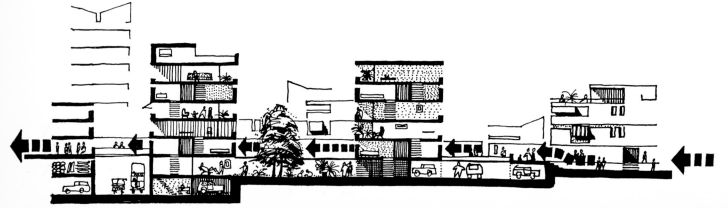

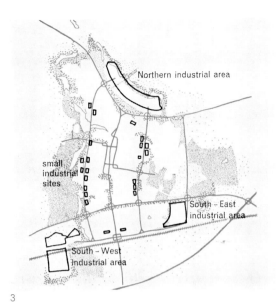

Northern industrial area

small industrial sites

South – East industrial area

South – West industrial area

3

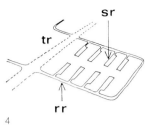

4

3 Position of the industrial areas
4 The road system in the residential areas
tr Town road, sr Service roads (culs-de-sac), rr Residential distributor road

3 Die Lage der Industrien
4 Das Straßensystem in den Wohngebieten
tr Stadtsammelstraße sr Stichstraße rr Wohnsammelstraße

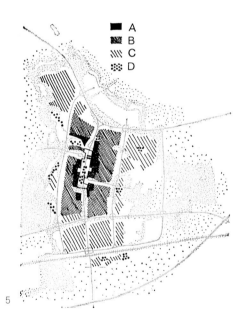

A
B
C
D

5

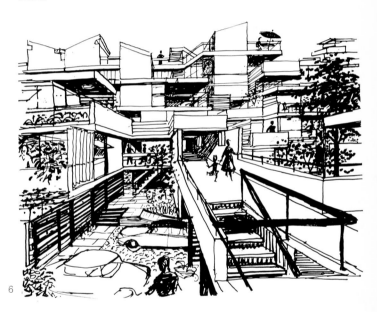

6

6/7 Two views of the town, conveying an impression of the manifold and variegated possibilities of development

6/7 Zwei Ansichten der Stadt, die einen Eindruck von den vielfältigen Bebauungsmöglichkeiten geben

7

5 Deliberately rejecting the radial system which is no longer suitable for modern urban conditions, the plan provided for a linear city along a public open space in the west, and an oblong commercial centre followed by residential zones with different densities
A Housing in the central area, B Inner residential zone, C Outer residential zone, D Special types of dwellings

5 In Abkehr von dem für die Bedingungen einer Stadt heute unbrauchbaren Radialsystem entstand der Plan einer linearen Stadt entlang einem Grünraum im Westen und mit einem längsgestreckten Geschäftsviertel, an das sich Wohnzonen verschiedener Dichte anschließen
A Wohnen im Kerngebiet, B Inneres Wohngebiet, C Äußeres Wohngebiet, D Sonderwohnformen

Searching for the New Town

Housing cannot be discussed without also discussing its town planning implications. Any simplifying model designed to demonstrate the inter-relations and complications of urban life is bound to fail. A schematic classification such as "traffic", "work", "housing" and "recreation" may do at the outset; it may even remain valid for the less inter-related activities in the country. But as a point of departure for town planning investigations, such a classification is too crude. A classification based on average values without taking into account the negative and positive extremes is always unrealistic, and therefore dangerous in that it tends to falsify facts. One of these over-simplifications which may have disastrous results is, e.g., that of regarding a dwelling as having a merely dormitory function. If such one-sided notions were accepted as a basis of the projects for the regeneration of European cities, this would make the evil ten times worse. Just as housing must be associated with many forms of work (with the obvious exception of heavy industries or plants with nuisance characteristics), with education and recreation, the workplace must become a special type of dwelling: an office worker may "dwell" in his office more intensely, and for a longer time of the day, than at home. Points of contact – and this is not meant in any derogatory sense – such as coffee bars, restaurants, pubs are just as important to the working area as they are to the residential or recreational areas. To find, despite this vitally necessary blending, a form of organisation for the town space as a whole which will provide centres of gravity, yet avoid excessive centralisation – this will be the task for the decades to come.

Auf der Suche nach der Neuen Stadt

Über Wohnungsbau läßt sich nicht reden, ohne auf städtebauliche Zusammenhänge einzugehen. Jedes vereinfachende Denkmodell versagt, mit dem die Verflechtung und Kompliziertheit des Lebens in einer Stadt erfaßt werden soll. Das schematische Einteilen in Verkehr, Arbeiten, Wohnen und sich Erholen ist für den Beginn einer Analyse allenfalls noch brauchbar, es mag auch für die sich wenig überschneidenden Lebensbereiche auf dem Land Gültigkeit haben, als Ausgangspunkt für städtebauliche Untersuchungen ist ein solches Gitter zu grob. Eine Einteilung nach Durchschnittswerten ohne Spitzen nach der negativen und positiven Seite ist immer lebensfremd und daher gefährlich in ihrer Verfälschung des Tatbestandes. Die Gleichsetzung von Wohnung und Schlafplatz ist z.B eine dieser Vereinfachungen mit verheerenden Folgen. Die Übernahme derartig einseitiger Vorstellungen in die Projekte zur Regenerierung der europäischen Städte würde das Übel verzehnfachen. Ebenso wie das Wohnen verknüpft sein muß mit vielen Formen des Arbeitens (Schwerindustrie oder störende Betriebe natürlich ausgenommen), der Erziehung und des Erholens, wird der Arbeitsplatz oft zu einer speziellen Wohnform: ein Büroarbeiter »wohnt« in diesem Büro intensiver und länger als zu Hause. Kontaktstellen, und das ist nicht abschätzig gemeint, wie Cafés, Speiselokale, Kneipen sind im Arbeitsbereich ebenso wichtig wie in den Wohn- oder Erholungsbereichen. Trotz dieser lebensnotwendigen Vermengung eine Organisationsform für den Gesamtraum der Stadt zu finden, die Schwerpunkte setzt, eine einseitige Zentralisierung aber vermeidet, ist die Aufgabe für die nächsten Jahrzehnte.

1 View of the Wolfsburg housing area near Fallerslebener Strasse, situated on the south bank of the Mittelland Canal opposite the Volkswagen Works
2 Parkland in the centre of the area

1 Ansicht der Siedlung an der Fallerslebener Straße, die dem Volkswagenwerk gegenüber am südlichen Ufer des Mittellandkanals liegt
2 Der Grünraum im Kern des Baugebiets

Wolfsburg (Germany), 1956/57 · Housing scheme of the Volkswagen Works
Architect: Paul G. Baumgarten

The long block of flats was developed in the nineteen-twenties and was then fitted into road networks originally designed for conventional street block type development. With its rigid pattern of, as it were, infinitely extensible concatenation, the long block is no longer acceptable. Even so, its advantages over the street block type of development practised in the 19th century are worth preserving: an opening up of the constricted street corridors; a better orientation of the dwellings; the union of two blocks by an intermediate park-strip which runs along the blocks right up to the road.
In post-war Germany, any rigid pattern was bound to be rejected. There was a general tendency to loosen up by arranging the blocks informally in staggered, fan-shaped patterns. Though identically orientated, the different dwellings are thus in different relationship with the environment.
The types of dwellings in this housing scheme at Wolfsburg are fairly akin; they meet the requirements of the sponsors, i.e. the Volkswagen Works, whose primary interest understandably lies in housing their own employees who make similar or identical demands on their dwellings.

Wolfsburg (Deutschland), 1956/57 · Siedlung des Volkswagenwerkes
Architekt: Paul G. Baumgarten

Der Zeilenbau wurde in den zwanziger Jahren entwickelt und man bediente sich der für blockweise Randbebauung gedachten Straßensysteme. In seiner Starrheit, der sozusagen unendlich fortsetzbaren Reihung wird er nicht mehr akzeptiert. Dennoch sollten die Vorteile bewahrt bleiben, die sich gegenüber der Randbebauung des 19.Jahrhunderts ergaben: Öffnung der beengenden Straßenschluchten, bessere Orientierung der Wohnungen, Verbindung zweier Zeilenreihen durch einen jeweils dazwischenliegenden Grünbereich, der entlang der Hauszeilen bis an die Straße heranreicht.
In der Nachkriegszeit mußte in Deutschland jede strenge Reihung auf Ablehnung stoßen. Allgemein wurde eine Auflockerung durch fächerförmige, teilweise versetzte Anordnung der Baukörper angestrebt. Die in der Orientierung gleichartigen Wohnungen stehen so zum Außenraum in jeweils unterschiedlicher Beziehung. Die Wohnungstypen dieses Wolfsburger Siedlungsteils sind alle relativ ähnlich; sie genügen den Ansprüchen des Volkswagenwerks als Bauherrn, das verständlicherweise in erster Linie an der Unterbringung von Betriebsangehörigen interessiert ist, die ähnliche oder gleichartige Ansprüche an die Wohnung stellen.

3 Compared with the four-storey blocks, the proportions of the three-storey rows are more pleasing. Because of the poor building soil, some of the blocks were given a facade cladding consisting of small-size asbestos cement boards
4 Section, 1 in 200. The bright staircase, receiving daylight from above and through the rear walls of the loggias, has induced the tenants to grow climbing plants on all the staircase landings
5/6 Plans, 1 in 200. Because of the wide span of the floors between the cross-walls, it seemed advisable to strengthen the structure by making all the party walls 4.$^3/_4$" thick

3 Gegenüber den meist viergeschossigen Bauten heben sich die Proportionen der dreigeschossigen Zeilen vorteilhaft ab. Ein Teil der Häuser erhielt wegen des schlechten Baugrunds eine Fassadenverkleidung aus kleinformatigen Eternitplatten
4 Schnitt, 1:200. Das helle, von oben und von den Loggia-Rückwänden her belichtete Treppenhaus hat die Bewohner animiert, auf allen Treppenabsätzen rankende Grünpflanzen zu ziehen
5/6 Grundrisse, 1:200. Die weit gespannten Decken des Querwandtyps ließen es ratsam erscheinen, alle Zwischenwände 12 cm dick aufzumauern, um eine bessere Aussteifung zu gewährleisten

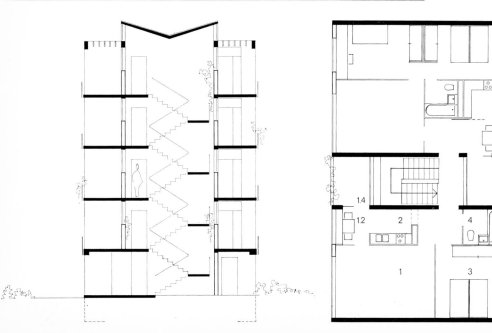

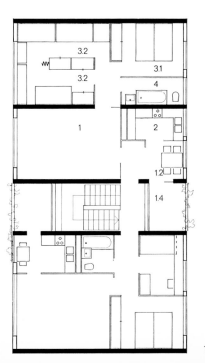

7   Site plan, 1 in 5000. North is at top. A Home for the aged,
numbers = storeys

7   Lageplan, 1:5000, Norden ist oben. A Altenheim,
Zahlen = Geschoßzahlen

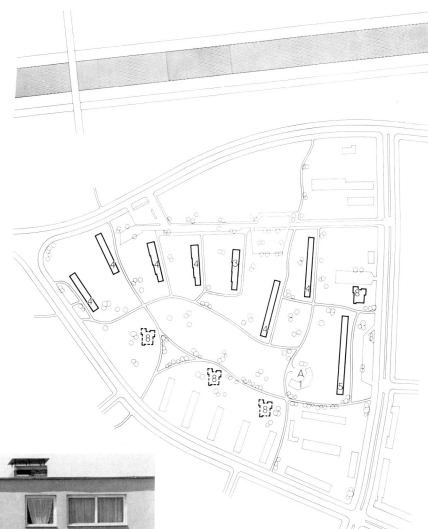

8   Depending on the purpose of the rooms, the windows
differ in size and shape. The additional lighting for the
staircase across the loggia has not been found disturbing

8   Die Fenster sind dem Zweck der Räume entsprechend
in Größe und Form unterschiedlich. Die zusätzliche Be-
lichtung des Treppenhauses über die Loggia hinweg hat
sich nicht als störend erwiesen

Bron-Parilly, Lyon (France), 1959
Town planning consultant: René Gagès
Architects: René Gagès, Frank Grimal, Pierre Bourdeix

For the City of Lyon, with a home population of 700,000 and serving as the capital of a conurbation of about 5 million, a programme has been developed for creating new urban districts in the outskirts.

The first of these, developed by consulting architects appointed by the Paris Ministry of Reconstruction, covers an area of approx. 75 acres, housing 10,000 people in 2607 dwellings. It is bordered on the west by an amply laid out boulevard, and is crossed by a highway with heavy traffic, leading to the Alps. The southern boundary is formed by woods and heath. The blocks are grouped so as to form three school areas and a shopping and cultural centre which adjoins the old suburb of Bron (in the north-east). This old suburb with low and irregularly placed houses – rather "unorganized", to talk in architects' language – is completely cut off from its surroundings by the high blocks of flats on its west and south sides. This unorganized zone has been given an unmistakable boundary by a nearly 1000 ft. long multi-storey block, flanked by point blocks.

Lyon Bron-Parilly (Frankreich), 1959
Städtebauliche Planung: René Gagès
Architekten: René Gagès mit Frank Grimal und Pierre Bourdeix

Für Lyon, die 750000 Einwohner zählende Hauptstadt einer Agglomeration von etwa 5 Millionen Menschen, wurde ein Programm zur Schaffung neuer Stadtviertel in den Außenbezirken entwickelt.

Das erste Gebiet, das unter der zentralen Leitung des Pariser Wiederaufbauministeriums durch von diesem eingesetzte beratende Architekten entstand, beherbergt auf einer Fläche von 30 Hektar in 2607 Wohnungen etwa 10000 Einwohner. Es wird im Westen von einem großangelegten Boulevard begrenzt und von einer stark befahrenen Ausfallstraße zu den Alpen durchquert. Im Süden grenzt es an ein Wald- und Heidegelände. Bei der mit den Gebäudemassen vorgenommenen Komposition entstehen drei Einzugsbereiche für Schulen und ein Geschäfts- und kulturelles Zentrum, das an der Nahtstelle zum alten Ortsteil Bron (im Nordosten) liegt. Dieser alte, niedrig und offen bebaute, wie die Architekten sagen, »nicht organisierte« Ortsteil wird nach Westen und Süden durch die Hochhausfassaden völlig von der Umgebung abgeschnitten. Die im Westen liegende, von Punkthäusern flankierte, 300 m lange Fassade soll dieses »Unordnungsgebiet« eindeutig begrenzen.

1 Site plan of the Bron-Parilly housing area
A Schools, B Cultural institutions, C Administration,
D Shops and market square

1 Lageplan des Neubaugebietes Bron-Parilly
A Schulen, B kulturelle Einrichtungen, C Verwaltung,
D Läden und Marktplatz

3–6

2 Aerial view of the area seen from northwest

2 Luftbild der Siedlung, von Nordwesten gesehen

3–6 Monumental effects are created, mainly, by the abrupt
rise of the multi-storey blocks

3–6 Monumentale Wirkungen werden vor allem durch das
übergangslose Aufsteigen der Hochhausscheiben hervorgerufen

7 Detail of facade / Fassadendetail

8–12 Plans of the six types of dwellings, 1 in 200. 520 single-room flats (with kitchen and bath), 802 two-room flats, 720 three-room flats, 324 four-room flats, 158 five-room flats, 83 six-room maisonettes. The six standard plans can be combined in many different ways around the access gallery, which is generally provided on every third floor. A notable feature is the high proportion of dwellings with four, five or six rooms, which is in keeping with French family planning policy. The basic plan unit is a space of 2.5 metres (8'2") height, 5.3 metres (17'5") length and 2.4 metres (7'10") width, flanked by bearing crosswalls

8–12 Grundrisse der Wohnungstypen, 1:200. Grundelement der Planung ist ein von tragenden Querwänden begrenzter, im Licht 2,5 m hoher Raum von 5,3 × 2,4 m. Sechs Typengrundrisse eignen sich zu vielfältigen Kombinationen um den meist in jedem dritten Geschoß gebauten Laubengang herum. Beachtlich ist der hohe Anteil an Vier-, Fünf- und Sechs-Zimmer-Wohnungen, der in Übereinstimmung mit der französischen Familienpolitik notwendig wird. Die Siedlung enthält 520 Ein-Zimmer-Wohnungen, 802 Zwei-Zimmer-Wohnungen, 720 Drei-Zimmer-Wohnungen, 324 Vier-Zimmer-Wohnungen, 158 Fünf-Zimmer-Wohnungen und 83 Sechs-Zimmer-Wohnungen

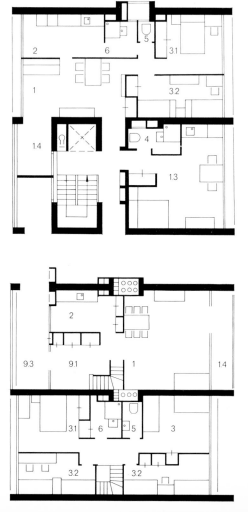

Park Hill, Sheffield (England), 1961

Project: The Sheffield Corporation City Architect's Department
City Architect: J. L. Womersley, assisted by W. L. Clunie and U. F. Warren
Project Architects: J. Lynn, A. V. Smith, J. S. Smith, G. I. Richmond
Structural engineers: Ove Arup and Partners

Park Hill can be regarded as a small-scale forerunner to what is being planned at Le Mirail, Toulouse. The living habits of the population are to be preserved by the 'decks' and courtyards; to replace the terrace-house streets which have been demolished, pedestrian precincts are being formed. In due course, the sense of common ownership, at present non-existent, is to be fostered; only then will it be possible, for instance, to plant trees in the courtyards. The rather hard and, in its over-concentration, seemingly inhuman rehousing scheme must be regarded as an attempt at converting the single-family slums into a townscape whose residents are to gather their first experience of joint amenities so that they can escape from the irritating isolation of their previous environment.

Sheffield-Park Hill (Großbritannien), 1961

Entwurf: The Sheffield Corporation City Architect's Department
City Architect: J. L. Womersley, Mitarbeiter: W. L. Clunie, U. F. Warren
Project Architects: J. Lynn, A. V. Smith, J. S. Smith, G. I. Richmond
Ingenieure: Ove Arup und Partner

Park Hill kann als Vorläufer »im kleinen Format« für das angesehen werden, was in Toulouse Le Mirail geplant ist.
Die Lebensgewohnheiten der Bevölkerung sollen mit den »Decks« und Höfen erhalten bleiben; wie in den abgerissenen Reihenhausstraßen bilden sich bekanntere, vertrautere Zonen. Allmählich soll sich der zur Zeit nicht vorhandene Sinn für gemeinschaftliches Eigentum herausbilden; erst dann können beispielsweise in den Höfen Bäume gepflanzt werden. Das hart und in seiner starken Konzentration »unmenschlich« erscheinende Sanierungsprojekt muß als ein Versuch gewertet werden, die Einfamilienhaus-Slums in eine Stadtlandschaft zu verwandeln, deren Bewohner erste Erfahrungen mit gemeinsamen Einrichtungen sammeln und so der provozierenden Isolierung ihrer bisherigen Umgebung entrinnen.

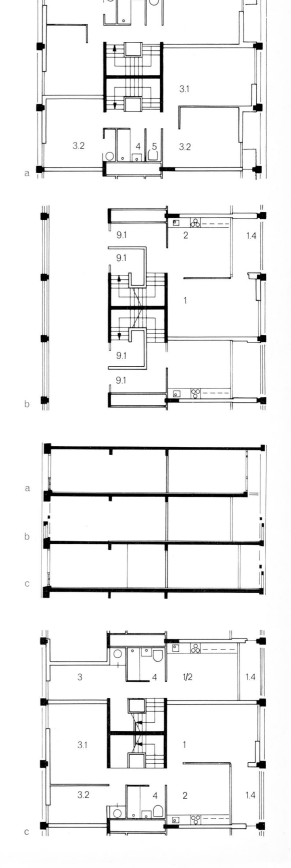

1 Typical plans and part-section, 1 in 200
a Upper floor of maisonettes, b Access level and lower floor of maisonettes c Living room floor below entrance level

1 Typische Grundrisse und Teilschnitt, 1:200
a Obergeschoß der Maisonettes, b Zugangsdeck und unteres Maisonette-Geschoß, c Wohngeschoß unter dem Zugangsdeck

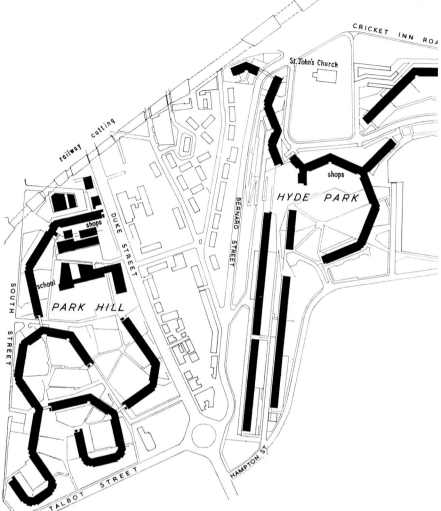

2 Corner of one of the courtyards, with access gallery and a fire escape which, leading to the adjacent maisonette, meets the official requirements

3 Site plan, 1 in 5000. The slope falls northwards, but the cornice level of the Park Hill blocks remains the same throughout; with the thus increasing height of the blocks, the courtyards are expanded. In the southern part, they merely contain playgrounds and lawns; at the northern end, however, they enclose a shopping centre and a school. Some 2900 people can be housed in households of normal size, and 3448 if all households were of maximum size. The maximum net density is 190 persons per acre or, if the park is included, just over 100 persons per acre

2 Detail einer Innenhofecke mit dem Laubengang und einem Austritt, der als Fluchtweg zum benachbarten Maisonette die Bestimmungen erfüllt

3 Lageplan, 1:5000. Der Hang fällt nach Norden ab, die Traufhöhe der Bebauung ist einheitlich; die Innenhöfe werden mit wachsender Gebäudehöhe immer größer. Sie umschließen im Südteil nur Spiel- und Rasenflächen, am Nordende dagegen ein Ladenzentrum und eine Schule. Bei Normalbelegung 2900, bei äußerster Belegung 3448 Bewohner. Dichte maximal netto 475 Einwohner je Hektar, einschließlich der Parkanlagen 256 Einwohner je Hektar

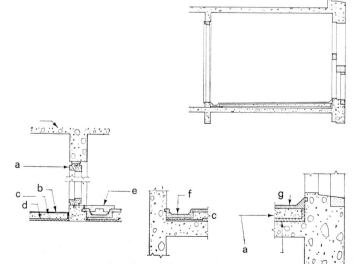

4 Details of access gallery, 1 in 10, with section, 1 in 100.
a Door, b Plastic tiles, c Screed, d Insulation, e Sill, f Gutter, g Mastic asphalt

4 Details des Zugangsdecks, 1:10, mit Übersichtsschnitt, 1:100
a Türe, b Kunststoff-Fliesen, c Estrich, d Isolierung, e Schwellenplatte, f Rinne, g Gußasphalt

192

5 View of the Park Hill scheme from the east, across one block of the adjacent Hyde Park scheme now under construction
6 One of the access galleries which is much more akin to a street than, e.g. the lifeless nightmarish corridors in Le Corbusier's housing units
7/8 Courtyards in the southern and central parts. The access galleries which are, on the hill side, connected by ramps, bridge the gaps between the different blocks

5 Ansicht der Park-Hill-Baugruppe, über eine Zeile der anschließend begonnenen Hyde-Park-Bebauung hinweg (von Osten)
6 Ein Zugangsdeck, das viel mehr Straßencharakter aufweist als etwa die leblosen, unheimlichen »Innenstraßen« in Le Corbusiers Wohneinheiten
7/8 Die Innenhöfe im Süd- und im Mittelteil. Die Zugangsdecks, die an der Bergseite über Rampen erschlossen sind, überbrücken die Lücken zwischen den einzelnen Hauskörpern

Le Mirail, Toulouse (France), 1962
Architects: Georges Candilis, Alexis Josic, Shadrach S. Woods

French history has created a centralism resulting in such an over-concentration of activities in the Paris region that it is now intended, with the aid of the Fourth Plan, to relieve the Paris area by shifting economic activities to the regional centres throughout the country and to other areas scheduled for special development. If this decentralisation is not also extended to all the administrative processes and to the responsibilities of the Departments, these attempts may well be doomed to failure.

Toulouse is to become the administrative centre for the Languedoc Departments and is, according to plans obtained from a competition, required to house another 100,000 people.

The consultant architects entrusted with the development plan are working in excellent co-operation: Woods acting as general staff, Josic as aesthete, and Candilis as a mighty advocate have been able to gather the enthusiastic youth of many countries. The creation of an urban unit of such a size within a period of ten years depends on the elimination, made possible by new legislation, of ground speculation and on a financial backing totalling more than £ 100 millions. At the future sale of the low buildings and shops, 40 per cent. of the purchase price will have to be covered by private mortgages.

The basic idea of the scheme is described by Candilis as follows:

"However high the quality of major urban development schemes may have been in the past, experience has shown that the intrinsic idea has often gone astray because, over a lengthy period of time, the work had to be carried out by different teams, governed by often changing constraints. We therefore tried to create, for Le Mirail, an urban structure which can easily be adapted to changing conditions by being built in stages. It consists of three basic elements: a concentration zone serving as the main venue of public activities; the traffic network ensuring access and distribution; the public open space. All these elements are connected with each other directly or indirectly, run parallel to each other or are superimposed on each other. They extend in ribbons over the entire development area and jointly form the heart and body of the future conurbation. This is our basic idea."

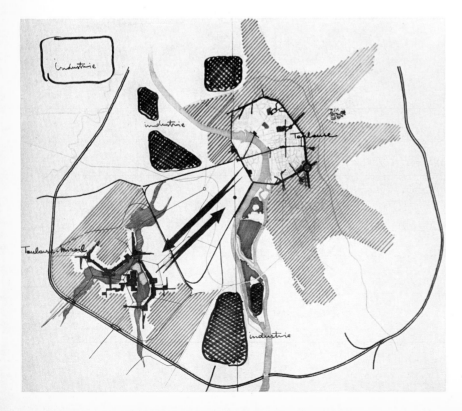

1 Sketch: Toulouse, old and new

1 Skizze: Toulouse alt und neu

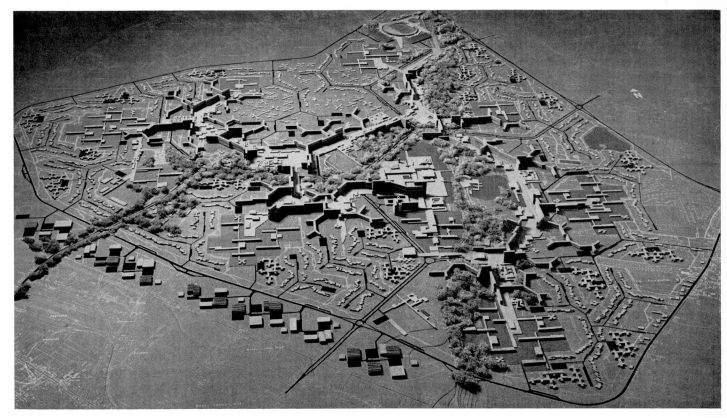

Toulouse Le Mirail (Frankreich), 1962
Architekten: Georges Candilis, Alexis Josic, Shadrach S. Woods

Die historische Entwicklung hat Frankreich einen Zentralismus beschert, der eine derartige Überbelastung der Pariser Region hervorgerufen hat, daß man heute mit Hilfe des »4. Planes« durch Verlagerung der wirtschaftlichen Aktivkräfte in die regionalen Zentren des ganzen Landes und in andere, unter bestimmten Gesichtspunkten zu fördernde Gegenden Entlastung für Paris schaffen will. Solange nicht eine Dezentralisierung aller Verwaltungsvorgänge und eine Verlagerung der Kompetenzen in die Departements folgt, sind diese Versuche wohl erfolglos.
Toulouse soll Verwaltungszentrum des Departements Languedoc werden und nach den in einem Wettbewerb ermittelten Plänen 100000 Einwohner mehr aufnehmen.
Das Büro der mit der Planung beauftragten Architekten zeigt eine glänzende Zusammenarbeit: Woods als Generalstäbler, Josic als Ästhet und Candilis als sprachgewaltiger Anwalt konnten die begeisterungsfähige Jugend vieler Länder um sich versammeln. Die durch die Gesetze mögliche Ausschaltung der Bodenspekulation und die Finanzierung des Gesamtaufwandes von über 1,2 Milliarden DM sind Voraussetzung für den Bau einer derart großen Stadteinheit innerhalb von 10 Jahren. Beim späteren Verkauf der Flachbauten und Läden sollen 40% der Summe durch private Hypotheken gedeckt werden. Candilis beschreibt die Planung wie folgt:
»So gut auch die Pläne für größere städtebauliche Einheiten sein mögen, die Erfahrung zeigt, daß die ihnen innewohnende Idee oft verlorengeht, weil sie in einem längeren Zeitraum mit häufig wechselnden Einschränkungen von verschiedenen Teams ausgeführt werden. Wir versuchten darum für Le Mirail ein urbanes Gerüst zu schaffen, das sich den wechselnden Bedingungen bei der Realisierung in Bauabschnitten leicht anpassen läßt. Es besteht aus drei Grundelementen: einer Hauptverdichtungszone als dem Kraftfeld des öffentlichen Lebens, dem Verkehrsnetz, das Zugang und Verteilung regelt, und der Grünzone. Alle diese Elemente sind miteinander mittelbar oder unmittelbar verbunden, gehen parallel oder überlagern sich; sie entwickeln sich bandartig über das zur Verfügung stehende Gelände und bilden als Ganzes Herz und Körper der künftigen städtischen Agglomeration. Das ist unsere Grundidee.«

2 Comprehensive view of the new development area, seen from the south. The hexagonal road system is independent of the meandering lines of the blocks of flats and offices

2 Gesamtansicht des Neustadtgebietes von Süden gesehen. Das in Sechseckformen aufgebaute Straßensystem ist losgelöst vom System der schlangenartigen Wohnblöcke und Geschäftshäuser

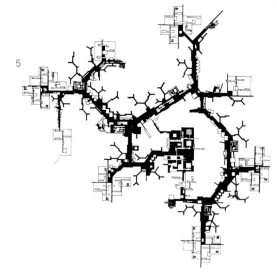

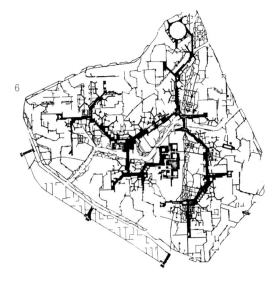

3 Part-view of the model. The open spaces embody existing parks and small housing units
4 The same part of the town, seen against the background of surrounding buildings

3 Ausschnitt aus der Planung. In den Freiräumen vorhandene Parkanlagen und individuelle Wohnbebauung
4 Der gleiche Teil der Stadt im Zusammenhang mit der umgebenden Bebauung gesehen

5 Diagram showing the distribution of walkways in the central zone, 1 in 50,000. It is hoped that Languedoc temperament will see to it that the vast pedestrian precincts are filled with life
6 The walkways throughout the new development area, 1 in 50,000
7 General plan, 1 in 25,000, omitting the low housing units within the open spaces. The old City of Toulouse is situated in the north-west. On the south-western side, at the edge of the new redevelopment area, a ribbon of light industry

5 Schema der Verteilung der Fußwege in der Mittelzone, 1:50000. Man hofft, daß südfranzösisches Temperament die ausgedehnten Fußgängerebenen mit Leben füllen wird
6 Die Fußgängerwege im Gesamtbereich der Stadt, 1:50000
7 Generalplan, 1:25000, ohne die Flachbauten in den Freiräumen. Die alte Stadt Toulouse liegt im Nordwesten. Im Südwesten am Rand der Neustadt eine Zone für Leichtindustrie

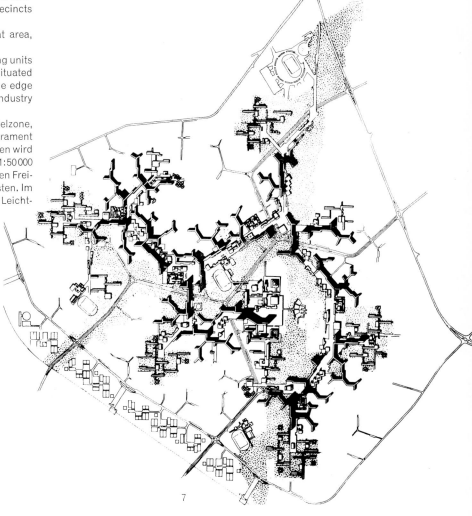

7

8 The traffic separation system: From the car parks, walkways lead to the open ground floors of the blocks of flats (thin arrows). At the shopping centres are underground car parks
A Shopping centre, B Schools, C Cars, D Car park, E Offices and light industry, F Parkland

8 Das System der getrennten Verkehrswege: Von den Parkplätzen aus Fußwege im Stützengeschoß der Wohnbauten (dünne Pfeile). Bei den Einkaufszentren unterirdische Garagen
A Einkaufszentrum, B Schulen, C Autos, D Parkplatz, E Handel, F Park

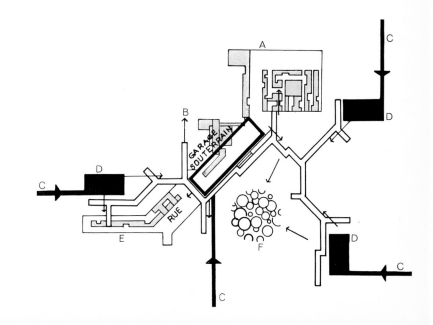

Genoa (Italy), 1951–1954 · "Villa Bernabò Brea" INA Casa housing scheme
Architects: Giulio Zappa, Giovanni Grossi Bianchi, Luigi Carlo Daneri

This housing estate, erected in an old park, comprises some 1800 dwelling units.
Making the most of the unique position offering a southwards view on the Mediterranean, the blocks follow the contour lines up the hill. Block E, which forms as it
were a bridge across the dale, contains a number of shops facing a covered passage-
way which links up with the ground floor level on either side. Block C likewise contains shops as well as a welfare clinic. A kindergarten is huddled into the dell just
above the 'bridge' house, an elementary school is placed at the southern tip of the
park. In the 'duplex' type maisonettes placed below the "street level floor" of Block E
(which call for effective sound insulation), straight flights of stairs can be placed
at right angles to the cross-walls despite the small wall spacing (4.0 metres or, say,
13 ft.).
With their identical details and their chessboard pattern of retracted wall units and
parapets, which would be unsuitable for a harder, more northern climate, the blocks
are embedded in the green luxuriance of the park in which the gaiety of Mediterranean joie-de-vivre is symbolized and harmonized.

Genua (Italien), 1951–1954 · INA-Casa-Siedlung »Villa Bernabò Brea«
Architekten: Giulio Zappa, Giovanni Grossi Bianchi, Luigi Carlo Daneri

Die in einem alten Park gebaute Siedlung umfaßt etwa 1800 Wohnungen. Unter
Ausnutzung der einzigartigen Lage mit dem Blick nach Süden auf das Mittelmeer
staffeln sich die Baukörper, durchweg den Höhenlinien folgend, den Hang hinauf.
Haus E, das sich wie eine Brücke quer über das Tal legt, enthält in einem beiderseits ebenerdig auslaufenden Stützengeschoß Läden; im Haus C sind ebenfalls
Läden und eine Station zur sozialen und ärztlichen Betreuung eingebaut. Ein Kindergarten schmiegt sich in die Talmulde oberhalb des Brückenhauses, eine Volksschule liegt im Südzipfel des Parkgeländes. Bei den unter dem »Straßengeschoß«
in Haus E angeordneten Reihenhauswohnungen mit versetzten Geschossen (die
eine gute Schalldämmung voraussetzen) können gerade Treppenläufe trotz des
geringen Wandabstandes (4 m) in Deckenspannrichtung eingebaut werden.
Die Gleichartigkeit der Detailformen und das, in einem härteren nördlichen Klima
unzweckmäßige, Spiel der schachbrettartig zurückspringenden Wandteile und
Brüstungsflächen sind eingebettet in das Grün der Parkbäume, das die Munterkeit
südländischer Ausdrucksfreude zusammenfaßt und harmonisiert.

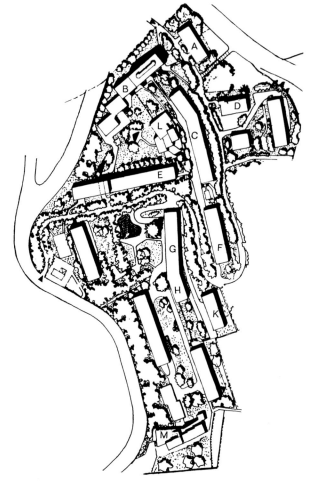

1 Site plan, 1 in 2000. Shops and welfare clinic are placed
in Block C, further shops are in Block E.
L denotes the kindergarten, M the elementary school
2 A view in the same direction as fig. 3 but seen from
Block E. In the foreground is the kindergarten, on the right
Block C, on the left Block B, in the background Block A

1 Lageplan, 1:2000. Läden und Räume für ärztliche und
soziale Betreuung sind in Haus C, weitere Läden in Haus
E eingebaut.
L Kindergarten, M Volksschule
2 In der gleichen Blickrichtung wie in Bild 3, jedoch vom
Haus E aus gesehen: der Kindergarten, rechts Haus C,
links Haus B, im Hintergrund Haus A

3 View towards north-east, with Block E in the foreground
and the multi-storey block, marked B in the plan, in the
background

3 Blick nach Nordosten auf Haus E im Vordergrund und
das Hochhaus B

4 The southwards view from the roof of Block E shows how the blocks, following the contour lines, recede to permit the sea view. The public open space, otherwise often neglected in Italian housing schemes, here retains a connection down the valley with the adjoining gardens

4 Vom Dach des Hauses E aus nach Süden gesehen geben die den Höhenlinien folgenden Hauskörper den Blick auf das Meer frei. Das sonst in italienischen Siedlungen meist stiefmütterlich behandelte Grün bleibt hier in Talrichtung mit den benachbarten Gärten verbunden

5

5 North side of the access gallery type (Block D)
6 Plans of the two lower floors of Block E, 1 in 500. The maisonette entrances are on the hill side, a few steps above the bottom of the valley
7/8 Upstream and downstream sides of the 'bridge' house (Block E). Below the floor containing the shops are the maisonettes shown in the plans

5 Nordseite des Laubenganghauses D
6 Grundrisse der beiden unteren Geschosse in Haus E, 1:500. Die Wohnungseingänge liegen an der Bergseite, wenige Stufen über der Talsohle
7/8 Die Berg- und die Talseite des »Brückenhauses« (E). Unter dem Ladengeschoß die im Grundriß gezeigten Wohnungstypen

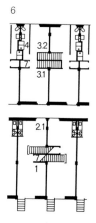

6

7

8

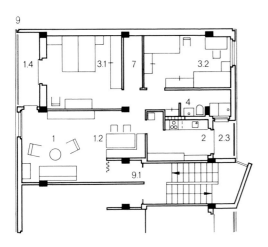

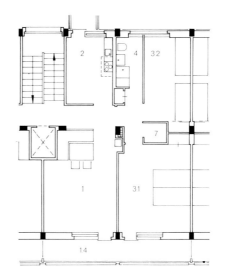

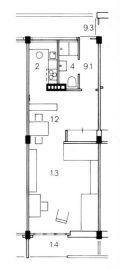

9 Plans, 1 in 200; left to right: Blocks F, B and D
10 A view up the valley showing, from left to right: Blocks B, G, H, F and K

9 Grundriß, 1:200, von links nach rechts Haus F, B und D
10 Blick talaufwärts, von links nach rechts Haus B, G, H, F und K

1 View of model / Modellfoto

LSM Slowacki, Lublin (Poland), under construction 1965
Architects: Oskar Hansen, Zofia Hansen, Bohdan Ofnalewski
Structural engineer: Jerzy Dowgiallo

The development scheme is planned for a population of 104,000 and will, apart from the dwellings, contain three schools, four kindergartens, two creches, a shopping and trading centre, a clinic, and a district heating plant. In planning the layout, it is necessary to take into account not only the traffic noise but, in particular, also the prevailing winds which come from the west or west-south-west. Long blocks, forming obtuse angles in the plan, afford protection to a zone open to the south and south-east which contains parks, play and sports grounds and other civic amenities.
On the west side are the access roads, car parks and garages. Pedestrian access is through the "wind protection wall" to the shorter blocks of graduated height where a "micro-climate" is being created, on all sides except the south. This quiet residential zone is followed by a ribbon of playgrounds for toddlers, and finally by the more noisy sports grounds for school children (Fig. 2).
The concrete structure, consisting of a longitudinal centre wall, floor slabs and outer wall stanchions, is to be supplemented by light-weight components so as to obtain the greatest possible flexibility in the layout of the dwellings.

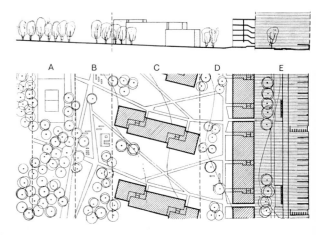

2 Schematic plan of the different zones, 1 in 2000
A Noisy zone for young people, forming part of the open space, B Children's playground, C Quiet residential zone, D Elderly people and toddlers, E Noisy zone along the road and garages, slightly mitigated by a row of trees in front of the blocks

2 Schema der verschiedenen Zonen, 1:2000.
A Lärmzone der Jugend im Parkstreifen, B Kinderspielplätze, C ruhige Wohnzone, D Alte und Kleinkinder, E Lärmzone der Straße und des Garagenstreifens, durch eine Baumreihe vor den Häusern etwas abgeschwächt

Lublin-LSM Slowacki (Polen), im Bau seit 1965
Architekten: Oskar Hansen, Zofia Hansen, Bohdan Ofnalewski
Ingenieur: Jerzy Dowgiallo

Das Quartier ist für 104000 Einwohner geplant und soll außer den Wohnungen 3 Schulen, 4 Kindergärten, 2 Kinderhorte, ein Einkaufs- und Handwerkerzentrum, eine Gesundheitsstation und eine Heizzentrale erhalten. Neben dem Verkehrslärm muß bei der Anlage der Siedlung vor allem der vorwiegend aus Westen oder West-Südwest wehende Wind berücksichtigt werden. Langgestreckte, in stumpfen Winkeln gebrochene Baukörper schirmen eine nach Süden und Südosten offene Zone mit Parkanlagen, Sport- und Spielflächen und Gemeinschaftsbauten ab.
Im Westen liegen Zufahrtswege, Parkierungsflächen und Garagen. Die Zugänge führen durch den »Windwall« hindurch zu den kurzen, abgestuften Zeilen, zwischen denen in geschützter, nach Süden offener Lage ein »Mikroklima« geschaffen wird. Auf diese ruhige Wohnzone folgt ein Streifen mit Spielgelegenheiten für die Kleinen und anschließend die Lärmzone mit Sportflächen für die Schuljugend (Bild 2). Die Betonkonstruktion, bestehend aus Mittelwand, Decken und Stützen entlang der Außenwand, soll durch leichtere Bauteile ergänzt werden, um eine möglichst große Variabilität in der Anlage der Wohnungen zu erreichen.

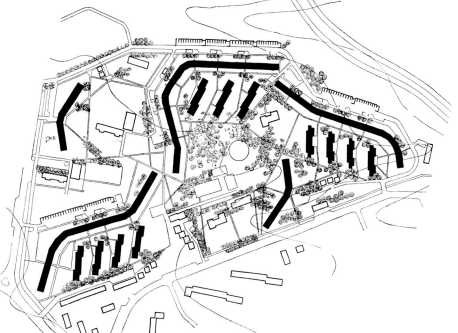

4   The building site. One can almost feel the wind sweeping over this bare hilltop
5   Artist's impression of the proposed buildings
6/7   Schematic presentation of plans and sections, 1 in 1000. The structural principle permits different layout combinations; because of the centre wall, however, not one of the rooms in the flats facing north can receive direct sunlight

4   Das Baugelände. Man meint den Wind zu spüren, der über diese kahle Kuppe fegt
5   Skizze der geplanten Bebauung
6/7   Schematische Darstellung der Grundrisse und Schnitte, 1:1000. Das Konstruktionsprinzip erlaubt unterschiedliche Grundrißkombinationen, verhindert durch die Mittelmauer jedoch, daß die Nordwohnungen wenigstens einen besonnten Raum erhalten können

4

5

6   7

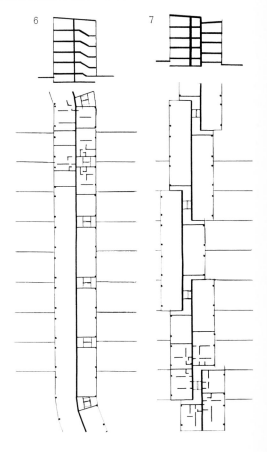

Siemensstadt, Berlin, 1956–1962 · Extension of the ring-shaped estate
Architect: Hans Scharoun

Due to the progressive views held by the head of a housing association, the planning of this estate was preceded by consultations with a competent authority, viz. the Institute for Town Planning at Berlin Technical University. A detailed survey provided data concerning population structure, traffic facilities, relationship between the redevelopment area and the larger metropolitan and regional units, population trends, income and professional grouping, the resulting types of dwellings, and the necessary service amenities. The results were embodied in an overall plan (Fig. 3) and in a development plan on a scale of 1 in 1000 where it was possible to align the roads in accordance with the pre-existing mains system. For a short while after the war, Berlin would have been able, on the basis of such ingenious planning, to take a step forward in a town planning effort which would have been of an exemplary and pioneering character, at least for Europe. But neither the planners nor the housing association were powerful enough to obtain the approval of the omnipotent authorities for more than a small fraction of their plans. As a result, the sewers were covered by a poplar plantation whilst the few housing units actually built were intersected by a loop road in such a way that the original idea behind the plan is nearly obscured. Moreover, the housing estate has sunk behind a mountain of walls and concrete structures of the urban motorway ring which rises to a height of almost six storeys and is, as it happens, in keeping with Speer's fateful concept of a ring road system. What is still left is a comparatively great variety of types of dwellings, and the proof that building activities freed from the strait-jacket of rectangular mannerism are no more expansive than the cheerless monotony of schematic production-line housing. What also remains is the knowledge, obtained from the surveys, that all the housing demands can be combined in a healthy mixture in a group of 450 dwelling units.

Berlin-Siemensstadt, 1956–1962 · Erweiterung der Ring-Siedlung
Architekt: Hans Scharoun

Dem einsichtsvollen Leiter einer Wohnungsbaugesellschaft war es zu verdanken, daß vor Beginn der Bauplanung eine kompetente Stelle, das Institut für Städtebau an der Technischen Universität Berlin, zu Rate gezogen wurde. Eine gründliche Planungsanalyse gab Aufschluß über die Besiedlungsstruktur, die Verkehrserschließung, die räumlichen Zusammenhänge zwischen dem Planungsgebiet und den übergeordneten Einheiten der Stadt und Region, die Bevölkerungsentwicklung, die Berufsstruktur, die daraus resultierenden Wohnungstypengruppen und die erforderlichen Dienstleistungsbetriebe. Die Ergebnisse wurden in einem Rahmenplan (Bild 3) und in einem Bebauungsplan 1:1000 niedergelegt, in dem die Straßenführung sich an bereits vorhandene Kanalisationsstränge anlehnen konnte. Einen Augenblick lang stand für Berlin die Möglichkeit offen, auf der Grundlage dieser geistvollen Planung den nächsten Schritt in die Zukunft eines zumindest für Europa vorbildlichen und wegweisenden Städtebaus zu tun. Weder die Planer, noch die Baugesellschaft hatten jedoch die Kraft, mehr als einen kleinen Teil der Pläne gegen die Ämterallmacht durchzusetzen. So entstand über den Kanalisationssträngen eine Pappelplantage, während eine Straßenschleife die wenigen gebauten »Wohngehöfte« derart in Teile schneidet, daß die Planungsidee kaum mehr wahrzunehmen ist. Zudem versinkt das Siedlungsgebiet hinter einem sich fast sechs Geschosse hoch auftürmenden Gebirge von Wällen und Betonkonstruktionen des Schnellstraßenringes, der unausgesprochen dem verhängnisvollen Speerschen Ringstraßenkonzept folgt. Geblieben ist eine noch verhältnismäßig große Vielfalt der angebotenen Wohnungstypen und der Beweis, daß aus den Zwangsjacken des rektangulären Manierismus befreites Bauen nicht teurer zu stehen kommt als die trostlose Langeweile schematischer »Wohnungsproduktion«. Geblieben ist ferner die mit den Analysen erarbeitete Erkenntnis, daß sich in einer Gruppe von 450 Wohnungen alle vorkommenden Wohnungsansprüche in einer »gesunden« Mischung vereinigen lassen.

3 Overall plan prepared by Scharoun at his Institute for ▶
Town Planning (1955), 1 in 40,000. It covers an area from the River Havel near Spandau in the west to the Wedding district in the east.
1 Spur road to Avus motorway, 2 Siemensdamm and Nonnendamm Allee, 3 Goerdelerdamm, 4 Kurt-Schumacher-Damm, 5 Tegeler Weg, 6 Access road, 7 Walkway through the park on the north side of the housing estate, 8 Urban railway, 9 River Spree, 10 Jungfernheide Common, 11 Charlottenburg Palace, 12 Olympia Stadium

3 Der Rahmenplan, den Scharoun mit seinem Institut für Städtebau aufstellte (1955), 1:40000. Er reicht von der Havel bei Spandau im Westen bis zum Wedding im Osten.
1 Avus-Zubringer, 2 Siemensdamm, Nonnendammallee, 3 Goerdelerdamm, 4 Kurt-Schumacher-Damm, 5 Tegeler Weg, 6 Erschließungsstraße, 7 Fußweg im Grünraum nördlich des Wohnbandes, 8 S-Bahnen, 9 Spree, 10 Volkspark Jungfernheide, 11 Schloß Charlottenburg, 12 Olympia-Stadion

Residential areas / Wohnen

Trade and commerce / Gewerbe

Industrial areas / Industrie

Open spaces / Grünflächen

1 Site plan, 1 in 40,000. The types of housing characteristic for the years 1900 (left), 1930 (centre) and 1960 (right)
are marked by heavy lines

1 Übersichtsplan, 1:40000. Herausgehoben sind die für
die Jahre 1900 (links), 1930 (Mitte) und 1960 (rechts) typischen Bebauungsformen

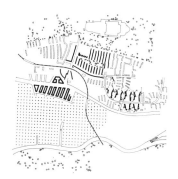

2 Westward view from one of the studios on the Spandau
road and the industrial estate

2 Blick aus einem Atelier nach Westen auf die nach
Spandau führende Straße und die Industriegebäude

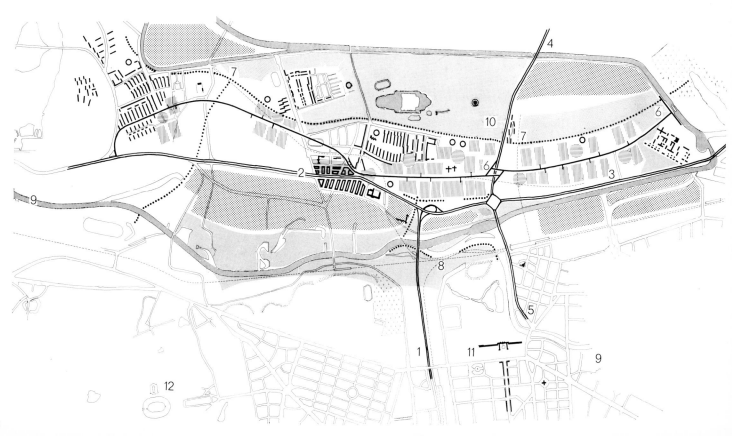

4 Site plan, 1 in 5000, showing the original plan of the housing units between the access road in the north and the walkway in the south. The margin of freedom in choosing the type and size of the dwellings was greater than in the housing estate actually built. In the event, it was necessary to omit six-room flats, single-family houses and "symbiotic" dwellings (for young and old people together)
5 Connection of the area developed in 1957/62 with the "ring" estate of 1930 (background left)

4 Lageplan, 1:5000. Ursprüngliche Planung der Wohngehöfte zwischen der Erschließungsstraße im Norden und dem Fußweg im Süden. Der Spielraum für die Art und Größe der Wohnungstypen war größer als in der ausgeführten Siedlung. Sechs-Zimmer-Wohnungen, Einfamilienhäuser und Symbiosetypen (für jung und alt) konnten nicht gebaut werden. Zahlen = Geschoßzahl
5 Der Anschluß der Erweiterung von 1957/1962 an die »Ring«-Siedlung von 1930 (links im Hintergrund)

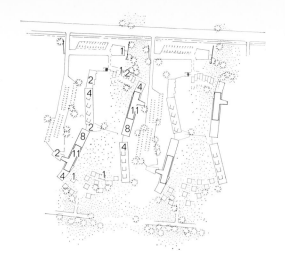

6 The vivid skyline of the new estate is in contrast to the notions of orderliness governing the "ring" estate of 1930 where the primary consideration was insistence on hygienic conditions – "air and light for every dwelling"
7 Site plan of the housing estate, 1 in 5000. The hatched and cross-hatched areas mark blocks of different height in the part of the estate designed by Scharoun

6 Die bewegte Silhouette der Wohngebirgslandschaft steht in Kontrast zu den Ordnungsvorstellungen, die 1930 das Gesicht der Ring-Siedlung prägten, bei der es zunächst nur um die Durchsetzung hygienischer Verhältnisse ging – »Luft und Licht für jede Wohnung«
7 Lageplan der Wohnsiedlung, 1:5000. Schraffiert und gerastert: verschieden hohe Bauteile des von Scharoun entworfenen Teils der Siedlung

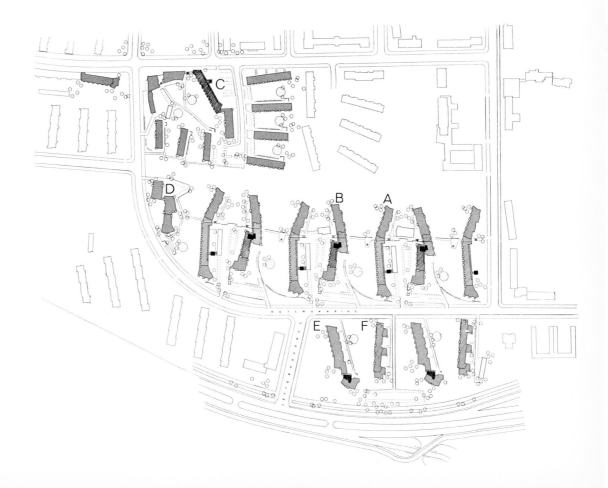

8

B 1

A 1

A 2

B 2

B 3

A 6

A 3

A 5

A 4

8   Second floor plan of one of the housing units, 1 in 1000
9   Spree Valley near Siemensstadt, with some fragments of the "housing unit" idea in the foreground. On the right, Block A; on the left, Block B; beyond the road on the extreme left, Block E and, further to the right, Block F

8   Ein Wohngehöft, zweites Obergeschoß, 1:1000
9   Das Spreetal bei Siemensstadt, im Vordergrund Teilstücke der Wohngehöftidee. Im Vordergrund rechts Bauteil A, links vorn B, jenseits der Straße E (links außen) und F

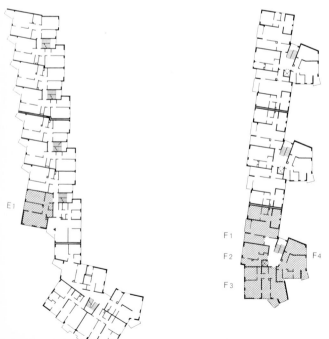

E 1

F 1

F 2

F 4

F 3

9

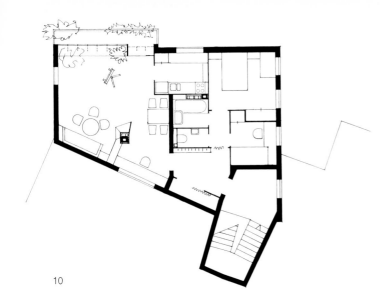

10

11

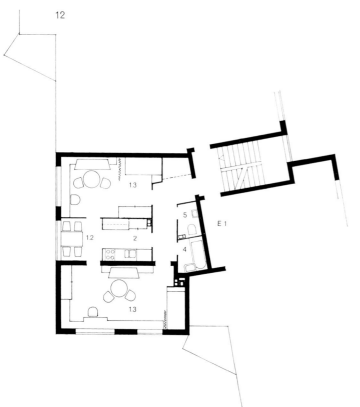

E 1

12

13

F 1

F 2

F 3

F 4

10 Plan of a studio flat (Block E), 1 in 200
11 Southern end of Block E, containing a studio flat
12/13 Plans of the different types of flats (cf. Fig. 8), 1 in 200

10 Atelierwohnung, Grundriß, 1:200
11 Ansicht des südlichen Kopfbaues E, der eine Atelierwohnung enthält
12/13 Grundrisse der Wohnungstypen, 1:200, vergleiche
Bild 8

14 Block A, seen from north-west. Note the access galleries in the centre and the studio window on top
15 Seen from the children's playground (between Blocks E and F), the blocks still seem to show the originally intended cohesion of a single housing unit; but the open space is cut into two by the road embankment
16 Diversity of heights at the southern end of Block A; in the background, the access gallery type block (Block C)
17–20 Plans of different types of dwellings, 1 in 200, (cf. page 208, Fig. 8)

14 Bauteil A von Nordwesten gesehen. In der Mitte zeichnen sich die Laubengänge, oben das Atelierfenster ab
15 Vom Kinderspielplatz (zwischen E und F) aus gesehen bilden die Baukörper eines Gehöftes noch den geplanten räumlichen Zusammenhang, die Grünräume werden jedoch von dem Straßenwall zerteilt
16 Die Staffelung der Bauhöhen am Südende des Bauteiles A. Im Hintergrund das Laubenganghochhaus C
17–20 Grundrisse der Wohnungstypen, 1:200, (vgl. Bild 8, Seite 208)

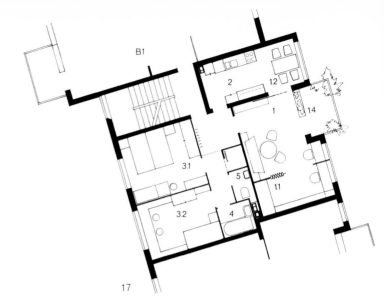

17

14

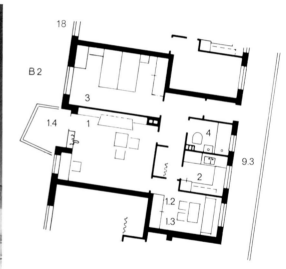

18

15

16

21

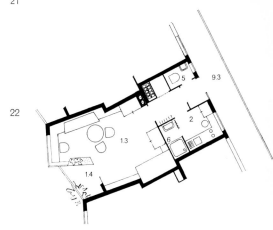

22

19

20

A1

A2

A6

A3

A5

A4

21/22 Flat with furniture provided by the tenant in the access gallery type block (Block C) with a plan, 1 in 200
23 South-west front of the access gallery type block (Block C)

21/22 Wohnung mit »Mietermöblierung« im Laubengang-haus C. Darunter ein Grundriß, 1:200
23 Südwestseite des Laubenganghochhauses C

Legends

Number	Description
1	Living room
1.1	Study
1.2	Dining area
1.3	Bed-sitting room
1.4	Balcony
1.5	Terrace
1.6	Air-raid shelter
2	Kitchen
2.1	Dining kitchen
2.2	Scullery
2.3	Kitchen balcony
3	Bedroom
3.1	Parents' bedroom
3.2	Nursery
3.3	Spare bedroom
4	Bathroom
5	W.C.
6	Shower or washroom
6.1	Sauna
7	Cupboard or boxroom
8	Ancillary premises
8.1	House entrance
8.2	Basement
8.3	Laundry or drying room
8.4	Bicycles
8.5	Prams
8.6	Heating and/or air-conditioning
8.7	Refuse collection
8.8	Electrical installations
9.1	Entrance hall
9.2	Staircase
9.3	Access gallery
9.4	Ramp
10	Garage
11	Hobby room
12	Sports implements
13	Caretaker
14	Office
15	Shop
16	Doctor's surgery
17	Post office

Legende

Ziffer	Raum
1	Wohnraum
1.1	Arbeitsplatz/Studio
1.2	Eßplatz
1.3	Wohnschlafraum
1.4	Balkon/Loggia
1.5	Terrasse
1.6	Luftschutzkeller
2	Küche
2.1	Eßküche
2.2	Hauswirtschaftsraum
2.3	Küchenbalkon
3	Zimmer
3.1	Elternschlafzimmer
3.2	Kinderzimmer
3.3	Mädchenzimmer/Gastzimmer
4	Bad
5	WC
6	Dusche/Waschraum
6.1	Sauna
7	Schrankraum/Abstellraum
8	Nebenräume
8.1	Hauseingang
8.2	Keller
8.3	Waschküche/Trockenraum
8.4	Fahrräder
8.5	Kinderwagen
8.6	Heizung/Klimaanlage
8.7	Müllsammelraum
8.8	Elektrozentrale
9.1	Eingangsflur
9.2	Treppenhaus
9.3	Laubengang
9.4	Rampe
10	Garage
11	Hobbyraum
12	Sportgeräte
13	Hausmeister
14	Büro
15	Laden
16	Arztpraxis
17	Post

Index of Architects · Verzeichnis der Architekten

Photo Credits · Fotonachweis

Amerika Dienst, Berlin-Dahlem 114 (2)
The Architectural Review, London 192 (2), 193 (5–8)
Bauwelt, Berlin 157 (12)
Behr Photography, London 34 (35), 39 (52), 41 (61, 62)
De Benedetti 12 (13)
Jean Biaugeaud, Arcueil 35 (40)
Hans Werner Bobran, Stuttgart-Büsnau 55 (85)
de Burgh Galwey 192 (2), 193 (5–8)
Colour Applications, London 95 (1), 125
Foto Cresta, Genova 198 (2), 199 (3), 200 (4, 5, 7, 8), 201 (10)
Photo Cuyl, Lyon 189 (2)
Ernst Deyhle, Rottenburg 62 (107), 163 (3), 164 (6–9), 166 (2–5), 170 (12–14)
Hernan Diaz, Bogota 91, 151 (3), 152 (5)
Walter Ehmann, Köln-Klettenberg 96 (2), 106 (1), 107 (3), 108 (8), 181 (3)
Ä. Fethulla, Helsinki 88 (1, 2)
Fototecnica Fortunati, Milano 61 (102–104)
John D. Fowler 97 (3)
Reinhard Friedrich, Berlin-Lichterfelde 205 (2), 207 (6), 208 (9), 209 (11), 210 (14–16), 211 (21, 23)
Y. Futagawa, Tokyo 34 (36), 57 (89)
J. Gauss, Stuttgart 109 (1)
Otto Hagemann, Berlin-Friedenau 55 (84)
Hamburger Luftamt 66 (122, Freigabe Nr. 100 478)
René Hartmann, Zug 139 (7), 138 (6)
Robert D. Harvey, Boston 115 (5, 6)
Heikki Havas, Helsinki 85 (1)
K. Helmer-Petersen, Copenhagen 56 (86), 75 (4, 6), 76 (7, 9)
Eva und Pertti Ingervo, Herttoniemi 86 (3), 87 (7, 8)
Ishimoto 39 (50)
Karl E. Jacobs, Berlin-Lichterfelde 32 (23)
Jaenecke – Samuelson, Malmö 15 (23), 20 (41), 21 (45–51)
Pierre Joly – Véra Cardot 15 (25), 19 (40)
Ito Josué, St.-Etienne 188 (3), 190 (7)
I. Kalter, Tel-Aviv 32 (26)
Foto Kay, Hamburg 78 (2), 79 (6)
Foto-Kessler, Berlin-Wilmersdorf 185 (1), 187 (8)
Walter Köster, Berlin-Lichterfelde 26 (9), 27 (11, 12), 173
Karl Krämer Verlag, Stuttgart 145 (2)
Edmund Kupiecki, Warszawa 33 (31), 63 (110–114)
Larsen & Nielsen 15 (24), 77 (2)
Lewellyn Studio, Chicago 69 (128), 174 (1, 2)
London County Council 16 (26), 17 (28)
Studio Martin, Paris 99 (4), 100 (8)
F. Maurer, Zürich 126 (2), 127 (3), 128 (5, 8), 129 (9, 10)
Joseph W. Molitor, Ossining 114 (3), 117 (13)
Neue Heimat (Benecke), Hamburg 161 (5)
Photo-Atelier Obigt, Berlin-Friedenau 130 (2), 131 (4)
Hermann Ohlsen, Bremen 67 (123)
Lennart Olson, Stockholm 56 (86), 80 (1, 2), 81 (4, 5), 83 (7)
Orgel-Köhne, Berlin-Charlottenburg 185 (2), 186 (3)
Peter Pitt, London 56 (88), 102 (2, 3), 103 (5)
Heinz Rasch, Wuppertal 9 (5)
Simo Rista 110 (1, 2), 111 (3, 5)
Foto-Zentrale Röse, Berlin-Spandau 157 (13, 14)
Sallstedts Bildbyrå, Stockholm 60 (98, 99)
Photo Schlossar, Crailsheim 30 (17, 19, 20)
K. W. Schmitt, Berlin-Lichterfelde 34 (37), 67 (124), 105
Schou-Jo 77 (3)
Stenbergs Illustrationsbyrå, Malmö 20 (42)
Franz Stoedtner, Düsseldorf 38 (47)
Atelier Sundahl 18 (31, 34, 35), 60 (97)
Studio Swain, Glasgow 121 (1)
Teigens Fotoatelier, Oslo 132 (3), 133 (4), 134 (6, 7), 135 (8–11)
W. J. Toomey 119 (8)

Ullstein Verlag 24 (4)
USIS, Bad Godesberg 69 (130)
Victoriano de los Rios 9 (4)
Hartmut Vogler, Dortmund 112 (1), 113 (5, 6)
J. A. Vrijhof, Rotterdam 178 (2)
Olle Waller, Göteborg 13 (15, 16)
G. Forrest Wilson, Glasgow 10 (7), 11 (12)
Windstosser, Stuttgart 165 (10)
Photo Yan – J. Dieuzaide, Toulouse 195 (2), 196 (3, 4)
Fotoarchiv Zeiss Ikon AG. Goerzwerk, Berlin 165 (12)

Sources:
P. 25, Fig. 6, from: "Balkone im Wohnungsbau". FBW, Stuttgart, 1954.
P. 28, Fig. 14, from: "The Illustrated London News", No. 119, 10th August, 1844.
P. 54, Data concerning electric power requirements, from: Erichbernd Brocher, "Anforderungen an die Hausinstallation im Sozialen Wohnungsbau: Hanover, 1962.
P. 64, Aimé Césaire, quoted from: "Cahier d'un retour au pays natal – Back to the native country". Insel Verlag, Wiesbaden, 1962.
P. 64, H. G. Wells, quoted from: "A short History of the World". New York, The Macmillan Company, 1922.

Quellen:
S. 25, Bild 6, nach: Balkone im Wohnungsbau. FBW, Stuttgart 1954.
S. 28, Bild 14, nach: The Illustrated London News, Nr. 119, 10. August 1844.
S. 55, Angaben über Elektro-Anschlußwerte nach: Erichbernd Brocher, Anforderungen an die Hausinstallation im Sozialen Wohnungsbau. Hannover 1962.
S. 65, Zitat Aimé Césaire aus: Cahier d'un retour au pays natal – Zurück ins Land der Geburt. Insel-Verlag, Wiesbaden 1962.
S. 65, Zitat H. G. Wells aus: Die Geschichte unserer Welt. Artemis-Verlag, Zürich 1959.